OVER THE TOP

HUMOROUS MOUNTAINEERING TALES

THE MOUNTAINEERS ANTHOLOGY S·E·R·I·E·S

VOLUME III

OVER THE TOP

HUMOROUS MOUNTAINEERING TALES

EDITED BY PETER POTTERFIELD
FOREWORD BY GREG CHILD

THE MOUNTAINEERS BOOKS

Published by
The Mountaineers Books
1001 SW Klickitat Way, Suite 201
Seattle, WA 98134

First edition, 2002

Published simultaneously in Great Britain by Cordee, 3a DeMontfort Street, Leicester, England, LE1 7HD

Manufactured in the United States of America

Acquiring Editor: Cassandra Conyers
Project Editor: Kathleen Cubley
Cover and Book Design: Ani Rucki
Layout: Mayumi Thompson
Cover art: Ani Rucki

Library of Congress Cataloging-in-Publication Data
Over the top : humorous mountaineering tales / edited by Peter Potterfield ; foreword by Greg Child.— 1st ed.
    p. cm. — (The mountaineers anthology series ; v. 3)
Includes bibliographical references and index.
  ISBN 0-89886-889-0 (pbk.)
  1. Mountaineering—Anecdotes. 2. Mountaineers—Anecdotes. I. Potterfield, Peter. II. Series.
  GV199.82 .O94 2002
  796.52'2—dc21
                                        2002009091

CONTENTS

FOREWORD

It is flattering to be asked by Peter Potterfield to write the foreword to his compilation of humorous climbing writing, especially after having been told by Peter that my stories make him laugh. I hope he meant the funny ones, and not the ones in which I was trying to be serious. Either way, I feel I am in good company in this book as many of the stories selected for this anthology are also favorites of mine, written by writers who have made me laugh, too.

This is just my opinion, but humor in climbing literature is a strangely rare bird, given all the books about alpinism on the library shelves of the American Alpine Club in Golden, Colorado, or the Alpine Club in London. Climbing as presented in most of those books is a serious and dramatic business, especially when it comes to the literature of Himalayan expeditions, which often read like accounts of soldiers going into battle. I mean, even though Reinhold Messner climbed all the 8000-meter peaks, pushing the frontiers of high altitude climbing to visionary and heroic levels, and though he published more titles about his exploits than perhaps any other climber in history, his books just don't make you laugh. Like most books in the expedition genre, they are not intended to be funny.

So far as I can tell, the Brits were the first to get behind the climbing story as a vehicle for humor. If writers like Frank Smythe and Bill Tillman blazed the way to funny stories back in the thirties, the genre came of age in the sixties and seventies. Among the best of those humorists was Tom Patey (a Scot), who penned scores of irreverent tales and lyrics that parodied the British climbing scene. His stories in some way set the mark for climbing humor: gently and lovingly ripping apart one's climbing partners and exposing their weaknesses for all to laugh at, and admire. Patey was a good satirist with a gift for timing and pace. One of his best stories, "A Short Walk with Whillans," is included in this anthology. It records an outing on the Eiger North Face with the legendary Don Whillans, who was arguably the most caustic wit the British climbing scene ever produced. Patey's tale is a snapshot portrait of Whillans, and the author accurately renders this moody yet playful cynic who could craft masterful one-liners on the spur of the moment and deliver them with crippling impact. When Patey and Whillans are retreating down the Eiger in the face of bad weather and life-threatening stonefall, they encounter a team of Japanese who tell the Englishmen that they are, nonetheless, "going up." Whillans' reply—that they may be going up "farther than they think" (i.e., all the way to heaven)—is wise and ironic, and emblematic of Whillans's dark wit. Patey knows exactly how to deliver the remark to shock us and make us giggle at once.

Another landmark in the realm of climbing humor came around the same period with British writer W.E. Bowman's comic novel, *The Ascent of Rum Doodle*. While Patey parodied his real-life peers, Bowman used fiction to knock the stuffing out of the pompous pith-helmeted explorer-mountaineer, with his tale of a farcical British Himalayan expedition to a mythical peak. The expeditioners are incompetent, arrogant, and bombastic imperialists—not unlike many expeditioners of reality. The book seemed a presage of Monty Python's hilarious television spoof on climbing, the mockumentary of a hairdresser's expedition to Everest, led by a fop who directs the expedition from underneath a hair-styling machine in a base camp outfitted like a beauty salon.

The reason the Brits cottoned on to the climbing-is-funny idea so readily has a lot to do with the fact that British weather is so lousy, and British climbers are forced to spend most climbing weekends in the pub while it rains on the cliffs. A healthy and well-lubricated pub scene, with its witty and irreverent banter and practical jokes, cannot fail to spawn a good laugh. My own climbing writing, and whatever humor that I tried to craft into it, was born out of that sort of scene, during visits to Britain, and in my birthplace in Australia, which had a British sense of humor beaten into it by virtue of its origins in the 1700s as a penal colony where England's imprisoned riff-raff were dumped. In addition, the first few Himalayan expeditions I went on were with Brits. The jokes, sarcasm, and foibles of my companions on those trips provided me with an inexhaustible supply of material to parody, embellish, or simply tell-it-as-it-was. Funny moments from those expeditions got play in many stories I wrote during my years as a semi-regular columnist for *Climbing* magazine.

That column—titled "Postcards from the Edge," (later compiled in my book, *Postcards from the Ledge*)—was the idea of former editor-in-chief Michael

Kennedy, who let me run free and write all manner of gibberish so long as the stories hinged (a little) on climbing. The column-sized story proved to be the perfect vehicle for the humorous climbing vignette: just enough space to set a scene and deliver a punch line. "Postcards" gave rise to more recent humor columns in that magazine, by American writers John "Verm" Sherman, John "Largo" Long, and the anonymous and acid mini-columnist known as Master Beta.

But don't get me wrong, humor in American climbing writing has been there all along, and it has evolved indigenously from the British influence to which I give such credit. The late, great, Warren Harding, who was the driving force behind the first ascent of "The Nose" route on Yosemite Valley's El Capitan, wrote one of the quirkiest and most snidely funny books about climbing, ever, in 1975. *Downward Bound* is a montage of satirical interviews, plays, cartoons, and stories that are based on the early Yosemite climbing scene. Harding's stream of consciousness book isn't the easiest read, but it is the most surreal take on climbing I have come across. The first edition's inside-cover copy describes it accurately, as being a product of "a twisted mind and an hallucinatory imagination." Climbing could use a little more of that, these days.

So regard the stories in this anthology as an alternative to the side of climbing that dwells on the quest for harder routes and higher climbing grades, and on mountain epics in which, all too often, the outcome is tragic. Climbing is indeed a serious business, but sometimes we take it too seriously. These tales offer up the lighter side of a sport that most people who don't climb regard as a preposterous undertaking in the first place.

Greg Child
Castle Valley, Utah
May 2002

INTRODUCTION

For this, the third collection in The Mountaineers Books' ongoing series of anthologies featuring the best of mountaineering writing, the theme is a lighthearted one: humor. Much of climbing literature is preoccupied with the trouble, struggle, and even tragedy that so often follows human beings into the mountains. But things can go wrong in all kinds of ways, including comic ones.

The fact that there is not much hilarity to be found in climbing literature emphasizes that, in climbing as in stand-up, funny doesn't come easily. Climbing humor, particularly good humor, is rare. A sense of the comedic is most frequently found in the more self-deprecatory approach to climbing narratives, and only a handful of climbers seem sufficiently secure to make fun of themselves, or to emphasize comic elements when recounting their adventures.

This collection reflects seventy-five years of climbing narrative, and the full breadth of humor and wit that has emerged in that time. The nature of the humor found in these collected works is peculiar in its own right. With few exceptions, even these carefully culled climbing stories are not laugh-out-loud funny. Instead, they are more personal, and more subtle, reflecting the sensibilities mountaineers bring with them, or the defensive sort of humor useful in warding off physical suffering, or the challenges to ego that come so frequently when humans take their measure against a mountain, or a climb.

Frank Smythe worries both about being out of shape and the persistent weather jinx that seems to follow him around on his "mountaineering holiday," while David Roberts suffers under the barely tangible yet extremely discomfiting pressure subtly exerted by the local denizens of an artificial urban climbing venue. Greg Child writes about the weird milieu of modern-day sport climbing competitions, where the competitors vie for every advantage, including the psyche-out, before venturing onto the plastic and plywood for the main event. Tom Patey expertly chronicles time-honored ploys to dodge the hardest climbing, or avoid it altogether. Guy Waterman puts on his private-eye persona for a close-up look at the irrational attachment to equipment that seems endemic to climbers.

It's a varied lot, with voices as distinct as Kurt Diemberger's, the European climber with legendary longevity (on competing with Reinhold Messner), and John "Vermin" Sherman's, the master of taking the irreverent approach to climbing in general (on the historic early days of ice climbing in Valdez, Alaska).

If there is a universal thread running through these disparate pieces, it is this: We're all human beings, and even when engaged in physically demanding and potentially dangerous pursuits, the ability to laugh at ourselves dignifies our humanity.

Peter Potterfield
Seattle, Washington
May 2002

"THE INSULT OF INJURY"

FROM
Postcards from the Ledge
BY GREG CHILD

IN HIS FOURTH BOOK, *POSTCARDS FROM THE LEDGE,* GREG CHILD writes about a climb on Combatant, a neighbor to Waddington in British Columbia's Coast Range. A week into the climb, high on the route, Child is enjoying himself so much he speculates about a climb with no end—a hard, graceful alpine route that goes on forever. "Nothing in me wants the climb to end," he writes. "I feel content to keep going for another seven days, and maybe, another seven after that. . . ."

This innate love of climbing, and Child's unique ability to relate it in a humorous self-deprecating style, makes his books stand out from the current glut of mountaineering narratives. Child's skill as a writer combined with his irrefutable bona fides—K2 and Everest seem the least of his achievements when measured against his record of long, hard, mixed alpine routes on objectives such as Trango Tower, Shipton Spire, and various routes in Alaska— may make his the defining voice of climbing for a generation.

Child is the author of five books: *Thin Air: Encounters in the Himalaya, Mixed Emotions, Climbing: The Complete Reference, Postcards from the Ledge,* and *Over the Edge,* his account of a group of American climbers kidnapped by guerilla soldiers in Kyrgyzstan.

"The Insult of Injury," Child's droll examination of the tendency for climbers to become paranoid, even obsessed, by the nagging frustration of persistent injuries, is in *Postcards from the Ledge,* on pages 41–46.

A ll you guys ever do is talk about your injuries." That comment from a bored eavesdropper at a party.

True, we are standing around complaining again about the inexplicable, incurable aches that assail our wrists, elbows, shoulders, ankles, knees, and backs, our muscles, tendons, nerves, ligaments, cartilage, and bones. As it did for our grumpy, gouty, rheumatic, and bunion-plagued grandfathers, the onset of winter weather has multiplied the colonies of gremlins that infest our limbs and joints.

Yet we are not granddads, but in our thirties, not sedentary, but active. We run, cycle, pump iron, ski, stretch, eat well—all to train for climbing. Yeah, we like to climb a lot, climb anything: plastic, rock, mountains. But one day we awoke a day older, pulled on a hold a bit too hard, ran a mile too far, and from that moment on our aches became legion. We are the ibuprofen generation. This is the season of our discontent.

Standing in this circle of the walking wounded, it comes my turn to whine. I display my elbow, which sports a fresh scar from the surgeon's scalpel—the latest chapter in my battle with tendonitis. My problems began two-and-a-half years ago while I was lapping a juggy, overhanging traverse in a climbing gym. I crouched into undercling mode on two big buckets, and then, when I weighted my arms, I heard the faint rip of tearing fabric. The next instant it felt like someone was using my elbow to stub out the hot ember of a Camel. So this is tendonitis, I thought.

What had happened was this: my flexor muscles—developed to unnatural proportions by two decades of climbing—had played tug-of-war with the tendons connecting them to the bony nubs of the inner elbow, the medial epicondyl. The result: a colossal whupping of the zone where meaty muscle turns to Kevlar-strong tendon. So I rested my elbow, iced it, warmed it with hot towels, and wore a brace.

Elbow got worse.

"Rest won't cure tendonitis," someone advised. "You've got to train through it, pump blood into the injured area." This made some kind of sense, since tendons are poorly endowed with blood vessels, so I tried climbing again.

Elbow got worser.

Then some pill-head said in my third month of agony, "Take stronger anti-inflammatories." My guts already rattled with ibuprofen, but I upped the dose anyway, until I was warned, "Your kidneys will shrivel up if you take too much of that stuff." So I switched to aspirin, which, among other side effects, thins the blood. I took so many that I got paranoid I'd bleed to death if I cut myself shaving.

Elbow got worsest.

Next I tried a powerful prescription nonsteroidal anti-inflammatory. It caused depression and nausea.

Elbow cramped up and died.

Saw a doctor. Saw several doctors. "Describe the pain," said one. I wanted to scream, "Maggots with hacksaw mandibles gnawing rotted tendons, injecting them with acidic venom, laying eggs in my joints, the vile brood hatching, chewing tunnels through my muscles, spiraling in conga lines 'round my nerves, their thunderous footsteps charged with a thousand itchy volts."

Instead I told him I couldn't twist lids off jam jars, slice bread, change gears on my car, turn doorknobs, lift a suitcase. Pulling lint off my shirt hurt. Diagnosis: medial epicondylitis, commonly called golfer's elbow. "But I don't *play* golf," I whined.

Six months after the injury, I was injected with cortisone, a steroidal drug with legendary powers for reducing inflammation. That was the good news. The bad news was too much of the stuff corrodes the joint. But I was assured that one or two doses were harmless.

Did it work? Yo! That tendon shrank like an erection in an icy river. The pain faded as if I'd been hit with morphine. I started pulling at rock again. But eight months later, tendonitis crept back. This time, though, the stiffness consumed both elbows, and like some antibiotic-resistant virus, a second cortisone job barely quelled the inflammation. Modern medicine had failed me.

The months that followed were bleak as I watched my bouldering shoes gather dust and the calluses peel from my fingertips. I was a coyote caught in a bear trap, gnawing its leg off. I snapped and barked and begged for help.

Vitamin therapy was recommended, so I gobbled antioxidants like vitamins E, C, and B6, minerals like magnesium and calcium. I munched amino acids. I even tried powdered bovine trachea, the logic being that cow gullets are made of substances similar to tendons and ligaments. This sounds like the cannibalistic custom of eating the heart of your enemy to gain his strength, but I swallowed the stuff anyway. "Expensive urine," said one doctor, laughing and citing studies that showed virtually no supplements are absorbed by injured cells.

An acupuncturist stuck needles into my ear, neck, and arm to stimulate the flow of *chi* energy in my body. A chiropractor wrenched my neck and elbow until the joints made alarming clicks. Physiotherapists performed cross-tissue and deep-tissue massage. Herbal poultices and hot ginger compresses were applied. Homeopathic potions imbibed. I decreased my intake of coffee, liquor, meat, gluten; when nothing came of this, I increased my intake of liquor, meat, coffee, gluten.

Along the way I learned that doctors scoff at alternative cures, and alternative practitioners diss conventional medicine. Yet, who could heal me?

A hippie who suggested I lie in a circle of crystals and place magnets on my elbows advised me to adjust my attitude. "You won't get better unless you believe in the healing method," he said. My memory dredged up a scene from my childhood, of the old Presbyterian minister at school who preached that we'd never get through the Pearly Gates if we didn't believe in God.

Belief, the power of the mind. It is the key to the executive bathroom. A witch doctor can point a magic bone at a man, and because the tribe believes the bone has the power to kill, the man dies. "Visualize healing," the hippie said. "I'm trying," I replied, straining so hard on a mental image of my tendons being crocheted together that I wet my pants.

It was suggested that I find a practitioner to realign the plates of my skull. And one to replace my dental fillings with nonmercuric compounds. One climber claimed that a mystical therapist cured her tendonitis by looking into her mouth and finding root canal in need of repair. I told my dentist this. He looked at me to make sure I wasn't overdosing on his Novocaine, then characterized the notion as "crazy."

Someone else recommended an herbal enema to flush out my gripey bowels. Get hypnotized. "Your astrological chart predicts this injury," nodded a friend with a bent toward star gazing. Try electrotherapy to stimulate the muscles. Ultrasound to fibrillate the affected region. Visit a faith healer in the Philippines—yeah, right, watch him extract chicken gizzards from my elbow. Meditate. Yoga. Get worry beads. Apply leeches to the elbows to siphon off bad blood.

"See a shrink. Maybe your injury is the manifestation of some neurosis lurking in your psyche; maybe deep down you're trying to quit climbing, and your injury is a device of your subconscious," I was told. After hearing that, I walked around depressed for a week, convinced I was a hypochondriac.

I read about transferal technique, in which the patient writes an essay about his problem, then puts it in a box. That done, the ill is symbolically out of the body. I went further, I drove a hundred miles, dug a hole, buried the box containing the essay, then spat on the grave.

I also compared notes with others who had wrenched their bodies. Another climber solved his arm pain with an operation called a fasceotomy, in which a surgeon sliced open the Saran Wrap-like sheath surrounding his overly buff forearm muscles. The pent-up muscle oozed out, like the innards of an overcooked sausage on a barbecue. The relief, I understand, is like removing a too-tight climbing slipper from your foot on a hot day. Olympic runner Mary Decker had the job done on her ballooned-out calf muscles, and she still runs like a gazelle.

Another guy had nodules of cartilaginous grit that wandered around his elbow joints like mice, turning up in a different place every time he had an x-ray. Others had flexed so hard that a tendon had ripped off a sliver of bone—an avulsion fracture. Still others had a tendon snap like rubber and twang back up a limb, necessitating a surgical fishing expedition to find and reattach the tendon.

I met many victims of carpal tunnel syndrome, an exquisitely painful condition that occurs when a tendon located in a groove in the wrist inflames and rubs against bone. And there were dislocations; I once saw Henry Barber's shoulder slip out of place while he was climbing—the tendons strapping his arm into his shoulder socket got sloppy—and I watched him flip about on the ground like a trout plucked from a stream. Typists, keyboard operators, and women cradling babies were also among the ranks of the injured. They suffered from RSS, repetitive stress syndrome, caused by performing repetitious work tasks.

No one was safe from the tyranny of tendonitis.

Two-and-a-half years after the onset of my injury a surgeon cut open my elbow to see what could be done. He went in expecting to do a flex release, a serious procedure in which the tendons of the flexor muscle are cut and relocated to a less tightly strung position. Footballer Joe Montana had had it done, and he was throwing again; Jerry Moffat had it done too, long ago, and he cranks like the proverbial disease. In the end, my doc performed a cleanup job instead, slicing out a cubic centimeter of degenerated tendon and ripped-up fascia.

"Maybe it'll work for me, maybe not," I tell my fellow sufferers in the circle of injury, adopting a fatalistic tone that suggests I've tried it all.

Then Smith, a friend with a wretched hand ligament, corners me at the party and presents me with a small box. He'd recently had luck with a *milagro*, an amulet popular among Latino folk. Appropriately, Smith's amulet was shaped like a hand. I open the box. It contains a tiny metal charm fashioned into the likeness of an arm, elbow, and hand. Smith tells me he is contemplating having his *milagro* supercharged with the blessing of a Santeria priestess. Santeria is a mix of West African, Catholic, and West Indian faiths that incorporates ecstatic trances, magic, and animal sacrifice.

I cradle the tin charm in my palm, forming a mental picture of a big chanting Jamaican woman cutting the head off a chicken and spraying hot blood all over my elbow and amulet. A puzzled look crosses my face as I ponder the political correctness of this form of therapy.

"You've got to believe, Child," Smith says. My amulet sits on my bedside table. Lately my elbow has been feeling better. I think.

"A SHORT WALK WITH WHILLANS"

FROM
One Man's Mountains
BY TOM PATEY

TOM PATEY AND DON WHILLANS ARE BOTH ICONS OF THE BRITISH climbing scene of the 1950s and 1960s, but for different reasons.

Patey, the quintessential Scottish climber, cut his teeth as a teenager on crags such as Lochnagar, above Balmoral Castle, and then went on to set the hard-man standard for winter climbing in Scotland with routes such as the first ascent of Zero Gully and the first traverse of Creag Meaghaidh. Patey also made important first ascents in the Himalaya, such as the Mustagh Tower in the Karakoram in 1956 and Rakoposhi in 1958. He spent much of the 1960s putting up new routes in the Alps with Joe Brown. His is a resume of unrivalled pluck and versatility, and to it Patey added the role of participant-reporter and insightful satirist.

Then there's Whillans, the blunt and brilliant blue-collar climber, whose huge presence infused British mountaineering from his early days on local gritstone crags in the industrial North of England to landmark achievements in alpinism: the first ascent of the Central Pillar of Freney (hailed then as the "last great problem in the Alps") to the South Face of Annapurna in 1970, the most technical big route done in the Himalaya at the time. With a figure as legendary as Whillans, trying to winnow fact from fiction can be dangerous: as outspoken and accomplished as Whillans was, he has become even more so in the retelling, and "Whillans stories" are now a genre unto themselves.

With his place in history so secure, it's high praise that Whillans comes alive in Patey's story like no place else. This wonderful piece captures vividly the acerbic personality of Whillans, his bull's-eye one-liners, and the attitude both these pioneering climbers brought to the most difficult and dangerous routes of the day. In a marvel of writing short, the story is Patey's low-key description of the pair's attempt to climb the North Face of the Eiger, the infamous Nordwand, at a time when only two British teams had successfully reached the top of this the most deadly wall in the Alps.

Patey, who was killed roping off one of his beloved Scottish sea stacks in 1970, wrote this piece following the pair's Eiger attempt in 1963. It is in *One Man's Mountains*, on pages 183–192.

D id you spot that great long streak of blood on the road over from Chamonix? Twenty yards long, I'd say." The speaker was Don Whillans. We were seated in the little inn at Alpiglen and Don's aggressive profile was framed against an awe-inspiring backdrop of the Eiger Nordwand. I reflected that the conversation had become attuned to the environment.

"Probably some unfortunate animal," I ventured without much conviction.

Whillans's eyes narrowed. "Human blood," he said. "Remember—lass?" (appealing to his wife Audrey), "I told you to stop the car for a better look. Really turned her stomach, it did. Just when she was getting over the funeral."

I felt an urge to inquire whose funeral they had attended. There had been several. Every time we went up on the Montenvers train we passed a corpse going down. I let the question go. It seemed irrelevant, possibly even irreverent.

"Ay, it's a good life," he mused, "providing you don't weaken."

"What happens if you do?"

"They bury you," he growled, and finished his pint.

Don has that rarest of gifts, the ability to condense a whole paragraph into a single, terse, uncompromising sentence. But there are also occasions when he can become almost lyrical in a macabre sort of way. It depends on the environment.

We occupied a window table in the inn. There were several other tables, and hunched round each of these were groups of shadowy men draped in black cagoules—lean-jawed, grim, uncommunicative characters who spoke in guttural monosyllables and gazed steadfastly toward the window. You only had to glimpse their earnest faces to realize that these men were Eiger Candidates—martyrs for the "Mordwand."*

"Look at that big black bastard up there," Whillans chuckled dryly, gesturing with his thumb. "Just waiting to get its claws into you. And think of all the young lads who've sat just where you're sitting now, and come back all tied up in sacks. It makes you think."

It certainly did. I was beginning to wish I had stayed at Chamonix, funerals or no funerals.

---

* Eiger pseudonym coined by German Press—literally "Murder Wall."

"Take that young blonde over there," he pointed toward the sturdy Aryan barmaid, who had just replenished his glass. "I wonder how many dead men she's danced with? All the same," he concluded after a minute's reflection, "t'wouldn't be a bad way to spend your last night."

I licked my lips nervously. Don's philosophic discourses are not for the fainthearted.

One of the Eiger Candidates detached himself from a neighboring group and approached us with obvious intent. He was red haired, small and compact, and he looked like a Neanderthal man. This likeness derived from his hunched shoulders, and the way he craned his head forwards like a man who had been struck repeatedly on the crown by a heavy hammer, and through time developed a protective overgrowth of skull. His name proved to be Eckhart, and he was a German. Most of them still are.

The odd thing about him was his laugh. It had an uncanny hollow quality. He laughed quite a lot without generating a great deal of warmth, and he wore a twisted grin that seemed to be permanently frozen onto his face. Even Whillans was moved.

"You—going—up?" he inquired.

"Nein," said Eckhart. "Nix gutt! . . . You wait here little time, I think. . . . Now there is much vatter." He turned up his coat collar ruefully and laughed. "Many, many stein fall. . . . All day, all night. . . . Stein, stein." He tapped his head significantly and laughed uproariously. "Two nights we wait at *Tod Bivouac.*" He repeated the name as if relishing its sinister undertones. ("It means Dead Man," I said to Whillans in a hushed whisper.) "Always it is nix gutt. . . . Vatter, stein. . . . Stein, vatter . . . so we go down. It is very funny."

We nodded sympathetically. It was all a huge joke.

"Our two Kameraden, they go on. They are saying at the telescopes, one man he has fallen fifty meters. Me? I do not believe this." (Loud and prolonged laughter from the company.)

"You have looked through the telescope?" I inquired anxiously.

"Nein," he grinned, "Not necessary . . . tonight they gain summit . . . tomorrow they descend. And now we will have another beer."

Eckhart was nineteen. He had already accounted for the North Face of the Matterhorn as a training climb, and he intended to camp at the foot of the

Eigerwand until the right conditions prevailed. If necessary, he could wait until October. Like most of his countrymen he was nothing if not thorough, and finding his bivouac tent did not measure up to his expectations he had hitchhiked all the way back to Munich to secure another one. As a result of this, he had missed the settled spell of weather that had allowed several rivals to complete the route, including the second successful British team, Baillie and Haston, and also the lone Swiss climber, Darbellay, who had thus made the first solo ascent.

"Made of the right stuff, that youngster," observed Don.

"If you ask me I think he was trying to scare us off," I suggested. "Psychological warfare that's all it is."

"Wait till we get on the face tomorrow," said Whillans. "We'll hear your piece then."

➤   ➤   ➤

Shortly after noon the next day we left Audrey behind at Alpiglen, and the two of us set off up the green meadows which girdle the foot of the Eigerwand. Before leaving, Don had disposed of his Last Will and Testament. "You've got the car key, lass, and you know where to find the house key. That's all you need to know. Ta, for now."

Audrey smiled wanly. She had my profound sympathy.

The heat was oppressive, the atmosphere heavy with menace. How many Munich Bergsteigers had trod this very turf on their upward path never to return to their native Klettergarten? I was humming Wagner's Valkyrie theme music as we reached the lowest rocks of the Face.

Then a most unexpected thing happened. From an alcove in the wall emerged a very ordinary Swiss tourist, followed by his very ordinary wife, five small children, and a poodle dog. I stopped humming immediately. I had read of tearful farewells with wives and sweethearts calling plaintively, but this was ridiculous. What an undignified send-off! The five children accompanied us up the first snow slope scrambling happily in our wake, and prodding our rucksacks with inquisitive fingers. "Go away," said Whillans irritably, but ineffectively. We were quite relieved when, ultimately, they were recalled to base and we stopped playing Pied Pipers. The dog held on a bit longer until some well directed stones sent it on its way. "Charming, I must say," remarked Don. I wondered whether Hermann Buhl would have given up on the spot—a most irregular start to an Eiger Epic and probably a bad omen.

We started climbing up the left side of the shattered pillar, a variant of the normal route which had been perfected by Don in the course of several earlier attempts. He was well on his way to becoming the Grand Old Man of Grindelwald, though not through any fault of his own. This was his fourth attempt at the climb and on every previous occasion he had been turned back by bad weather or by having to rescue his rivals. As a result of this he must have spent more hours on the Face than any other British climber.

Don's preparations for the Eiger—meticulous in every other respect— had not included unnecessary physical exertion. While I dragged my weary muscles from Breuil to Zermatt via the Matterhorn he whiled away the days at Chamonix sun bathing at the Plage until opening time. At the Bar Nationale he nightly sank five or six pints of "heavy," smoked forty cigarettes, persuaded other layabouts to feed the juke box with their last few francs, and amassed a considerable reputation as an exponent of "Baby Foot," the table football game which is the national sport of France. One day the heat had been sufficiently intense to cause a rush of blood to the head because he had walked four miles up to the Montenvers following the railway track, and had acquired such enormous blisters that he had to make the return journey by train. He was nevertheless just as fit as he wanted to be, or indeed needed to be.

First impressions of the Eigerwand belied its evil reputation. This was good climbing rock with excellent friction and lots of small incuts. We climbed unroped, making height rapidly. In fact I was just starting to enjoy myself, when I found the boot. . . .

"Somebody's left a boot here," I shouted to Don.

He pricked up his ears. "Look and see if there's a foot in it," he said.

I had picked it up: I put it down again hurriedly.

"Ha! Here's something else—a torn rucksack," he hissed.

"And here's his water bottle—squashed flat."

I had lost my new-found enthusiasm and decided to ignore future foreign bodies. (I even ignored the pun.)

"You might as well start getting used to them now," advised Whillans. "This is where they usually glance off, before they hit the bottom."

He's a cheery character I thought to myself. To Don, a spade is just a spade—a simple trenching tool used by gravediggers.

At the top of the Pillar we donned our safety helmets. "One thing to remember on the Eiger," said Don, "never look up, or you may need a plastic surgeon."

His advice seemed superfluous that evening, as we did not hear a single ricochet. We climbed on up, past the Second Pillar and roped up for the traverse across to the Difficult Crack. At this late hour the Crack was streaming with water so we decided to bivouac while we were still dry. There was an excellent bivouac cave near the foot of the crack.

⋎　　⋎　　⋎

"I'll have one of your cigarettes," said Don. "I've only brought Gauloises." This was a statement of fact, not a question. There is something about Don's proverbial bluntness that arouses one's admiration. Of such stuff are generals made. We had a short discussion about bivouacking, but eventually I had to agree with his arguments and occupy the outer berth. It would be less likely to induce claustrophobia, or so I gathered.

I was even more aware of the sudden fall in temperature. My ultra-warm Terray duvet failed by a single critical inch to meet the convertible bivy-rucksack which I had borrowed from Joe Brown. It had been designed, so the manufacturers announced, to Joe's personal specifications, and as far as I could judge, to his personal dimensions as well.

Insidiously and from nowhere it seemed, a mighty thunderstorm built up in the valley less than a mile away. Flashes of lightning lit up the whole Face and gray tentacles of mist crept out of the dusk threatening to envelop our lofty eyrie.

"The girl in the tourist office said that a ridge of high pressure occupying the whole of central Europe would last for at least another three days."

"Charming," growled Whillans. "I could give you a better forecast without raising my head."

"We should be singing Bavarian drinking songs to keep our spirits up," I suggested. "How about some Austrian yodeling."

"They're too fond of dipping in glacier streams . . . that's what does it," he muttered sleepily.

"Does what?"

"Makes them yodel. All the same, these bloody Austrians."

➤   ➤   ➤

The day dawned clear. For once it seemed that a miracle had happened and a major thunderstorm had cleared the Eiger, without lodging on the Face. Don remained inscrutable and cautious as ever. Although we were sheltered from any prevailing wind we would have no advance warning of the weather, as our horizons were limited by the Face itself.

There was still a trickle of water coming down the Difficult Crack as Don launched himself stiffly at the first obstacle. Because of our uncertainty about the weather and an argument about who should make breakfast, we had started late. It was 6:30 A.M. and we would have to hurry. He made a bad start by clipping both strands of the double rope to each of the three pitons he found in position. The rope jammed continuously and this was even more disconcerting for me, when I followed carrying both rucksacks. Hanging down the middle of the pitch was an old frayed rope, said to have been abandoned by Mlle Loulou Boulaz, and this kept getting entangled with the ice axes. By the time I had joined Don at this stance I was breathing heavily and more than usually irritated. We used the excuse to unrope and get back into normal rhythm before tackling the Hinterstoisser. It was easy to find the route hereabouts: you merely followed the pitons. They were planted everywhere with rotting rope loops (apparently used for abseils) attached to most of them. It is a significant insight into human psychology that nobody ever stops to remove superfluous pegs on the Eiger. If nothing else they help to alleviate the sense of utter isolation that fills this vast Face, but they also act as constant reminders of man's ultimate destiny and the pageant of history written into the rock. Other reminders were there in plenty—gloves, socks, ropes, crampons and boots. None of them appeared to have been abandoned with the owners' consent.

The Hinterstoisser Traverse, despite the illustrations of prewar heroes traversing "a la Dulfer," is nothing to get excited about. With two fixed ropes of unknown vintage as an emergency handrail, you can walk across it in three minutes. Stripped of scaffolding, it would probably qualify as Severe by contemporary British standards. The fixed ropes continued without a break as far as the Swallow's Nest—another bivouac site hallowed by tradition. Thus far I could well have been climbing the Italian Ridge of the Matterhorn.

We skirted the first ice field on the right, scrambling up easy rubble where we had expected to find black ice. It was certainly abnormally warm, but if the weather held we had definite grounds for assuming that we could complete the climb in one day—our original intention. The Ice Hose which breaches the rocky barrier between the first and second ice fields no longer merited the name because the ice had all gone. It seemed to offer an easy alley but Don preferred to stick to known alternatives and advanced upon an improbable looking wall some distance across to the left. By the time I had confirmed our position on Hiebeler's route description, he had completed the pitch and was shouting for me to come on. He was well into his stride, but still did not seem to share my optimism.

His doubts were well founded. Ten minutes later, we were crossing the waterworn slabs leading on to the second ice field when we saw the first falling stones. To be exact we did not see the stones, but merely the puff of smoke each one left behind at the point of impact. They did not come bouncing down the cliff with a noisy clatter as stones usually do. In fact they were only audible after they had gone past—WROUFF!—a nasty sort of sound halfway between a suck and a blow.

"It's the small ones that make that sort of noise," explained Whillans, "Wait till you hear the really big ones!"

The blue print for a successful Eiger ascent seems to involve being at the right place at the right time. According to our calculations the Face should have been immune to stonefall at this hour of the morning.

Unfortunately the Eiger makes its own rules. An enormous black cloud had taken shape out of what ought to have been a clear blue sky and had come to rest on the summit ice field. It reminded me of a gigantic black vulture spreading its wings before dropping like lightning on unsuspecting prey.

Down there at the foot of the second ice field, it was suddenly very cold and lonely. Away across to the left was the Ramp; a possible hideaway to sit out the storm. It seemed little more than a stone's throw, but I knew as well as Don did, that we had almost 1,500 feet of steep snow-ice to cross before we could get any sort of shelter from stones.

There was no question of finding adequate cover in the immediate vicinity. On either side of us steep ice slopes, peppered with fallen debris, dropped away into the void. Simultaneously with Whillans's arrival at the stance the first flash of lightning struck the White Spider.

"That settles it," said he, clipping the spare rope through my belay carabiner.

"What's going on?" I demanded, finding it hard to credit that such a crucial decision could be reached on the spur of the moment.

"I'm going down," he said, "That's what's going on."

"Wait a minute! Let's discuss the whole situation calmly." I stretched out one hand to flick the ash off my cigarette. Then a most unusual thing happened. There was a higher pitched "WROUFF" than usual, and the end of my cigarette disappeared!

It was the sort of subtle touch that Hollywood film directors dream about.

"I see what you mean," I said. "I'm going down too."

I cannot recall coming off a climb so quickly. As a result of a long acquaintance Don knew the location of every abseil point and this enabled us to bypass the complete section of the climb which includes the Hinterstoisser Traverse and the Chimney leading up to the Swallow's Nest. To do this, you merely rappel directly downwards from the last abseil point above the Swallow's Nest and so reach a key piton at the top of the wall overlooking the start of the Hinterstoisser Traverse. From here a straightforward rappel of 140 feet goes vertically down the wall to the large ledge at the start of the traverse. If Hinterstoisser had realized that, he would probably not now have a traverse named after him, and the Eigerwand would not enjoy one half its present notoriety. The idea of "a Point of No Return" always captures the imagination, and until very recent times, it was still the fashion to abandon a fixed rope at the Hinterstoisser in order to safeguard a possible retreat.

The unrelenting bombardment, which had kept us hopping from one abseil to the next like demented fleas, began to slacken off as we came into the lee of the "Rote Fluh." The weather had obviously broken down completely and it was raining heavily. We followed separate ways down the easy lower section of the Face, sending down volleys of loose scree in front of us. Every now and again we heard strange noises, like a series of muffled yelps, but since we appeared to have the mountain to ourselves, this did not provoke comment. Whillans had just disappeared round a nearby corner when I heard a loud ejaculation.

"God Almighty," he said (or words to that effect) "Japs! Come and see for yourself!"

Sure enough, there they were. Two identical little men in identical climbing uniforms, sitting side by side underneath an overhang. They had been crouching there for an hour, waiting for the bombardment to slacken. I estimated that we must have scored several near misses.

"You—Japs?" grunted Don. It seemed an unnecessary question.

"Yes, yes," they grinned happily, displaying a full set of teeth. "We are Japanese."

"Going—up," queried Whillans. He pointed meaningfully at the grey holocaust sweeping down from the White Spider.

"Yes, yes," they chorused in unison. "Up. Always upwards. First Japanese Ascent."

"You-may-be-going-up-Mate," said Whillans, giving every syllable unnecessary emphasis, "but-a-lot-'igher-than-you-think!"

They did not know what to make of this, so they wrung his hand several times, and thanked him profusely for the advice.

"'Appy little pair!" said Don. "I don't imagine we'll ever see them again."

He was mistaken. They came back seven days later after several feet of new snow had fallen. They had survived a full-scale Eiger blizzard and had reached our highest point on the second ice field. If they did not receive a medal for valor they had certainly earned one. They were the forerunners of the climbing elite of Japan, whose members now climb Mount Everest for the purpose of skiing back down again.

We got back to the Alpiglen in time for late lunch. The telescope stood forlorn and deserted in the rain. The Eiger had retired into its misty oblivion, as Don Whillans retired to his favorite corner seat by the window.

"READY FOR THE SCRAP HEAP?"

FROM
My Life
BY ANDERL HECKMAIR

ANDERL HECKMAIR WILL FOREVER BE KNOWN AS THE MAN WHO first climbed the North Face of the Eiger, in the Bernese Oberland, even though he did it in the company of three other men. The July 1938 climb remains a milestone in mountaineering: Heckmair, using newfangled twelve-point crampons and climbing with Ludwig Vorg, soon overtook another party of two climbers, Austrians Heinrich Harrer and Fritz Kasparek, already on the famous face. The four climbers joined forces, but there is no doubt that through the unknown upper-route difficulties—the Traverse of the Gods, the ice field known as the White Spider, and the storied Exit Cracks—it was Heckmair's strength, determination, and superb routefinding that led the party out of certain death and into international acclaim.

Reinhold Messner called the climb one of the greatest ever, even a work of art. "It is," Messner said, "an expression of the serious and playful self-realization of four mountaineers who, trusting the strongest in the team, in fair partnership, managed a unique achievement."

Heckmair's success came despite a difficult childhood. He was sickly, poor, and orphaned at an early age, but a schoolboy trip to Switzerland exposed him to the joys of climbing. Soon he was spending all the time he could find in the Alps, the Dolomites, and other climbing areas near his Bavarian home. Even before he became famous as the conqueror of the Eiger, Heckmair had an impressive resume in the Alps, with bold attempts on the Grandes Jorasses North Face and an elegant new route on the Grands Charmoz to his credit.

An impecunious young climber, Heckmair's persistent lack of funds meant that he was forced to guide clients or teach skiing in order to finance his time in the mountains. Guiding in particular was a job he found distasteful, and one he sometimes executed with remarkable irresponsibility, abandoning a party of Danes on an Alpine glacier, for instance, or sandbagging one of his novice clients into trying a route that was difficult even for Heckmair.

The following excerpt from Heckmair's biography describes the climbing seasons leading up to his first ascent of the Eiger Nordwand in 1938. A series of personal misfortunes, including bad weather, missed connections, and a broken foot, had stymied his climbing plans. The thirty-year-old Heckmair had begun to fear that his career as a climber might be over. Feeling depressed by his bad luck, he eventually agreed to be hired out by a "lady schoolteacher" for some guiding in the Dolomites.

Heckmair's tale of how he accidentally ended up climbing the North Face of the Cima Grande three years before his Eiger triumph reveals a funny and mischievous side to a climber better known for his determination and strength under grim conditions. "Ready for the Scrap Heap?" is in *Anderl Heckmair: My Life*, on pages 62–67.

I had had enough of being a tourist guide. I also had some money. I could go back to the mountains again. I had a friend in Munich, Martl Maier his name was, who was one of the best climbers and whom I knew to be keen on the Grandes Jorasses. I told him about my plans and he was very taken with them. We agreed on the essentials and went our separate ways for a while.

In the meantime I had been given a guiding job in the Dolomites. Before leaving I went back to Munich to settle further details with Martl, but he was nowhere to be found. I was merely informed that he had gone traveling. Where and with whom, nobody knew. Deeply disappointed, I slouched off through the streets of Munich. Turning a corner I bumped into another climbing friend, Ludwig Steinauer.

"Weren't you interested in the Grandes Jorasses too?" I asked.

"With you I'd go any time. When are we off?"

"First I have to go to the Dolomites, but I'll be at the Leschaux hut on the third of August. I'll need an ax, crampons, and this and that."

"Agreed. I'll bring all the gear with me."

⟩   ⟩   ⟩

I headed off to the Dolomites in a happy mood, completed my guiding assignment and reached Courmayeur on August 1. Next day I wanted to walk up to the Torino Hut and down the Mer de Glace to the Leschaux hut, but did not feel too happy about crossing the glacier on my own. The idea of engaging a guide never entered my head. As I wandered around Courmayeur, I noticed a tent on the outskirts of town; perhaps it might be climbers also wanting to go over to Chamonix. They turned out not to be climbers but some young Danes who did indeed wish to visit Chamonix. "Then you're in luck. I'm a mountain guide and I'll take you over Mont Blanc," I announced. They had intended to do the modest walk over the Little St. Bernard Pass. At 6 A.M. they stood ready to receive their marching orders, and by noon we had reached the Torino hut. After a brief rest we were able to continue; despite their heavy packs they had really gone well. I did not allow the fact that they were only wearing shorts and thoroughly unsuitable footwear to bother me too much. Before setting foot on the glacier I roped them up and gave them the necessary instructions. We had not gone 500 meters before the one in front fell into a crevasse. Before long we had him out, looking rather pale. "Don't worry about it," I reassured them. "That kind of thing happens on glaciers all the time. That's why you're tied on." Secretly I was relieved to be tied on too. Despite several more little excursions into crevasses, I was able to see them safely on toward the Requin hut.

Another group came toward us, with a lone figure walking about 100 meters away from them. As they drew nearer I recognized Martl. We hugged each other with howls of joy.

"Why didn't you leave word for me in Munich?" I asked.

"But I did leave you a letter!"

"Well, I never got it, so I made an appointment to meet Steinauer at the Leschaux hut. He'll be there today or tomorrow with all my gear. There's nothing we can do about it. We'll just have to climb as a rope of three."

Martl was not exactly over-enthusiastic about the idea, but I tied him on close in front of me and let the Danes go ahead without paying much attention while we chatted. Presently we became aware that we had wandered into a frightful maze of crevasses. There was nothing for it but to abseil into a wide crevasse and clamber up the other side, which was more or less climbable.

The poor Danes, who were completely unaccustomed to such maneuvers, were completely at the end of their tether by the time we reached the Requin hut. From here on there was a path to Montenvers, so we left them there to spend the night and hurried on toward the Leschaux hut, where Steinauer was indeed waiting. The greeting between him and Martl was somewhat frosty, but he too had to accept the situation as it was.

First off, we had to spend a couple of days preparing for the climb. The

Leschaux hut was in the process of being renovated, so we moved house to a convenient shelterstone some 100 meters above. Then competition appeared on the scene in the form of two other Munich climbers, Peters and Harringer, who pitched a tent 100 meters below the hut on a slab of rock. Each party kept a close eye on the other. I made an attempt to establish diplomatic relations by undiplomatically suggesting to Peters that they should wait and see how we got on. Peters commented that he had his own ideas as to what he should do, and I withdrew in a huff. In any case the weather was so bad that with the best will in the world it was impossible to try anything at all. One day it got so unpleasant that the workmen invited us to leave our cave and join them in the hut. We accepted gladly, and the workmen indicated that we should also fetch our friends from the tent. I scrambled down and called out: "Don't be so stubborn. The workmen are letting us use the hut. Come on up, all your gear is floating away." Harringer responded, but not so Peters, who remained sulking in the tent. For this breach of good manners we begged the pardon of the kindly French workers. They believed that we must have had an almighty quarrel.

The storm raged around the hut as it only can in the mountains. We were happy to have a dry corner and could not understand Peters's attitude. Suddenly flames flared up below the hut as Peters's tent caught fire. His petrol stove had exploded. We ran down and helped him to stamp out the blaze.

"Now you'll come up and join us, surely?"

"Why on earth? I can sleep in the bushes. I still have a sleeping bag, and I'm not bothered about the wet."

I doubted his sanity, but he steadfastly held out and remained in excellent humor even though the bad weather continued for several days.

I had other duties to attend to, and as it would take a good week or ten days for conditions on the face to get back to normal I suggested to my friends that they should take a look at it without me. They were not exactly enthusiastic, but had to admit that my arguments were logical.

Once I had departed, Steinauer and Maier grabbed the first available opportunity to attack the face, so that Peters and Harringer should not get in before them. They bivouacked on the top of the first buttress to the right of the central gully. During the night Martl got hungry and tucked into the provisions; his actions caused a dreadful bout of cursing from Ludwig in the morning. They quarreled; there could be no question of going on and they came back down. Steinauer left, but Martl remained in the hope of joining forces with Peters and Harringer. Peters had no intention of climbing as a threesome, so he left Martl where he was and set off up the face with Harringer. Conditions were still bad, and on the third day they decided to turn back. As they were preparing their bivouac, Harringer, who was unbelayed, slipped and fell wordlessly to his death, taking with him the rucksack containing the bivouac equipment.

Peters spent a terrible night, and the next day continued to abseil down with the remaining length of rope. As time went on he became snowblind. In this state he reached the big ice slope, where he was observed by climbers at the Leschaux hut who hurried to his rescue, among them Martl Maier. Only now was Peters willing to join forces with Maier and took him on his now-vacant pillion back to Munich. In the summer of 1935 they succeeded in making the first ascent of the North Face of the Grandes Jorasses together.

That year I was continually dogged by bad luck. I nurtured no grudge over Maier and Peters teaming up together; all that mattered to me was to find a new climbing partner and to get in ahead of the competition. The companion was soon found in the person of Hans Lucke from Kufstein, a climber with whom I had already done many climbs in the Kaisergebirge and whose unshakable good humor made him always ready for any adventure. We had plenty of time ahead of us to make our preparations and organize our finances. I earned my money in Switzerland working as a ski instructor for the travel agency where I had played at being a tourist guide. Every mark, every franc I earned I saved, as we could not expect to receive any kind of grant. I had connections with several very wealthy people, but was unwilling to saddle them with feelings of moral responsibility in the event that it all went wrong.

It was mid-June, still quite early in the season, when we left for Courmayeur, this time by train. On the way up to the Torino hut we ran into snow even below the level of the Pavilion de Mon Fréty. It was so slushy that we decided to bivouac there. In the morning, however, there was breakable crust over the slush, which was even worse, so we waited for another day. To cap it all, the weather turned bad too. "You know what?" I said. "We're three or four weeks too early. Let's go down and catch a train to Portofino. I know some people who have a little house there. We can stay there until conditions improve." Hans was all for it, so we headed off to Genoa and Portofino, where our skis, ice axes, and nailed boots excited no little attention.

We were welcomed with open arms. Our hosts believed that they could talk us out of our foolhardy project, but we were happy to let them spoil us and passed three marvelous weeks swimming, walking, and even climbing, as we found some excellent rocks in hidden bays where we could train in complete privacy.

We had now fixed the day of our return to the Mont Blanc range, and out of sheer high spirits we dashed down to our training crags the afternoon before we were due to leave. That was when it happened. I jumped off and broke my foot. It was a bitter blow. Instead of Courmayeur it was back to Munich after ten days with my leg in a pot. I had written to a friend in Munich to tell him of my misfortune. He met me at the station with a slightly anxious smile on his face and a newspaper under his arm bearing the headline: "Grandes Jorasses North Face conquered by Peters and Maier." So they had done it! My friend tried to comfort me. "Don't let it get you down," he said. "Who knows, your bad luck may have been a blessing in disguise. In any case, you'll be thirty soon. It's time to join the ranks of the has-beens. Find yourself a steady job and give up all this frantic competition." His blunt words were well meant, but they hit me hard.

I had to spend the next few weeks in the hospital until my foot was all right again. I was not very talkative but lay all day in tortured self-examination, staring at the ceiling. Was I a failure? Was my place really with the has-beens? Well, if so, there was nothing I could do about it. I would just go on being a mountain guide, living in the mountains and doing the climbs I enjoyed, and leave off harassing myself with ambitious projects. As time wore on I became bright and cheerful again and not only my broken leg healed but my spiritual wounds too, of which the good doctor knew nothing.

Hardly had I been discharged from the hospital than I was engaged by a lady schoolteacher to do some guiding in the Dolomites. On our way up to the Lavaredo hut we encountered a couple of friends from Nuremberg, beaming with joy at having done the fifteenth ascent of the north face of the Cima

Grande. Originally climbed by Comici, in those days it was reckoned to be the hardest route around. Instantly I began to feel twinges of that very ambition which I had so solemnly renounced while in hospital. Secretly, I began to size up my schoolteacher, wondering whether I could talk her into trying the face. But no, it would have been too insane. I put away the thought and steeled my will to be a staunch, honest guide who would never encourage a client to attempt anything beyond his or her ability.

The hut was not too busy, and I noticed a lanky, pleasant looking young man wolfing down a triple-sized evening meal with evident relish. Drifting over in his direction, I opened with the question: "Did it taste good?" He glanced at me in surprise and simply nodded. I tried another tack. "Did you get hungry doing a hard route?" Now at last he deigned to answer: "My friends have left. I had another day's holiday left and was just using up the last of my lire." As soon as he spoke I detected his Nuremberg accent. He had been with my friends and was rather put out at missing out on the north face. "Then we could go and do it together," I exclaimed. He accepted with delight, and my teacher readily agreed to a day or two's rest.

I was brimming with enthusiasm and could hardly wait for the next day. But the next morning the rain was drumming on the roof of our attic dormitory. Paradoxical as it may sound, mountain climbers in general like their comforts and are often even lazy, qualities to which I am by no means immune. If bad weather thwarted my plans to climb, I could always sleep through the whole day with pleasure and a clear conscience. On this occasion, however, I was so vexed that I could not sleep another wink. Toward seven o'clock the rain eased, and an hour later nothing worse than cold, damp clouds drifted around the mountains.

My companion, who went by the name of Theo Erpenbeck—we had finally got around to introducing ourselves—had already packed his sack to go down to the valley, remarking: "You can't do a climb like that in this kind of weather, and anyway it's much too late." I begged him just to walk up to the foot of the face and do the first two or three pitches with me, after which I would feel satisfied and we could abseil off. Thus it was that at 9:30 A.M. we stood at the start of a climb that had never been done without a bivouac. As we tied on to the rope above the first easy rocks I reassured him that I would just do two or three pitches, then I got to grips with it. There was no need for me to place any pitons; there were far too many already for my taste. I wasted no time trying to take any of them out, but simply did not bother to clip in to all of them. In any case, I did not have enough carabiners. After three pitches I had no thoughts of turning back. Theo had no say in the matter; no sooner had he reached the stance than I whipped off the belay and climbed on.

Only once, after climbing at least fifteen meters without seeing any pitons, did I feel that something might be amiss. At this point I noticed a whole row of pegs running up a slightly overhanging corner about five meters off to one side. Without any protection at all the traverse across to the corner was far from easy, but if I had hammered any in my companion would also have been obliged to deviate from the proper line. As I reached the stance and shouted to him to come on, I heard a reproachful voice saying: "Have you given up clipping in at all now?"

Shortly before the gully in the upper part of the face there was a roof about half a meter across. I had heard that at this point others had used a sling for aid. As I had no slings I leaned out backwards in desperation and found a fantastic hold, big enough to get both hands on while I leaned back in tension from the rope. On the command "slack" my legs swung clear of the rock. It was lucky that I had been a good gymnast in my youth. A quick pull up and a mantelshelf and I was up. In the gully above I would gladly have taken off the rope, but as poor Theo's arms had no more feeling left in them that would not have been right at all. The real difficulties were over now, and there was no more talk of turning back. By three o'clock in the afternoon we were sitting on the summit. Theo pulled a flask of red-wine tea out of his sack that he had only intended to take up as far as the foot of the face. I have hardly ever tasted anything quite so delicious.

By now we were firing on all four cylinders, and like mad dogs we tore back down to the hut, where we were greeted with the question: "Where did you turn back?" Once again I was stared at with patent suspicion as I replied: "We've climbed the whole face, and we can't help it if we're back already." My peace of mind was restored; I knew now that I had no need to fear the scrap heap along with the rest of the old has-beens, and patiently led my schoolmistress up all the routes she wished to do. Theo left for home the next day, and I first saw him again several decades later, after he had recovered from a serious illness. He wanted nothing more to do with climbs of such severity. I, on the other hand, could not get enough of them.

One face above all still remained unconquered and now that I had got back my self-confidence, I concentrated all my thoughts and all my will on the North Face of the Eiger.

"BAD DAY AT PRACTICE ROCK"

FROM
*Moments of Doubt and Other Mountaineering Writings of
David Roberts*
BY DAVID ROBERTS

ROYAL ROBBINS, THE PIONEERING YOSEMITE BIG-WALL CLIMBER, once wrote of David Roberts's skill as a writer: "He commands our respect apart from his climbing accomplishments."

Roberts has become one of America's most prolific climbing writers, but his climbing credentials are what gave him credibility with what can be a skeptical audience. Achievements such as his 1965 ascent of Mount Huntington in Alaska proved Roberts had a passion for difficult climbs, and the skill to pull them off.

Roberts's Huntington experience provided him with something else: the impetus to begin writing. The result was *Mountain of My Fear*, and since the publication of that book, Roberts has gained a following in the world of nonfiction journalism, whether he is writing about the Anasazi culture, profiling a well-known climber, such as John Roskelley, or examining an historic expedition, like the 1950 French climb of Annapurna. To date, Roberts has written more than a dozen volumes.

"Bad Day at Practice Rock" is another matter. It's a humorous look into an arcane microcosm within the much larger universe of climbing, the home turf of committed regulars not unlike a close-knit band of surfers whose hostility to outsiders is a way of proclaiming ownership of the beach. This examination of a distilled essence of climber culture is perhaps a little dated now in terms of shoes, cultural references, and level of difficulty, but it remains sharply insightful in regard to human behavior.

The climbing rock in question has long been supplanted in Seattle by other artificial climbing venues—the city was a pioneering place for indoor climbing gyms. But "the rock" still has its devotees and its distinct microculture. The scene, which Roberts compares to that of a local basketball court in Manhattan's Harlem neighborhood, is still true to form: play here, and your moves are going to be judged harshly by the locals, even if the put-down is never overt. It's a psych-out zone, big time, and the author eloquently feels the pain.

Written in 1985, "Bad Day at Practice Rock" first appeared in *Ultrasport* magazine, July/August 1985, and is in *Moments of Doubt*, on pages 77–80.

[Author's note: It felt weirdly conspicuous to be jotting notes on a piece of paper while I hung out at the Seattle Practice Rock, and indeed, one athlete, having asked me what I was doing, delivered a hearty obscenity my direction when I gave him a straight answer. Despite the new faddishness of our sport, climbers still like to think of themselves as purists.]

was in Seattle visiting an old climbing friend, with whom in more tigerish days I had assaulted distant precipices. "Want to go bouldering?" he asked me. It was a complicated question. Bouldering used to be fun—the idle base camp play of mountaineers waiting for the weather to turn good up high. With your boots half-tied, you ambled over to some glacial erratic deposited on the meadow by the last ice age, fondled the rock, and improvised routes upon it. "Try this one," you said, and actually summoned up magnanimous pleasure if your buddy got up it as well.

The bouldering scene today remains a playground of sorts. My friend's invitation could be likened to that of a New York City basketball enthusiast who says, "Want to go shoot some hoops? I know a court up around 110th Street where there's usually a game."

With a glum sense of duty, I agreed to go bouldering. The action in Seattle centers around an outcrop euphemistically named the University of Washington Practice Rock. It is an artificial cliff made mostly of cement, and I was curious to see it. We drove over to the campus, paid fifty cents to park, and strolled over to the Rock, which stands just behind the much larger massif of the football stadium where the Washington Huskies do battle.

The Practice Rock amounts to seven Stonehenge-like slabs set on end. For holds, pieces of real stone have been cooked into the concrete, like raisins in a pudding. The slabs tower as high as thirty feet off the "deck," and a thoughtful architect has added metal loops that protrude from its top edges, to which ropes may be attached for safe top-rope belays. My comrade informed me, however, that you would be sneered off the Rock if you brought a rope— even though it was evident that you would cream yourself if you fell the wrong way off the wrong corner of the edifice.

A coterie of regulars was at work, identifiable by their snazzy shoes, their chalk bags, and their office-clerk air as they trudged from one problem to the next. Despite their blasé manner, these veterans seemed to average about eighteen years of age. They had the politely punk look of today's lost generation, the youths who line up the night before for Circle Jerks concerts, eschew beer, and are sixty-odd percent in favor of Reagan.

The shoes are Spanish Fires (pronounced "Fee-rays") and Calmas, or Italian Skywalkers, with soles so sticky they have revolutionized rock climbing. Chalk is a conceit borrowed from gymnasts: each athlete hangs his bright-colored bag like a sixshooter from his waist loop, with a hold-open device facilitating a quick draw from the most precarious positions. Chalk has become so vital to the sport that entrepreneurs peddle it like marijuana at campgrounds. My friend had once seen John Bachar, the brilliant solo climber, being offered a sample at Joshua Tree National Monument in California. Bachar dipped a hand, rubbed his fingertips together, and said, "You call this chalk? This stuff is shit."

I ventured timidly into the playing area and made a few tentative moves, trying to act as if I were just doing stretching exercises. At once my premonition was confirmed: everything on the Rock was hard. The structure had been built in 1975 with the intention that many of the "lines" would be about 5.4 in difficulty, but somebody goofed. There is, in fact, a fifty-six-page guidebook to the Practice Rock, and almost every route listed in it is 5.10 or harder. The laconic flavor of the route names gives a clue to the ambiance of the place: "Iron Cross Traverse," "Left Cement Problem," "The Gong Show," "Dan's Heel Hook," "Smoot's Reach" (Smoot being the author of the guide), "No-Rocks Face."

As desperate as even the more obvious boulder problems seemed to me, they were beneath the attention of the regulars. If you climb at one place for long, you get the sequences of moves down pat, or "wired," in the lingo of the sport. To spice up their play, the eighteen-year-old perfectionists had made ground rules that created tougher challenges. They declared the reassuringly protruding stones out of bounds (whence "No-Rocks Face"), instead pinching and wedging on irregularities of cement alone. They had no-hands problems. They insisted on fifteen different varieties of hand jams in a fifteen-foot crack. As I watched, several diehards started a route not by standing at the base of it, but by sitting in a yoga position on the ground, just to eke a few more feet of difficulty out of it.

My companion was in good shape, had been climbing on the north face of the Eiger only months before, and was still in the prime of manhood, but he couldn't touch the hardest problems which the crewcut teenagers were flashing through. I watched as a regular coached him on a one-rock problem: "Smear with your left," his advisor coaxed, "lay with the right, and throw to the block." I could decipher that injunction, but it soon became clear to me that along with the expertise of bouldering has evolved a whole argot to narrate it. If one youngster said to another, "Yeah, I threw a 'mo to what looked like a bomber jug and it was a rude hit—rounded and way greasy," what he meant to convey was something like the following: "At that point I made a dynamic move—i.e. a controlled lunge—toward what looked from below like a large, solid handhold, only to find when I grasped it that its edges were rounded and it was slippery from other people's sweat. That was quite a shock, let me tell you."

It was a lovely, brisk afternoon in Seattle, and I was feeling miserable. The trouble with bouldering is that the put-down is never overt. No one really pays much attention to what you do, but if you are a climber, simply to be awash in such a sea of invidious comparison is, as the boys say, a rude hit. For a climber of my generation, who grew up believing that bouldering was mere casual training for the real thing—big-range mountaineering, of course—a visit to the University of Washington Practice Rock is like one of those nightmares in which you have gone back to your first grade classroom but forgotten to put on any pants.

I was able to take faint comfort from watching the subtle mind games the hard core were playing with each other. There was a lot of gentle sandbagging going on—the offhand recommendation as a "nice little problem" of some piece of terrifying muscular arcana which had probably cost the recommender sleepless nights to solve. Chalk and Fires may be *de rigueur* for the well-dressed boulderer of today, but one hotshot was upstaging everybody by solving the hardest problems barefoot and with clean hands. He had his nonchalance wired, as well as the moves, for he seemed to imply that he had just happened to drop by without his usual paraphernalia and thought he'd give a few of the routes a go all the same.

Then, just as I was ready to go home, I saw a girl of ten, apparently touring the campus with her mother and father, break free of them and come running over to the Rock. She shouted back, "Just a sec, OK?" The point of the playground was instantly obvious to her. In her scuffed sneakers she cavorted at the bottom of a route. She got about two feet up, fell off, and squealed with delight. The hard young men gazed on in approbation. She was ready to try another move, but her parents scolded her back to responsibility, and she reluctantly left. My whole day brightened: I had seen bouldering innocence, and could almost remember what it felt like.

"CHALK"

FROM
Stone Palaces
BY GEOF CHILDS

THE WRITING OF GEOF CHILDS TENDS TOWARD HUMOR OF THE understated variety, as he takes the longer view on how we might live and where climbing might fit in. But "Chalk" is something else again, an overtly funny examination both of how controversies come and go (remember when reaching into a chalk bag was considered akin to cheating?), and of his own personal epiphany in the use of magnesium carbonate.

Childs knows what he's talking about. He lives in one of the most remote corners of the Lower 48, and has worked as a professional mountain guide for more than a quarter century. And while the North Cascades are where he lives and works, he's been farther afield to take on what some people might consider bigger challenges, such as the west face of Makalu. More than a hundred first ascents on rock and ice in his native Cascades, along with a few decades of traveling around the world, skiing and snowboarding, have given Childs a wide perspective and strong sense of irony.

"I wrote 'Chalk' in the late '70s," Childs remembered, "just about the time chalk had ceased being an issue anymore. It must be hard for climbers now to imagine the level of controversy involving its use back then."

This story takes place in the mid-1970s, a time of EBs and heavily decorated chalk bags, and it begins on the climbing crags of Maine. Sam Streibert, the man who freed the VMC route on Cannon Cliff, and Childs head out for a climb on an obscure crag known as South Bubbles. Childs's goal is a first ascent of some moment, but he gets even more than he bargained for when he reaches for the chalk.

"Chalk" can be found in *Stone Palaces*, on pages 20–25.

We have only one person to blame, and that's each other.

—Larry Beck, New York Rangers
(on the reason for a fight)

There are few things that are harder to sympathize with than the moral broodings of a generation past. Chlorinated water and trade unionism, for example, hardly strike us as major issues any more. But there was a time when people were happily willing to shoot holes in each other over the right to whiter teeth and fair wages. In climbing, the parallels are many. Gymnastic chalk and the machine driven bolt are two.

It was not that long ago that the bolts that have now become a feature at almost every crag in North America were a source of widespread controversy. Reputations were ruined and routes vandalized by zealots on both sides of the issue. So fresh are the wounds left by bolting that it is easy to forget there was a time when chalk was a topic of almost equal gravity and concern.

I was living on Mount Desert Island, Maine, the first time I ever used chalk, and I remember the circumstances well. The surf-washed cliffs and roadside crags of Acadia National Park, at the island's center, were largely unknown outside of Maine in those days, a circumstance that left its sea stacks, splitter cracks, and untraveled faces largely in the hands of us locals. We knew this happy idyll could not last forever, and by the summer of 1975 the pressure from outsiders was already beginning to mount. Climbers from Boston, North Conway, and Connecticut were showing up in greater numbers than ever. Determined to grab as many lines for myself as possible, I was enjoying a particularly energetic season when the weather went bad. Bad as in hot. And hot in the way that only coastal New England can be hot. Week after week with temperatures in the high nineties, the sky cloudless, and the zephyrs that dragged themselves in off the North Atlantic so sodden with humidity that with every move you made it felt as if you were lifting the whole weight of the sky. Our bodies shone with sweat, our feet baked through the black soles of our EBs, and lichen fell from the walls like spindrift. It was enough to keep even the least sensible at home, but my ambitions drove me to climb. A chemistry of vanity and desire that set me to thinking about chalk.

I had first witnessed the use of magnesium carbonate in Boulder, Colorado. Sitting on the stairs at a sunken fire escape on the campus of CU called the "Pit," I had watched in awe as locals scampered the dank sandstone walls belayed by nothing but an occasional dip into the handsomely embroidered bags carried at their waists. Though I knew the practice to be controversial, I was struck by its practicality. Clearly, chalk offered a significant advantage in dealing with the humidity of the human hand—exactly the characteristic I had in mind when I entered a local drug store and asked if they had any. The druggist eyed me quizzically and then found a single block on the bottom of a long-forgotten shelf. He charged me 25 cents for it and told me that, to the best of his knowledge, it was a laxative for babies.

Back in my apartment I unwrapped the block and examined it closely. Its appearance was inoffensive, deceptive, clean. I ran my hand over the surface of the cube and rubbed my fingertips together. The sudden stickiness of my grip was both stunning and unsettling. Surely, I thought to myself, no one who is less than a 5.11 leader has any justification for using this magical substance. But then, massaging the block and placing my hand against the wall, I quivered at the thought of clinging upside down to a wall of tenuous friction. It was with this image in mind that I replaced the block in its bag and shoved it to the far corner of a drawer.

Less than a week later Steve Shea, an Aspen climber, and I were trying to free a short, poorly protected aid route when he pulled a chalk bag out of his pocket, dipped, and then danced where I later struggled hopelessly to follow. Returning home I immediately transferred the chalk from the back of my drawer to the bottom of a small stuff sack. Then, for practice, I clipped the string through the snap on the front of my shorts and, stemming between the baseboards in one corner of the living room, carefully bouldered to the bathroom and back stopping every few feet to dip my fingers into the bag. The rush of power that coursed through my body obliterated any moral concerns. In a flash of light I suddenly realized that all that had ever stood between me and raising my standard was chalk! Stepping down, I placed the stuff sack with my climbing gear, opened a can of beer, and solemnly vowed never to use it on anything less than 5.10 . . . or maybe hard 5.9—unless, of course, I was really, really scared or feeling kind of off-form or something like that, in which case I could probably use it down to, oh, say 5.6 or something.

›   ›   ›

Without a doubt the transcendent event in Eastern rock climbing that summer had been Sam Streibert's and Bob Anderson's freeing of the VMC route on Cannon Cliff. Having done the route on aid, this achievement struck me as more impressive than days two, four, and five of Creation and, frankly, not that far behind the advent of fire. So when the phone rang and I heard Sam on the other end of the line asking if I wanted to go climbing, it was as if divine convergence had settled any qualms I might have had about the use of chalk. I knew immediately what route we should do: an obscure corner hung well up on the side of a cliff called the South Bubbles. I told Sam about the route and explained to him that it didn't look that hard—maybe 5.9 or easy 5.10. I also told him that it got sun in the late afternoon and that we might find it a little "sweaty." Sam immediately agreed to an attempt, and we made plans to meet the next day.

As I hung up the phone my mind did cartwheels. A vision of Sam—trembling at his belay stance, hands held together in prayer as I pulled through the crux—formed in my imagination. The climb was a setup, of course. It would be scorching hot up there and Sam, I knew, did not use chalk. Slave to the myths and rituals of another generation, he wouldn't have a chance. It was with more than a certain sadness that I tucked the bag inside the top flap of my pack and opened another bottle of beer.

The next day, as Sam uncoiled the rope, I snapped my chalk bag into place above the zipper of my climbing shorts. Then, seizing the host's initiative, I shoved the sack in my front pocket and took the lead, quickly scrambling the initial problems with a bulge in my trousers that must have looked like I was wearing a codpiece.

While I do not recall the pitch in much detail anymore, I do remember that I rapidly reached a point where an awkward traverse was required to attain the crux corner. I hesitated before the traverse, placed a shaky wire at waist level, and then stemmed out on a pair of uninspiring knobs. Above and just out of reach was a fracture I felt certain would provide better holds and solid gear. Shifting my feet and searching for something to get my hands on I came to the realization that, as in all climbing stories, I had reached the point where to proceed meant there would be no option of retreat.

Carefully adjusting my weight, I began to explore the smear I'd have to stand on in order to launch myself toward the crack. After several moments of moving back and forth I at last felt confidence enough in these holds to release a hand. As I reached down and pulled the stuff sack out of my pocket, I quickly stole a glance at Sam. Thank God, he was looking at the view. Then, as rehearsed, I opened the bag, fluttered my fingers inside its depths, and withdrew them. I switched hands and whitened the other. The increased tackiness of my grip was subtle—but satisfying. By this time, however, the hand I had originally dunked was utterly pumped and in need of a second trip to the chalk bag.

What followed was a drama of diminishing returns. Each time I chalked one hand the other would become increasingly fatigued and in need of re-chalking. This was obviously not a situation that could go on indefinitely. As my level of exhaustion increased so did my level of alarm. Now, instead of gently massaging the block, I was thrashing at it, whipping my hand back and forth with a vigor that sent small puffs of carbonate into the air and filled my nostrils with dust. Sweat dripped into my eyes. My feet began to tremble. Sensing that it was clearly time to move on, I thrust my hand back into the bag, shook it energetically, and had just begun to withdraw it when I felt the gentle, indescribably awful pressure of the stuff sack closing around my wrist.

Good Lord!

Trapped! I looked down in horror. The throat of that sphinctered sack had clasped my hand, sheathing it completely in nylon and leaving me feeling very much like that portion of the human anatomy that it most resembled. Using my hips to hide my struggles from Sam I immediately began pulling the sack up and down against my swami harness. I can only imagine what he must have thought I was doing! Yet the thing still refused to budge. With a growing sense of anxiety I began pawing more aggressively at the bag, flinging my hand left and right, yanking and torquing my wrist, spinning my arm in circles. None of which seemed to help in the least. Finally resorting to brute force, I jerked back on the bag sharply. There was a muted "pop" and my hand came away free though still shrouded in the upturned chalk bag. Unfortunately, in liberating my hand I had snapped the button off my shorts which now, unrestrained, began a southward journey in the direction of my ankles, A long leader fall and the possibility of death suddenly paled at the thought of being found that way! Quickly, I threw my knees apart and squatted—a maneuver that stopped my shorts from falling any farther but left me in the posture of a sumo wrestler purging himself of raw fish.

Frankly, I didn't care. Dignity was no longer of any concern to me. Whatever small flame of self-esteem still burned in my breast was rapidly suffocating in the billowing smog of magnesium carbonate that formed around me as I began frantically whipping my arm back and forth in an attempt to throw off the bag. From below, I must have appeared like the prophet Elijah ascending through a layer of strato-cumuli into heaven. In fact, so impressive was this display that several cars pulled over to the side of the road and I could hear people shouting, "Up there! Look up there!" Blinded and choking, I decided to risk one final gambit. Reinserting my hand into the pocket of my shorts, and distending my stomach, I trapped the sack between gut and thigh, and then, with a loud scream, yanked backward.

The applause and exclamations that came from the road following this maneuver were recounted to me later by Sam. So great was the cloud of particulates that erupted from the sack, he explained, that the entire lower portion of the cliff was thrown into shadow. Seventy feet above him, the sight of my now naked fingers appearing through the haze very nearly brought me to tears. Despite the fact that chalk now so thoroughly covered the rock that I probably could have lain down without sliding off, I elected to retreat. Reversing my moves to the corner looked hard enough; continuing upward while holding my shorts with one hand struck me as unfeasible. Thus, it was as a thoroughly broken man that I worked my way back across the slab and then down through the intermediate moves. Sam, watching all this from his belay stance, must have thought that I had aged fifty years during my spell at the sharp end. Like some geriatric Icarus, my face, hair, arms, legs, and clothing had all turned completely white. My voice, as I called to him for a tightrope, was tremulous and weak. Once I reached the bottom of the difficulties I found an alternative route to the top and hastily established a belay.

⁊   ⁊   ⁊

Sam came up the crack. He assured me that it was hard. At least 5.10, he said, though I knew he was being generous. And to tell the truth, I have never been back to confirm his rating. In fact, I left Maine shortly after our climb and now live on the opposite side of the continent. I have never seen Sam again; never been back to the South Bubble. I do still climb. And, like everybody else, I carry a chalk bag. It's different now, though. Nobody cares about a little white powder on the rock. Besides, winters are hard here and the muck that collects on our local classics is almost always gone by spring. The residue that clings to the overhangs goes undiscussed. With so much rock to climb it seems like a small thing. The same with bolts. People come into the sport with different expectations and different desires these days. So, slave to the myths and rituals of another generation, I hold my silence and my chalk bag tight.

"A LESSON IN FRENCH"

FROM
Summits and Secrets in *The Kurt Diemberger Omnibus*
BY KURT DIEMBERGER

KURT DIEMBERGER HAS ONE OF THE MOST EXTENSIVE BIG-MOUNTAIN climbing resumes of any living climber. He is the only person alive to have made the first ascent of two of the world's 8000-meter peaks: Broad Peak in 1957 (where he partnered with Hermann Buhl) and Dhaulagiri in 1960. The only other person to have accomplished that feat was Buhl himself, who perished by falling through a cornice as he and Diemberger descended the Karakoram peak, Chogolisa, together but unroped.

Diemberger had similar success in his native Europe, climbing not just the ultimate set piece, the Eiger, by its fearsome Nordwand, but putting up impressive new routes on the north faces of Lyskamm, the Matterhorn, and the Königspitze.

While the bulk of Diemberger's Himalayan activity took place before 1960, he returned to the big mountains of Asia in the 1970s. After a hiatus of almost ten years, Diemberger continued to attempt—and to succeed—on the world's highest peaks: Makalu, Everest, Gasherbrum, and K2, where Diemberger was to go on three separate expeditions and where he would experience his ultimate test. His active climbing on 8000-meter peaks ended in 1986, during a tragic season on K2, when his wife, Julie Tullis, and four other climbers perished when they were trapped by storm at Camp 4. Diemberger himself barely survived.

The story that follows, from Diemberger's first book, *Summits and Secrets*, is "A Lesson in French." It is a charming story far different from the high-mountain epics most readers associate with Diemberger. After his ascent of the Eiger Nordwand in 1958, Diemberger and his longtime climbing companion Wolfgang Stefan, were in need of a sunny holiday. So off to France they went, where "A Lesson in French" begins.

The story relates how a French climbing friend of Diemberger sends the Austrian climber and Stefan to a "favorite" climb in the Calanques, the famous limestone cliffs near Marseilles. The Germans, laden with ropes and pitons, are innocently looking for warm limestone to climb, and they are unaware of the mischief their French comrade perpetrates on them, routing them through a beach frequented by bathers who prefer to swim *au natural*. The story comes from *Summits and Secrets*, first published in 1971, and reprinted in *The Kurt Diemberger Omnibus*, pages 161–164.

What does an Alpine climber do when it is raining in Chamonix? He drives to Georges Livanos in Marseilles, or rather to his practice-climbing ground. Practice ground? An understatement for the Calanques; they are a climber's paradise. For these are limestone cliffs, some of them hundreds of feet high, rising sheer from the sea; and there are some you can only get to in a boat.

In addition to all this, there are Morgiou and Sormiou, two small fishing villages, with idyllic and alluring names; the only two places, locked in their dreams, on that twelve-mile-long coast—a hem of the land which is uncrossed by any road, and deeply indented by innumerable bays. Cactuses blossom there, and the hot sun beats down on a turquoise sky, perfectly mirrored in a seabed covered with red starfish, while shoals of glittering fishes flash in the crystal-clear water above it. There is no road to those two hamlets, only two potholed tracks, extremely difficult to find. This is a landscape in its original, primeval state.

Who would not wish to pitch his tent there? So—let us go.

⸙   ⸙   ⸙

We were at Livanos's home in Marseilles. We had actually tracked it down, and even found him there—a miracle, in view of our scanty acquaintance with the language, and a miracle in respect of the man himself, for he is never *at* home. This salesman, always on his travels, this specialist in Grade VI climbs, always on "extreme" faces, takes his wife with him when he goes. Yet here they were, both of them, lively, gay, relaxed, as if we had always known them. Very soon eggs and tomatoes were sizzling in the kitchen, while Livanos cracked jokes and talked about the Calanques.

Later, over a strong cup of espresso coffee, he asked us what exactly we were looking for. Sipping the aromatic beverage reflectively, I told him: a climb on firm limestone, with a view of the sea, in some deserted corner, and redolent of the warm south. Livanos grinned. "You German romantics!" he said and promptly drew a bold sketch, laughing happily as he did so, really enjoying himself. "It's Morgiou you want," he said. "The *Grande Chandèle,* our tall candle. That's the best climb round there; highly romantic. And don't forget to do it by its Marseilles ridge—it's much the best thing on the Chandèle." He hummed a few bars—could it have been the Marseillaise?—handed over the sketch, and off we went.

ⅉ   ⅉ   ⅉ

We had a job to find Morgiou, but we did, thanks to the sketch-map. One can rely on Livanos: from the Marseilles suburbs onwards, every road was correctly marked. We would have been completely lost without it, for I know about twenty words of French and Wolfi commands less. So we would have been hard put to it to find a recondite fishing harbor.

Morgiou, a bay with brightly colored boats in it, under the hot sun. We decided to have a look at the Chandèle straight away and find a place for our tent. The scenery was savage, a coast of precipitous cliffs, below which we made our way; there were shrubs and trees growing out of the rock, and the air was keen with the tang of the sea.

It grew more and more lonely; the sea was glittering and moving; there were cactus flowers—and nobody. Just a small fishing boat out there between the islands. In the middle of all this solitude, stood a notice board—how very odd! It said: *"Occupé—les naturalistes de Marseille."* It was all French to us, so we went on. Then we turned a corner. "Oh . . . !" we said, and fell into a temporary silence.

The accent was unmistakably French: stalking gazelle-legs, swinging hips, and a lot of other things besides . . . at a distance, but not so far away as all that.

"H'm!" I remarked and looked at Wolfi, whose mouth was still wide open, whose eyes shone with the light of a boyfriend in a television commercial. . . . "H'm," he said, clearing his throat, for he had taken note of my look and had immediately assumed his toughest north-face expression: "The 'Naturalistes' must be nudists, then . . . " Was it only my fancy, or had his Viennese accent suddenly acquired a French *timbre*? "Obviously," I replied and, unhurriedly, took stock of the impressive landscape. It was a marvelous bay.

"What do we do now?" asked Wolfi as the next contribution to our voluble dialogue; moved no doubt by his mountaineering conscience, and pointing to the rock-tower of the Chandèle, beyond the marvelous bay . . .

"A typical Calanques feature, on superb rock, with views far out to sea, a magnificent climb": thus Livanos's description before handing the route guide over to us. Oh, that Livanos . . . !

So much for the description. (This is where it ended.) Now what? Before our eyes, lovely, happy nudity and, by heaven, this was obviously France!

"It's the only way through," I said, summing up the situation, and trying to sound objective. To our left was a cliff, barring the way, with the breakers creaming at its feet—then a strip of sand, and sharp-edged, sloping slabs— the only sharp-edged objects to be seen in that direction . . .

That Livanos! I could just imagine him grinning over his "route description," specially designed for "Romantics."

"We must get across—but how?" growled Wolfi, wrinkling his forehead. We had never met a mountaineering difficulty of this kind before, and there is no mention of it in Paulcke's textbook on alpine dangers. But it has never been our habit to beat a retreat.

"There are only two ways about it," I philosophized. "To be noticeable or not to be noticeable. With, or without . . . "

Wolfi scratched his head. "Oh, well," he said, smiling contentedly. We decided for "with." The alternative would really have been too much bother, with all this climbing gear of ours. . . .

We were certainly noticed. The first looks cast upon us went through us like gimlets. We thought hard of the Grande Chandèle and continued on our way.

Now everybody was staring at us, the intruders, with many an inquisitive glance. Could we be members? Blushing, we looked, as indifferently as possible, away beyond slim shoulders, feeling the while appallingly "dressed-up." None the less we accomplished that exciting traverse. With stride unfaltering, our pitons clinking among French bosoms, our bodies hung about with ropes and climbing hammers among French buttocks, dazzled by graceful contours, our pulses racing, but undeterred, we made our way through that shapely panorama set in the graceful coastal scenery of the Calanques; two tough sinewy alpine figures, their thoughts fixed only on the summits, the cynosure of all eyes, like models on a catwalk . . . Suddenly, Wolfi began to hum a Parisian ditty, unmusically, out of tune. I too slowed my pace as I crossed the big, sharp-edged, sun-drenched limestone slabs, with their out-crop of sheer loveliness. I had to, of course, because of the sharp edges . . .

I wondered if mountaineers could qualify for membership. My pace grew still slower. After all, Paulcke's book on alpine dangers says: "Go slowly and you go well, and if you go well you go far."* And if you go well . . . ! Ye gods, I was fairly dazzled the next moment; if I could only address that gorgeous creature! I groaned—oh, these language difficulties!—and passed on in silence, brokenhearted. Passed on, left her . . . and if you go well—that ass Paulcke had no idea what "well" means. "Well" didn't mean the same thing, here and now. No, here, if you go slowly, all that happens—unfortunately—is that you still get on far too quickly. At this moment a deep sigh next to me announced the end of the "Song of Paris." If you go slowly, you get along too quickly and much too far; there was no doubt that we had irretrievably completed the traverse. I sat down, exhausted, on a boulder. Wolfi said not a word and passed the flask of peppermint tea across to me; then he took a swig himself. From the last slab of paradise the strains of the Marseillaise came wafting over to us.

It was only later, from much higher up, that we observed quite a different approach route to the Grande Chandèle. Livanos again—he never mentioned it!

Oh, well . . .

       ＞   ＞   ＞

Sun, sea, and sand—and, of course, rock. The weather had long ago turned fine again on Mont Blanc; but it was fine here too, and here stood our tent, on the seashore.

We balanced our delicate way up that lovely ridge. Down below lay the island-studded sea; a gentle breeze blew in from the distant horizon, the rock was firm, the water rippled and glinted, more than 1,500 feet beneath our feet. A splendid cliff, this Grande Chandèle, a marvelous tower, set in an enviably beautiful practice ground, in the midst of a region that has neither roads nor houses—almost as it was in the beginning of things. . . .

We sat on top, blinking up at the sun, down to the sea.

"*C'est très joli ici,*" remarked Wolfi, for once in unexceptionable French.

"*Tu as raison,*" I replied. Then we went off for a swim.

* "Che va piano, va sano: che va sano va lontano."

"DAVI"

FROM
The Burgess Book of Lies
BY ADRIAN AND ALAN BURGESS

ADRIAN BURGESS AND HIS IDENTICAL TWIN BROTHER, ALAN, WERE born in the Pennine Moorland of Yorkshire, England. They began climbing in England at the age of fourteen, but soon moved on to the greater challenge of the Alps. During the 1960s and early 1970s, the twins made more than fifty major alpine ascents in summer and winter. Since the mid-1970s, Adrian and Al have ranged farther afield, participating in expeditions from Alaska and South America to the Himalaya.

The pair has seen its share of epics, summits, and big mountains, from Everest to Manaslu to K2. Both climbed Dhaulagiri and Annapurna IV, the latter a rare Himalayan success in winter. They attempted Everest in winter as well, something almost unheard of, with Joe Tasker, a year before Tasker and Peter Boardman were killed high on the mountain. Both brothers attempted the unclimbed Northwest Ridge on K2 in 1986 with Alan Rouse, but they left for home before the tragic events of that climb ensued. Adrian reached the summit of Everest in 1989, in a rapid three-day ascent with less than eighteen hours of climbing. His account is one of the most moving and honest in recent years.

"Davi" is the story of the Burgess brothers' friendship with Davi Vevar, the "delinquent son of a Welsh parson . . . a wild man both in appearance and actions." The friendship began in the late 1960s, when both the Burgess brothers and Davi were teaching school in Scotland.

"'Davi' was a chapter that I wrote for *The Book of Lies*," Adrian said. "At the time it took place, we were just out of college and were poorly paid teachers. Unlike most other teachers of our age, we slept on friends' floors or in really cheap apartments packed together. The aim was to save enough money to climb as much as possible without giving up our partying lifestyle. Davi was just one character who colored our lives, but he was just that bit more colorful than most and quite dangerous to be with."

The story is the hilarious chronicle of how the twins introduce Davi to climbing and become immersed in the man's unbridled lust for life. Whether climbing hand over hand up the rope or mixing a gin and tonic between his knees while driving through the fog of France, Davi is a larger-than-life character whose story is both a cautionary tale and a ribald comedy. The story is in *The Burgess Book of Lies*, on pages 103–115.

There are times in life when you meet a person who forever changes your outlook. The mingling of adventures and experiences with such a person allows no retreat. For us, that person was Davi Vevar.

It was difficult to believe that anyone could be so crazy. We constantly found ourselves trying to protect him from himself. He would sit on the branch of his life and hack at it while daring the ground to come up and get him. All of this helped us to feel pretty normal by comparison.

Davi (DAH-vee) was the delinquent son of a Welsh parson and a year or so younger than us. While Al and I were living in Chester, he was attending Chester College. He was a wild man, both in appearance and actions. I first met him as I was about to enter a party, and he materialized out of a dark November night and stopped me.

"That will be a quid to help pay for the keg," he said. "The ladies get in free."

He was dressed in a dark-gray trench coat with a woolen hat covering most of his black, curly Hendrix-style hair. His heavy Welsh accent was gruff and intimidating. I paid up.

"Ta very much," he said and melted back into the night.

He didn't climb but he liked the parties, and that's how our lives became entwined. We'd climb all day and Davi would watch from the safety of a can of ale. Then one day the inevitable demand: "Take me on a climb." Al roped him up and away they went.

There were no easy beginnings for Davi. He wouldn't have entertained the idea of an easy climb. The climb was called Tensor and difficult enough for Al to treat it with respect. It starts in an exposed position a hundred feet off the ground, and the first moves are a trying traverse left underneath overhangs. Then it weaves through the overhangs to the top of the cliff.

Davi took one bold step left, promptly fell off, swung out like a spider on a thread and shouted up to Al: "A've lost me fags!" He began to climb hand-over-hand up the single rope, a large loop of slack building up the farther he climbed.

"Don't do that, Davi! You'll fall!" I bellowed up. But it was too late. He was moving as fast as a rat up a flue. When he reached a pin, he swung up on it, sheer terror giving him untold strength, and Al took in all the slack. Davi had become a climber.

He had so much natural finger-strength (I suspect from crushing empty beer cans), combined with a fearlessness bordering on crazy, that he quickly fitted into the mold of a climber.

>   >   >

One day he came up with a crazy scheme to visit an old girlfriend in the south of France. We'd drive the thousand miles each way. Al and I would climb, and he would . . . well, he wouldn't climb. All this would happen in the space of six days. He thought we were crazy for even going along with him.

We were heading south on the autoroute, Davi at the helm. A thick mist had cut visibility to a hundred yards, but that didn't stop him driving at eighty miles an hour. What scared me was the way he was trying, at the same time, to mix himself a gin-and-tonic between his knees. The small hole in the can of tonic kept missing the large neck of the gin bottle, but he persevered unswervingly—literally. I shut my eyes and tried to sleep.

The week was almost over, and we'd all had our own brand of fun. I counted the cash in the communal purse.

"Davi, where's all the money gone?" I asked. "There's only ten francs left."

"We spent it all on wine. Don't you remember?" He paused to consider the honor at stake, and added: "Don't worry, Aid. I'll borrow some from Noelle (his girlfriend)."

What little money we borrowed—well, had been given—had run out by the time we were north of Paris. It was midnight when we pulled into a gas station and began pumping gas. A sleepy attendant ambled toward us as I zeroed the pump, smiled, and pretended I was just beginning.

"*Combien franc de gasoline?*" I asked. "How much gas?" he asked back. I stuck up two fingers. He stared at me in disbelief. I'd asked for half a pint. Then we were on our way to the night ferry and another scam.

"Davi, we don't have enough money for three tickets," I said. "You'll have to hide in the back."

We covered him with sleeping bags and junk.

"Stay still, Davi, we're almost at the ticket office."

He was wriggling about, and the whole pile of junk was moving.

"Turn the fucking heater off! I'm frying!" was his muffled answer, followed by a string of Welsh curses.

"Davi, stay still! The customs people are there, too. We're going to have to smuggle you in."

We had taken a step from a small crime to a critical one. Smuggling people into England is taken very seriously. We made it safely on board and prowled the decks looking for food.

"I'm so hungry I could eat a horse between two mattresses," I growled.

"How about a protein roll?" asked Davi.

"What's that? Where is it?"

"Up in the lifeboat. Won't be a minute."

He began climbing up the superstructure in the pitch-black night, the flitting shadow of a cat burglar.

A whisper came down out of the swinging hull: "Aid, catch!"

A package flew through the air and was under my jacket within a second. He clambered back down. Mission completed. The three of us grouped in the corner of the well-lit bar, saliva building in our mouths. I slowly brought the package out into the light and let out a moan: "Davi, it's a hank of fucking rope!"

>   >   >

When I moved into his rented townhouse, I could hardly believe the mess. Books and climbing gear lay strewn in every room. The first night I laid out my sleeping pad among the jumble and swore that things would have to change. To get Davi to clean the place up was a major step forward, though his motives were different than mine.

"The chicks'll love a clean place, eh, Aid?" he said.

I didn't tell him they might not wish to share the place with me as well, because we both slept in the one room.

He was teaching biology at a nearby school, while I taught outdoor education at another. Some of my plans involved taking eight children up to Scotland to climb some snow gullies and do some winter hill-walking. Davi wanted to come but first had to figure out how to get time off work. The morning we were due to leave, he went into school as usual but with a crazy plan in mind.

He put on a tie around his neck next to his skin. Then he dressed normally in a white shirt and second tie. Just before going to report sick to the headmaster, he tightened the first tie to a point of near-strangulation. His face turned bright red and his eyes almost leapt from their sockets. All the veins in his neck and face dilated. The headmaster thought he was about to have a heart attack and sent him home immediately. And that's how Davi first went to Scotland.

That week was the first time he'd climbed on snow and ice and was as strenuous a time as he'd had in the mountains. However, it was after the day's efforts that the fun really began for him. He would sit by the open coal fire in the Glencoe bunkhouse and relate story after story to open-mouthed teenagers. He became their Superman, their Robin Hood, and their Rambo. But never their saint. Enamored by his wildness, they decided to play a prank on him. While he lay on his bunk, they held him down and cocooned him with a climbing rope—strapped him to his bed. Davi played the game and allowed it to happen. After he'd twisted and writhed to free himself, he set out on the chase. He found them safely locked in the mini-bus, jeering at him through the windows.

By this time I'd joined in the chase and decided I'd flush them out. With a butane-gas stove in hand, I casually poked the burner head through an open window and turned on the gas. Every head turned to watch. Noses began to twitch. Some clever joker began to open windows. Oxygen began to mix with the butane. They thought they'd won. Fingers pointed in glee. I showed them my final card—a cigarette lighter held ready by the hissing jet. The doors burst open and Davi grabbed the culprits.

When he began to tie their hands together, they relaxed. After all, it was all in fun. Wasn't it? . . . When he led two of them like mellow ponies to the back of the van, they raised their heads in suspicion. I herded the rest of the kids into the bus and Davi, giving the two boys twenty feet of slack rope, tied it off to the back seat. We were ready to go for a run. Or should I say, they were.

I drove very slowly out onto the narrow lane, around the winding corners—four miles per hour. Davi stood on the tailgate like a fisherman with a delicate catch. The boys were striding out well. Long loping gaits showed power and confidence. Half a mile later their expressions were not quite so confident. How much farther was this going to go on?

Davi was shouting instructions to me: "Ease off a bit, Aid. We don't want them coming down with 'road rash,' do we?"

Deep laughter roared out from the rear of the bus. Suddenly, horror of horrors, the local cop car emerged from a shaded bend up ahead.

"Shit! Stop!"

I slowed to a careful halt while Davi put his arms around the two runners and drew them toward the van. The bobbies were smiling. I gave them a wave. They returned it and went on their way.

＞   ＞   ＞

About that time Davi met a girl who owned a Morgan sports car. She was gracious enough to let Davi drive it, and he liked to go fast, very fast. We'd flash off down to Wales in a little over an hour, climb all day and burn back again. I have a vivid recollection of being a passenger in the roaring machine with my behind little more than nine inches from the passing road. The long hood that stretched out before me looked like it was taking aim at the oncoming traffic circle. Would we make it? We were doing a hundred and twenty! The smell of burning oil and the trembling of the whole frame had me speechless, when Davi growled out: "Just like a fucking Spitfire, Aid!"

He loved to point out to other riders a couple of marks on the dash. He called them "Aid's teeth marks!"

During this time, the Chester constabulary received orders to trail Davi and observe his movements. He must have unknowingly led them a fine chase, he in the Morgan and they in their small underpowered minivans. It all began in a Cheshire country pub, full of white-shirted Chester businessmen. Davi's girlfriend, Sean, had a large, aging St. Bernard dog who suffered from an arthritic hip. She'd been injecting the poor animal with a morphine derivative and had forgotten to throw away the syringe. A few beers down the line, Davi had begun to use it to squirt beer at unsuspecting locals. For him it had been clean fun and harmless enough. He'd dumped the syringe in an ashtray when he left, and the suspicious publican took it to the police.

From then on, the wonderfully ingenious minds that run the long arm of British law had decided that Davi was dealing in drugs obtained through his girlfriend's father, who was a doctor. He fit their profile so closely that he had to be guilty. Wild curly hair; an obvious disregard for authority; a penchant for parties; loud music and friends with long hair. Plus, how could a lowly teacher afford a flashy sports car? One summer evening Davi left his girlfriend at her parents and headed home, his hair blowing in the wind as he tore, carefree, along the winding country lanes. He was having fun. Unbeknownst to him, the cops thought no one in their right mind would ever drive like that, unless they were carrying a load of drugs.

He pulled into his driveway and found Al Rouse, Brian Hall, and Daphne all using an overhanging balcony to train on pullups and other climbing moves. Five minutes later three strangers, one a woman, walked purposely toward them, following an overly eager Alsatian dog.

"Who you looking for?" asked someone.

"Get inside! Police!" was the response. One pulled a gun.

They were all taken inside and told to strip naked while the officers searched for needle marks and other signs of drug addiction. Davi stood sheepishly, dressed in only his girlfriend's underwear. The cop wondered what kind of person stood before him. Davi explained: "Must have grabbed me girlfriend's undies by mistake this morning." After the embarrassingly obvious blunder, the cops left. Even the dog had its tail between its legs.

⚓   ⚓   ⚓

To report Davi's conversations fully is not easy. He had spoken only the Welsh language until age eight and so brought a completely different slant to the English he spoke. I never knew a person who could fit so many four-letter words into one sentence. He'd slip two between article and subject, then one for the verb and another one to qualify it and likewise for the object. All this with the sing-song lilt of the Gaelic.

He was becoming an accomplished climber, and to some degree this kept him out of trouble. He poured his vast energies onto the rock, but you still couldn't keep him out of the pub in the evenings. I remember returning to the house one night after all the pubs had closed and Davi was starving. He would often forget to eat because he'd be so busy just doing . . . something.

The cupboard held a couple of slices of stale bread, a blob of butter, and nothing else. Imagine my surprise when I see him scouting out for anything edible and his gaze stops at a friend's tropical-fish tank. Inspired by the wriggling and darting goldfish, his hand dips quickly and comes up with a prize. Onto the toast and under the grill it goes. There's a scream as his girlfriend comes in and snatches it off, to plop it back into the water. It sank.

⚐   ⚐   ⚐

In those days the Chester party scene was pretty active. We'd often meet in some classic old Cheshire country pub before going out on the town for the evening. When Sean invited a group of us back to a birthday party at her parents' home, we gladly accepted. It would naturally be a posh affair and so an invitation meant we'd been accepted, even if it was on a trial basis, into the upper echelons of the local who's who.

As Davi perceived it: "The food'll be good, and they think climbers are exotic, so don't get caught scratching yer arse."

The evening passed with the chink of fine crystal and many a fine conversation about why we clung to greasy rock faces and endured nights out tied onto tiny ledges.

"Why do you do it?" was a common question, and one of us would always answer something like: "Well, it seems to make all this," eyes dropped to an almost empty glass, then a pause, "so worthwhile." The host would then glimpse the dregs and scurry away to correct the balance. From the kitchen a plop reached trained ears, a satisfying sound.

After everyone had left, I asked Sean if she had a sleeping bag I could use. She told me her sister's room was empty and that the bed was big enough for me and Davi. She was playing it pretty cool in front of Dad.

"Fancy bedroom," I commented. "Where's her sister now?"

"Off visiting some rich boyfriend. She's going to get married in St. Paul's Cathedral in London."

I stood over a dressing table full of expensive-looking perfumes and deodorants.

"Fair number of smelling stuff here, Davi," I said.

"Yeah, look," he replied.

I turned my head into a fine spray of French perfume. He was using it like fly spray and I was the fly. "Bastard! I'll smell like a Parisian hooker."

Come morning we sat in the airy country kitchen, warm coffee before us. Sean had left to make toast. Davi looked over at me with a slightly guilty expression.

"Fucking hell, Aid," he said. "I woke up last night and smelled that perfume. Didn't know where I was and thought you were Sean's sister. I caught myself just in time. Bloody embarrassing."

✱　　✱　　✱

Davi seemed the most dangerous after the pub. On one occasion, we went back to his girlfriend's country cottage. He'd just bought a new chainsaw to help in his part-time firewood business and was anxious to show me see how it worked, so he fired it up with a deafening roar in the dining room. My memory flashed back to the movie, *The Texas Chainsaw Massacre*. In the next minute—after a "Watch this, Aid"—he raised the blade, shredding the wire and paper lampshade, and continued to cut off a big chunk of the country-style dining table. His girlfriend's country-style dining table! Not long after, he lost the use of the Morgan car—and girlfriend, too.

Urged on by tales of fighting and plunder, he'd like to get into the occasional brawl to keep his hand in. One time in Glencoe we'd been out ice climbing all day in nasty, snowy weather. The climbers' bar at the Clachaig Inn was elbow-to-elbow standing-room-only, with the faintly musty smell of sweat and drying clothes. Ian Nicholson, a giant of a man and local climbing expert, was behind the bar, collecting empty glasses at closing time. Al, Davi, and I were nearby, finishing the dregs of a heavy beer. A young, leather-clad biker lass stepped up to the bar and demanded another beer in no polite fashion. When she was refused, she smashed a glass defiantly but had not counted on Ian's rapid reflexes. He has the largest hands I've ever seen and to have one of those clip a fast backhander must have hurt.

Forward moved the boyfriend to avenge her pride, but quick as a flash, Al and I had his arms twisted in half-nelsons and he was thrown out the door.

We really didn't think too much about the incident until moments later the sea of bodies hurriedly parted to form a ten-foot-wide swath: we at one end and the bike-chain-swinging boyfriend at the other. Davi was primed. He, Al, and I stood shoulder to shoulder while the guy advanced to the far side of a billiard table. Whack!! Down slammed the chain. Thick oil was imprinted on the green baize.

There was an explosion of action as Davi leapt from the table before the guy could rearm. A bone-shattering crunch as fist met skull. We quickly followed as arms reached out to stop us. Davi was a blur of fists and ducking head as he guarded our backs. The next thing I knew, the bar was empty and we were all three standing there grinning in a pile of broken glass. The inn owner ushered us into a smaller, private bar.

"Keep ahold of that biker until the local police sergeant comes," he said and then turned to us. "And in the meantime, wot all ye be havin'?" he asked.

"Glen Morangie will go down just fine, thanks," said Al, ordering the first of many free Scotches.

          ➤   ➤   ➤

I only ever climbed one alpine route with Davi, but it was a day to remember. He'd just returned from an attempt on the South Face of the Aiguille de Midi with an attractive girl called Muriel.

"There were too many people all over the route, Aid. Ropes crossing every which way," he said. However, I'd seen his pack before he'd left. He had so many bottles of wine and wedges of Camembert that I could see he had very different ideas about the climb than she.

We were hanging out in the Chamonix campground and Davi had nothing to do. So I asked him: "Al, Bob Shaw, and I are going up to do a rock route on the Forgotten Pillar on the Argentière. Do you want to come?" The route had had one ascent by a French friend, Georges Bettembourg. He was a great Chamonix climber and wanted us to confirm the difficulty of the climb.

The next day we roped up at the bottom of a thousand-foot pillar of beautiful granite. Though I normally climbed in boots, we'd all decided the Alps warranted using rock shoes. From the beginning, the climbing was classic. There were thin cracks and delicate traverses, all at about 5.9 standard. Davi climbed quickly without bothering about much protection. It was a real pleasure to see him so at home and in perfect control. He'd not climbed many long routes and I remember him commenting, "Aid, it's much bigger than Tremadoc (a Welsh cliff)."

"Sure is, Davi."

"How we going to get down?" A crag rat's question.

"We'll rap back down."

We reached the top of the pillar at mid-afternoon. While I searched around for some good anchors, I heard Davi driving a pin.

"I'll rap from this, Aid." The rope was already threaded, and he was about to lean back on it.

"Wait a second, Davi! I want to test it," I said, pulling him back onto the ledge. I gave the pin a sharp tug downwards, and it dropped an inch in the crack.

"Oh, Davi," was all I could say. I quickly chose a fatter pin and pounded it home. Then I made a back-up anchor by slotting a small wired wedge into a constriction.

"OK Down ya go."

On a small ledge, Davi leaned out to look down a huge corner with two sets of overhangs. The exposure was extreme.

"There'd be nothing fucking left," he said.

"What?"

"If you fell. There'd be nothing fucking left."

"Shut up, Davi! You're getting me scared. You go first, but watch your head as you drop over the lip of the big roof."

I watched his yellow hard hat getting smaller.

CLUNK! His head connected with the rock. "Fucking overhang!"

He never would pay attention.

⚐   ⚐   ⚐

Davi is constantly meeting life head-on without thought for the consequences. He's also very creative. He finally seduced his wife-to-be by climbing up the outside of her hotel with a bottle of champagne in hand, broke into her room and was sitting there, complete with cheesy grin, when she returned to her room.

When he married Gail, his life changed. Not that he wasn't still crazy, but now he mixed it with elegance. He would sip wine from the best crystal instead of a cup, eat steaks from a plate rather than mashed potato from the electric kettle, and wait until 9:30 before leaving for the pub instead of going at 6:00.

He wished to introduce Gail to some of his climbing friends, and so together they went to a Christmas party being hosted by a North Wales climbing club. The gathering was held in a granite-block fortress of a hotel in some quaint Welsh village. Davi was on his best behavior and even wore a suit given to him by Gail's first husband. The evening progressed with plenty of joviality, and Davi sank untold pints of the local brew. Then the happy couple retired to their room, which, as in many Welsh hotels, did not have its own bathroom. That facility lay just down the hallway. In the middle of the night, Davi awoke with stretched bladder and a desire to relieve himself. He groggily dragged himself out of bed and staggered in a befuddled state to the toilet. Then, during his return to their room, he miscounted the doorways, unknowingly got lost and entered another room. Settling himself beneath the warm sheets he was soon asleep, far into the Land of Nod.

Morning arrived with a rude awakening for Davi.

"What the hell are you doing here?" barked an angry guy, lying on his side in the other half of the bed, less than two feet from Davi's sleep-encrusted eyes. Davi awoke with a start, furious.

"What the fuck are *you* doing here?" said Davi. "Get out! Where's Gail? Hey, get lost, you faggot!"

"It's *you* who must leave. This is *my* room. I'm the hotel manager!"

"Ugh! What? Are you sure?" Davi was waking up fast. "Oh, sorry about that." Then Davi left, wrapped only in a towel.

One spring we decided to climb on the granite of the Cornish coast. There was a comfortable climbers' hut down there, but as we weren't members, we used names of people we knew who were. After a hard day's climbing, the evening lengthened into late night. Al Rouse showed us a climbing challenge which involved wriggling between the ceiling and a steel supporting girder. One by one we tried the problem and everybody was laughing at the efforts. It held quite a lot of danger because if you squeezed part of your shoulders through and then slipped, there was a high chance of snapping your neck. At this point we'd forgotten that people were trying to sleep upstairs.

Then Davi tried. Both shoulders were locked in between joists and his feet were swinging free when he decides: "A'm fuckin' stuck!" said from the depths of flattened lungs. We roared with laughter. Gail, dressed in the finest silk, began to look a bit worried.

"Don't be daft, Davi," she said. "You got in. You can get out."

"A tell ya, woman, A'm fuckin' stuck!" Another roar of laughter. Then came a string of Welsh expletives that would have made his father blush, and he moved a few more inches through the gap. Finally, after another great heave, he was through and he swung down to the floor. The uproar was tremendous.

Then a man appeared at the door. "If you lot don't bloody shut up, there's going to be a big problem," he said. "A very big problem."

I could have guessed the next thing that would happen. Davi moved quickly to the door and began poking a straightened finger into the guy's chest.

"Don't ya come in here fuckin' shouting yer fuckin' abuse in front of my bloody wife or I'll fuckin' put you outside and lock the fuckin' door!" Davi looked terrifying. The man slunk away without another word.

Whenever we pass through England, we always look up Davi. He doesn't climb any more, now we're not around.

"It's just not the fuckin' same. Aid. All these poncy bastards dressed in their pink tights passin' 'round their diseases. They don't even like to fight. . . . "

Gail is just as beautiful as ever, and they have a young son called Jan. You can see he's proud of his dad, and I guess he's heard a lot of stories.

Sometimes, when Davi's had a couple of pints, you can spot a wistful look in his eyes. They tell of the past and think to the future. Who knows, maybe he'll climb again yet.

"THE SPORTING LIFE"

FROM
Postcards from the Ledge
BY GREG CHILD

"I LOVE TO CLIMB, I ALWAYS HAVE," GREG CHILD TOLD ME YEARS AGO. "It's a pretty simple thing. For all the complexities that exist in climbing, it's actually a very primal thing. Climbing meets some kind of basic need in me. All I know is that if I get too busy and can't go climbing, I start to go a bit stir crazy. It's an essential part of my daily diet, it's an important part of my make-up, probably because I've done it since I was thirteen or fourteen years old."

Over the years, few practitioners have taken climbing to a higher level than Child. From El Capitan to Mount Everest, Trango Tower to Baffin Island, and with more remote successes in between—Shivling, Lobsang Spire—Child has climbed at the rarefied top of his profession. It's a situation that makes "The Sporting Life" so much fun to read. Because after a life in the high mountains, Child finds himself in an alien world, climbing not on one of the world's famous or hidden peaks, or wildest faces, but on a set of plastic knobs bolted to a seemingly endless sheet of plywood.

Child is no stranger to hard rock climbing, in fact his early years were spent pushing the limits of what was possible in Australia. But to return to his native country so many years later for some sport climbing—in competition, no less—was something else again. "The Sporting Life" tells the story of Child's first foray into competitive sport climbing at Mount Victoria, near Sydney, Australia, in the 1993 Australian National Sportclimbing Championships. There Child finds himself in a stressed and foreign environment, one in which every contestant is looking for an edge, while the author is considering wearing lederhosen and red knee socks to cement his portrayal of the "old fart from yesteryear."

He doesn't, though, and therein lies the tale. The fun is in the telling of it, and the style here is classic Child: self-deprecating and outwardly hilarious, but serious, and twisted, even important, if viewed without the comic overlay he so skillfully applies. Child's mastery of this genre shows why he was the recipient of the American Alpine Club's Literary Award.

This story is in *Postcards from the Ledge*, on pages 36–40.

Vanity got the better of me on a visit to my native Australia and led me to compete in the 1993 Australian National Sportclimbing Championships at Mount Victoria, near Sydney. I used the ploy that I was entering for academic reasons to see how I reacted under the pressure of rules and a competitive climbing atmosphere. It was a scientific experiment. I wasn't serious about trying to win, and to prove I was in it for a lark I joked that in the qualifying round I'd climb dressed in lederhosen and bright red socks, like some old-fart alpinist of yesteryear.

But I didn't.

Back in the isolation room, I got serious. I couldn't help it. The mood there was funereal. Competitors sat silently in the autumn sun like dour young lizards, stretching, meditating, plugged into Walkmen, or pacing like death-row inmates counting the minutes before the noose was fitted to their necks. Swept up in the nervy mood, like everyone else waiting those three hours for their ten-minute session on the wall, I made endless visits to the portable john. My bowels hadn't been so efficient since I had dysentery in Pakistan in 1985.

Out in the arena where the forty-five-foot wall stood, we heard the audience screaming for blood as competitors in the division before us climbed up and then lobbed off. Our sweat took on the acrid odor of tension. I tried making conversation with my companions. Chat, I knew from storm-bound mountain bivouacs and other scary alpine times, helps quell nervous jitters. But talk in the isolation tank consisted of lambasting the course setter and the moguls running the competition, and downgrading other climbers' routes, though I did strike up a conversation with a young skateboarder, who, with puffed pride, described his recent expulsion from high school for drug abuse.

Guards were posted everywhere, armed with boomerangs and muskets, to prevent us from sneaking around the back and peeking at the course. Nobody trusted us. Finally, our keeper got a message on the walkie-talkie to escort us to the wall for a three-minute preview of the route. We were paraded up to the wall past the suddenly silent crowd. It seemed a religious moment, as if the bulging plywood structure were a pagan edifice, the crowd a worshipful horde of pilgrims, and we the sacrificial lambs.

Our three minutes of route study began. Mark Baker, winner of most of the competitions Down Under, produced a pair of binoculars, no less, and began scanning the wall, inspecting holds and scribbling notes on a sheet of paper.

"Do the rules allow that?" I asked.

"Sure, they do it in France," he said. Then I noticed that other competition veterans were charting the wall with sextants, night-vision goggles, and X-ray specs and then speed-writing hieroglyphics and equations on notepads. Left to rely on my memory alone, which had been vaporized long ago from too many jaunts toward 8000 meters, I realized I had no chance. All I saw were random blobs of plastic on a sea of plywood.

Herded back into isolation, the initial qualifying round of the comp began, and we were led to the wall one by one. The longer one waited, I found, the greater the volume of nervous by-products one produced. It seemed that no sooner did I pee than my bladder would fill again. Where did it all come from? By afternoon the latrine was overflowing, and a nervous line of climbers blocked entry to it. Clearly, setting off on the wall carrying a dram of excess fluid would be disadvantageous. If an enema were available, we would have fought over it.

"Hey, Mister," I heard a young voice squeak from the sidelines, "are you one of the climbers?" Two kids on tricycles had evaded the guards and stood before me.

"Yes," I told them.

"What are you doing?" they asked.

"I'm peeing."

"Why?"

"Because I'm nervous."

"Do you think you'll fall?"

"Yes."

"Then what's the point?"

"Go away."

My turn to climb came. I got on the wall. My mind went blank for four minutes; then I found myself at the end of the route. Ohmigod, I thought, now I've got to go through this again for the finals.

Back in isolation, I sat with eleven contenders for the big finale. For this round I had contemplated pulling a can of beer from my chalk bag, popping it with a flourish of spraying foam, guzzling it down, and then chowing into a Dagwood-size burger before stepping onto the wall. Just to show I wasn't serious.

But I wouldn't.

Four hours passed before I got my turn to climb. I spent the time sitting silently, visualizing the layout of the plastic barnacles I'd soon be set adrift on. Thoughts of the route made my hands sweat furiously. Automatically, I began dipping into my chalk bag, even though I was sitting still. Before I knew it, the bag was half empty, and my hands were gummed with a white slime as viscous as a slug belly. I wiped it off and, in the process, noticed that my fingernails needed trimming. Fretting that my digits would have a micron less crimping area, I became neurotically body-conscious and detected another burgeoning reservoir in my bladder. But before I could rectify any of that, a guard connected me to a rope and pushed me onto the stage.

At the first Snowbird World Cup, in 1988, I had watched the Frenchman Patrick Edlinger stun the crowd and his peers when he sauntered to the top of a wall that had beaten the best that the world had to offer. Where others slapped for holds or quivered as they held on with gutbusting power, Edlinger danced catlike, weightless, and elegant with his blond shock of hair swaying in the breeze. Those who saw him climb that day learned the meaning of the term "poetry in motion," and they went away moist-eyed, convinced that climbing was, after all, art. In a climbing life, there are a few precious moments when everything comes together on a climb. It coincides with a heady electric tingle that you feel in every molecule of your body. Edlinger had it running through his veins that day, and whether your game was mountains or crags, big-wall routes or bolted sport climbs, 5.14 or 5.7, the Frenchman's fingers and feet tapped out a message that was the same for all: be there, be focused, be your best.

That was Edlinger, though, and this was me. Confronted by the wall and a cheering or jeering crowd—I couldn't tell which—my testicles retracted as if I were surrounded by a gang of skinheads armed with two-by-fours. A huge digital clock began counting out the first seconds of my climb. Keira, the four-year-old daughter of a friend, waved to me from the crowd. I took it as encouragement; she was too young to hold a grudge against me, and I'd read to her from her storybook that very week. Then I faced the plywood, latched onto a hold, and stepped into the fray.

Negotiating a route through judges, photographers, and TV cameramen dangling on ropes and from scaffolding, I climbed ten feet up and crouched beneath a four-foot roof. Clipping a quickdraw, I then began feeling out the first crux. Streaks of chalk and bloody bits of fingernail embedded in the plywood indicated my predecessors' high points and told me the move was burly. Gripping a troublesome pocket with one hand and a buttock-shaped plastic blob with the other, I eyed the hold I needed to crank to and began high-stepping toward it, concentrating for all I was worth.

The noise from the crowd intensified as the gap between my fingers and the hold shrank. It was a rousing sound, a positive note, and it coaxed my fingers a millimeter closer to their destination. Above this noise I heard the cheers of Keira: "Come on, Greg! Come on, Greg!" she yelled. Her voice caused images from the children's storybook that I'd read to her to cloud my thoughts. Instead of focusing on a precise crank, my mind's eye tracked the progress of a purple hippo in a tutu bouncing across the frontal lobe of my brain.

"Shut up, Keira. Shut up, Keira," I thought. Then I saw my reflection mirrored in a TV camera lens pointed toward me. "Shit," I thought, "I don't look like Patrick Edlinger at all. I look like the picture on my driver's license."

The blood rushed out of my hands, leaving them cadaverous and cold, and flowed into my forearms, which swelled like sausages. My legs wobbled, and my feet sketched about the wall. I felt suddenly very heavy, as if a brick had been slipped into my pants. It was do or die, so I flapped at the hold.

My fingers missed their rendezvous. I clutched a handful of air, then dropped onto the rope. A sad noise rose from the crowd, and then they applauded. It all happened in two-and-a-half minutes.

Soon after, Mark Baker took the title, the crowd went to the pub, and workers began dismantling the wall. I didn't place last, but I was a long way from the front of the pack. My experiment had been a success. For one thing, I learned that earplugs are essential equipment to block out the sound of noisy fans. Next time I'll bring a telescope, too. And to prove I'm not serious at my next comp, I'll embark up the wall with ice axes and crampons. I'm certain there's nothing in the ULAA rules forbidding that.

"BIRD"

FROM
Stone Palaces
BY GEOF CHILDS

GEOF CHILDS'S PROFILE OF JIM BRIDWELL COULD AS EASILY BE IN AN anthology of important biographies as in an anthology of humor. Bridwell is an outrageous character, surrounded by a full-blown mythology that happens to include incredibly comic incidents, along with heroic and frightening ones.

Childs himself concedes that a piece on Bridwell by necessity might be contaminated with components of the Bridwell legend: "The strongest ties we have in climbing are our myths," said Childs, "the fables spun from parking lot to bar, from one crag to another, from climber to climber until the details are so convoluted and confused that all that remains is the telling."

But the facts of Bridwell's life make a suitably noble backdrop to the funny fable Childs offers us, and he writes from a position of knowledge. Childs met Bridwell in 1975, the year the "dean of Yosemite" climbed The Nose on El Cap in a day (with John Long and Billy Westbay). The seminal accomplishment serves to vindicate Bridwell's twisted vision, his ability to see into the future in terms of what was possible, and to form a sort of dividing line between what was in Yosemite Valley—the Golden Age of Chouinard, Robbins, et al—and what was to come.

When you preside over a changing of the guard that saw "Beat poetry, mountain Chablis and the bongos of the fifties give way to the Maharishi Yoga and blotter acid," you're going to be at the epicenter of some weird stuff. Bridwell was the resident climber laureate of the Valley for so long that it was perhaps inevitable his legacy would be constructed out of equal parts mind-boggling climbs and outrageously funny dramas.

Childs does us all a favor by putting down in words the life of this climber who hung in for so long, who made such an indelible impression. Bridwell's "strides into the unknown" included not just The Nose in a day but the Pacific Ocean Wall, Sea of Dreams, Butterfingers, all in the Valley, and beyond, to Cerro Torre, Pumori, and the Moose's Tooth. You know you're in for a wild ride when Bridwell concedes on these pages, "I must have been a pretty strange kid…."

"Duane Raleigh and Greg Child first suggested I write about Bridwell," Childs said. "He is a guy I had always admired and wondered about and marveled at. I still feel the same way. He's still the man, in my opinion."

"Bird" is in *Stone Palaces*, on pages 109–127.

When the terrain borders on controlled hysteria, management of the
unfettered imagination can make everything logical . . .
                    —Lincoln Kirstein

Everybody has a Jim Bridwell story. My personal favorite takes place
sometime in the late 1960s. Bridwell and fellow Yosemite lifer Jim
Madsen have driven up to Glacier Point and are engaged in a bit
of pharmaceutically enhanced eco-tourism when a tourist approaches with his poodle. The dog snaps at Madsen's ankles and Bridwell
remarks to the owner that he should put his pet on a leash. Disgusted at having
to share the view with two such obvious degenerates, the owner refuses. The
dog snarls again. Madsen boots it over the edge.

"OK," Bridwell tells the dog's horror-struck owner, "you don't have to."

Whether your sensitivities let you laugh at that story, or whether the story is
even true—and Bridwell insists that it is not—is immaterial. What is important
is the tale. The strongest ties we have in climbing are our myths: the fables spun
from parking lot to bar, from one crag to another, from climber to climber until
the details are so convoluted and confused that all that remains is the telling.
The written word can't capture what it really means to climb. The things that
happen on rock are simply too visceral, too complex and personal to lay down
on a page. The best climbing stories are the ones told out loud. And no one
has had more stories told about him than Jim Bridwell.

The Bridwell legend is, of course, a caricature. Only slowly does the icono-
clast whose dry wit, supreme talent, and incurable wild streak that forever changed
North American climbing come into view. Part genius, part rowdy, the real Jim
Bridwell is a pastiche of contradictions, both more and less than the sum of his
tales. At fifty-four he is soft-spoken and reflective, still fit, and percolating with
plans. He is wary of interviews. Celebrity, he knows, is a double-edged sword:
an opportunity wrapped in heavy strands of adoration and vilification. Getting
to know him, like climbing a wall, is a long and complicated process.

I first ran into Jim Bridwell in 1975. It was a heady time for both of us. I
had just climbed the Regular Northwest Face on Half Dome in a methodical
two and a half days. Bridwell, partnered with John Long and Billy Westbay,
had made the first one-day ascent of El Cap's Nose and was preparing to tackle

the vast and uncharted real estate to the left of the North America Wall, a stretch that under Bridwell's tutelage would usher in modern-day big-wall climbing and be known as the Pacific Ocean Wall. I was quietly stealing a shower at the Curry Company employees' compound when the front door exploded open. "Bridwell's here!" someone shouted. Naked and soap-covered, I stepped out to have a look. On either side of the door stood a small group of sun-buffed minions. In the middle was Bridwell. He was leaning over the sink washing his face. He looked gigantic. Dusty-blond hair hung to his shoulders. The muscles on his back looked as if they were cut from stone. He was dirty enough to merit a shower, and perhaps just a little uncomfortable with all the fuss.

He is still uncomfortable with all the fuss. Reputation, he will tell you, is more important than recognition, and despite having one of the best-known names in American mountaineering, he is happy to move through crowds unacknowledged. Called a visionary by climbers as diverse as Royal Robbins and Jared Ogden, he is perhaps more gamesman than shaman. Like all great athletes, Bridwell's contributions to mountaineering have stemmed from a profound understanding of the game. He feels its currents and flow almost intuitively.

Midway through his fourth decade of hard climbing, Bridwell is still focused on the next step, which he says is "technical climbing at altitude." With little urging he will produce a photo of some Himalayan or Patagonian or Alaskan wall and trace a line where his route will go. He knows every challenge by heart. "We will climb this in the dark," he says pointing to a couloir. "This is where the big-wall section begins." At an age when most of his peers have settled down to career paths and pension plans, Bridwell is still hungry, still driven to make a statement.

He is probably the only one who thinks he has to. For most of us, Bridwell has already done enough. From the mid-1960s until the late 1970s when the best climbers in the world were American, Bridwell was the best climber in America. And whether it pleases you or not, Bridwell is about as quintessentially American as it gets. Obsessive and distracted, heralded and hated, he is what attitude looks like harnessed to the business end of a climbing rope.

"To put Bridwell into context," explains his longtime friend John Long, "you have to understand that the accomplishments of the generation that preceded us were mythical. We thought of guys like Robbins and Chouinard as icons.

But Bridwell told us there were no myths—there were just rock climbs. And Bridwell was no icon."

Indeed, as the heroic figures of Yosemite's Golden Age were abandoning the stage, it was Bridwell—wearing purple bell-bottoms, a paisley vest, and a tatty bandanna—who stepped up and showed the world that anything was possible, if you had enough courage. Bridwell widened the definition of "Yosemite style" to encompass everything that went into building a life around climbing. In his glory days you could feel his presence in Camp 4 like a jolt of electricity.

Jim Bridwell may not have invented the low-ride, but anybody who has been in Yosemite and pushed his or her personal limits, stolen food off a tourist's tray, offended public decency, got drunk at their picnic table, played out their stay on crackers and relish, or slithered onto a half-driven piton 2,000 feet above the barbecued air of El Cap Meadow has stood along the banks of the river Bridwell and wondered at his beauty.

Not that the waters have always run sweet and clear. Away from the cliffs and mountains, Bridwell has backwashed into eddies of failed schemes and indifferences. The stubbornness and why-not attitude that have served him so well on walls have hobbled him on the horizontal. Yet, as the current crop of young climbers goes out into the world to put up their own masterpieces, they do so in a landscape shaped by Bridwell's imagination. The Nose in a day, the Pacific Ocean Wall and Sea of Dreams, his ascents of Cerro Torre, Pumori, and Moose's Tooth were more than just routes, they were strides into the unknown that have inspired the brightest stars of a generation and left in their wake an unrivaled legacy of brilliant style.

➤   ➤   ➤

To Bridwell, adventure is style. His obsession with minimizing bolts, for example, is less about ethics than playing dice with the limits of possibility. He can be a stern taskmaster but, says Billy Westbay, "He was always pushing us to be our best."

But as with all great achievements, there has been a cost attached.

"People don't look at me and say, 'My, how normal you look,'" Bridwell has said. "You know why? Too many lines on my face! From too many days looking up into the sun, or over my shoulder at the storm clouds—of being terrified. But you have to deprive yourself to learn, to move ahead."

The deprivation is, at times, much more apparent than the learning. Strands of gray infiltrate his still dusty-blond hair. His gaze is less penetrating, wearier than it once was. The line of his shoulders has been stooped by years of carrying heavy packs and hauling loads. Shaking hands with Bridwell is like picking up the roots of an old tree. His skin is hard and taut. His expression is frequently that of vague distraction, a look that turns easily to anger. He is not glib. He does not hold disparate thoughts in mind easily, and the halting, off-track associations that spike his conversation, like the weathered texture of his face, are legendary. As with so many of the myths and rumors that surround him, the description "head of a seventy-year-old, body of a twenty-five-year-old, and attitude of an eleven-year-old" captures his appearance at the cost of understanding the content of his soul. Impatient and demanding, a man of towering ambition, Bridwell has never let hubris rob him of his ability to view mountaineering within the greater context of life. A father, a husband, a pirate, and a pioneer, he has dreamed big dreams and made them happen. He has rolled the dice and had them come up sevens. The stories, as rich as they are, only tell half the truth. When in the 1970s every other climber in the world looked up at El Cap's terrifying geography and sought out its avenues of escape, Bridwell reveled in its mysteries.

"I always tried to be open to things," he says. "A new route, a new piece of gear, different ways of doing things. I always liked the idea of trying to see things from a different perspective."

What the rest of us thought to be questions of gear and logistics he understood as a test of faith—that if you believed it could be done, then you could do it. When we looked up we saw granite. Bridwell looked up and saw the future. Then he went out, threw himself headlong at the impossible, and in so doing rewrote the history of climbing.

        ➢   ➢   ➢

James Dennis Bridwell was born on July 29, 1944, in San Antonio, Texas. His father, Donald, was a war hero and an officer in the Army Air Corps.

Like all military families, the Bridwells moved often. So often, in fact, that by the time Jim entered middle school he could more easily list the states he had not lived in than the ones he had.

Reclusive by nature, Jim spent much of his childhood alone, working on projects, playing with his toys, or exploring the woods. Later, as sports began to occupy a greater percentage of his time, he seemed to grow out of himself a little. A natural athlete, he excelled at everything and had it not been for yet another family move, Jim might have spent the 1970s dishing up split-finger fastballs for some triple-A farm team instead of putting up hard aid routes in the Valley. But arriving as a freshman at San Mateo High School in California, he discovered that the teams had already been chosen. Once again on the outside, he drifted away from sports and into falconry.

"I must have been a pretty strange kid," Bridwell laughs, thinking back to those days. "I was always hanging out in the woods, hiding in blinds, and reading books."

One of those books was a guide to the national parks. Under the title "Yosemite National Park" Bridwell found a two-page photograph of El Capitan. Even at age seventeen he was tantalized by its immense scale. A few weeks later he came across another article—this one of an ascent of the Fisher Tower's Titan featuring photographs of Layton Kor. "That was it, man!" Bridwell remembers thinking. "I was already climbing cliffs to capture birds. I figured, hell, I can do that, too."

The next day Bridwell and his buddies were rappelling dirt mounds on a manila rope stolen from a transmission tower. Recognizing the limitations of this setup, Bridwell soon enrolled in a Sierra Club basic climbing course. "I was pretty good at it right away," he concedes. "But what I liked best about climbing was that I was accepted as myself." As his skills grew, however, he realized that his instructors "were not the serious guys I had read about in *Freedom of the Hills.*" The real climbers, he knew, were in Yosemite.

A superb middle-distance runner, Bridwell was offered a track scholarship to Purdue University. He turned it down in order to follow his high school track coach to San Jose State. He enrolled intending to graduate, but climbing was already exerting an increasingly powerful attraction over him. During the summer of his freshman year he made his first trip to Yosemite

Valley. By the time he returned his interest in formal education was at an end. Bridwell lasted just four semesters. In the spring of 1964 he quit school and left for the Valley. "Hell," he explains, "I had important climbs to do."

Pitching his tent beneath the pines—not far from the location he would later make famous as the "rescue site"—the nineteen-year-old Bridwell looked around and took his bearings. Everything seemed inordinately rich and infinitely better than he ever could have imagined.

With Royal Robbins in Europe and Yvon Chouinard in the army, the reigning god of Camp 4 in the early 1960s was Frank Sacherer. "When I first arrived in Yosemite," Bridwell says, "there was no guidebook and no information. The only protection was pitons. Climbing was dangerous and people played it cautiously." Everyone, that is, except for Sacherer, who was insanely bold and emphasized a minimum of gear and a maximum of commitment.

Bridwell's natural athleticism and youthful boldness brought him immediate attention, and it took him just two weeks to elbow his way into the inner circle's pecking order. Jim Baldwin, a well-liked Canadian, was the first to call him by name, but it was Sacherer who saw his potential. When they finally climbed together the impression Sacherer left on his young protégé was to last a lifetime.

In Sacherer, Bridwell found someone for whom climbing was not just a pastime but the definition of who and what he was. The abandon with which Sacherer threw himself at routes opened Bridwell's eyes to the fact that pushing the limits meant stepping over the line, holding nothing in reserve. Tormented and intense, Sacherer asked just as much from his partners as he did himself. He pushed and bullied, turning free time into workout sessions and meals into rewards. By the end of his second season Bridwell had accompanied Sacherer on the first ascents of Ahab (5.10a) and the Crack of Doom (5.10d) as well as the first free ascent of a Yosemite Grade V—the North Buttress of Middle Cathedral (5.10a).

According to Bridwell, when Frank Sacherer left Yosemite in 1966 to take a job in Europe as a physicist, "He had free-climbed routes that the best climbers of the day said couldn't be done free. He had climbed routes in a day they said could not be climbed in a day. In the 1960s, Sacherer did more to advance free climbing as we know it today than any other single person."

Partnered by period luminaries such as Mark Clemens, Peter Haan, Jim

Pettigrew, Kim Schmitz, Madsen, and others, Bridwell now set about putting Sacherer's philosophy into practice. Relying on pitons hand forged by Yvon Chouinard in the Camp 4 parking lot and Austrian kletterschuhs, Bridwell and his cohorts practiced a ground-up ethic that outlawed previewing, hang-dogging, or resting on gear. Even short routes were ventures into the unknown. Of that period, Bridwell's ascents of Outer Limits (5.10c), Catchy (5.10d), Wheat Thin (5.10c), New Dimensions (5.11a), Butterfingers (5.11a), and the Nabisco Wall (5.11a) remain his greatest works.

By the summer of 1967 Bridwell had become one of the Valley's best known habitués. Spending his winters in Tahoe, where he worked as a ski instructor, he was invariably among the first climbers to return to the Valley in spring and among the last to leave in fall. It is an indication of the high regard in which his climbing ability was held that the park service placed him in charge of organizing and managing their high-angle rescue team. It was a move that would change the Valley's social structure forever.

Described by Doug Robinson as "the most trampled and dusty, probably the noisiest, and certainly the least habitable of all Yosemite campgrounds," the Sunnyside walk-in site—known to climbers as Camp 4—was the home of every climber who entered the park. Figures as diverse as John Salathé and Don Whillans had rolled out their sleeping bags on its hallowed ground. Dungy and loud, Camp 4 probably generated more stories per square foot than any of the vertical real estate surrounding it. Handing control of its choicest sites over to Bridwell, a future park superintendent would later confess, was "not the wisest policy decision we ever made."

Neither was it the worst. Lost amid the skewed tales of wild times and "living as one with the dirt" is the fact that Bridwell and his handpicked gang of rescue technicians actually took their duties seriously. Rappelling off the summit of El Cap to pluck an injured climber off a ledge and deposit him safely on the ground posed technical and logistical problems no one had ever grappled with before. Over the next ten years the confederation of park personnel and climbers that formed Yosemite Search and Rescue (YOSAR) laid the foundation for today's high-angle search and rescue techniques.

On the domestic front, it is probably not too big a stretch of the imagination to suggest that Bridwell also found in Camp 4 the neighborhood he had never known as a child. Like him, its eccentric retinue of loners and misfits had escaped the suburbanized wasteland and aching loneliness of middle-class America to throw up their sun-faded tents and live, as Doug Robinson so perfectly phrased it, "like hobos in a paradise of stone." Now, with the keys to the asylum in hand, Bridwell moved quickly to create the city of his dreams.

Peopling the rescue site with the cream of Yosemite climbers, Bridwell and his chosen few lived as beggar kings beneath the great sweep of the Sierra in a New Jerusalem of golden light and endless days. Secure from site fees and visitor permits, Bridwell, Schmitz, Madsen, Phil Bircheff, and a changing cast of others built a peasant meritocracy where the only things that mattered were how hard you climbed and the quality of your vibe, where anything was possible and the worst disappointments were quickly healed by the gentle hiss of an evening breeze and the deep relief of a morning cigarette.

Then, as now, days began with the dregs of any available liquid left over from the night before and a spoonful of whatever remained in the pot. By 8:30 A.M. the more industrious residents of Camp 4 would walk across the street to the cafeteria. Half coherent and with sticks and leaves clinging to their hair, they would then forage the abandoned foodstuffs of horrified tourists until security, satiation, or disappointment sent them home to engage in the perpetual discussion of routes, partners, gear, and weather. Optimists worked on their dilapidated cars, the intellectuals read Ginsberg and Ferlinghetti, folk music drifted in the breeze, and by 5 P.M. the secret expeditions to new routes were old news. It was the perfect idyll.

Outside the Valley, however, another revolution was taking place. The values that had stood one generation through depression and war were being tossed away. Riots, assassinations, and the insanity of Vietnam were rattling the streets. Everything was upside down. Authority was in retreat while psychedelics, free love, and social agitation were everywhere. Everywhere, that is, but Camp 4. A situation that was destined to be short-lived. After all, the climbers of Camp 4 were already leading a socially unacceptable lifestyle, it only led to reason that the drugs and free love could not be far behind. And when they arrived, "The Bird," as he was now called, was ready.

"Almost every climber I knew used drugs," says Bridwell of those days. "We didn't use them on routes. It wasn't like that. We were using hallucinogens to help us understand what we were experiencing from a point of view seldom visited by the western mind. We were trying to make sense of this new awareness. To unfold the mysteries. Drugs were equipment."

It was a difficult adjustment for the old guard. Their crew-cut and orderly world was gone. The momentum was changing. In Camp 4 the beat poetry, mountain Chablis, and bongos of the 1950s had been replaced by Mararishi Yoga, blotter acid, and fuzzy riffs on cheap guitars. Yvon Chouinard, Royal Robbins, Warren Harding, and their cohorts had set a high standard. But although their final statements—the Muir Wall, North American Wall, and the Wall of Early Morning Light—were grand gestures, when the end of the Golden Age came it was marked by petty disputes, chopped bolts, and personal vendettas. A gilded era was gone and, as Bridwell puts it, "the Gods were bitter in their demise."

By the time the 1970s dawned Camp 4 was a changed place. The dulcet good life was gone. Now it was louder, funkier, and much more crowded. Though the summers were still reasonably peaceful, spring and fall brought hordes of long-haired outsiders seeking to imprint themselves on the walls. The scent of Camp 4's wood smoke mingled with that of pot. The midnight intrusions of bears foraging for leftovers were drowned out by arguments over chalk and passive protection. Coming to the Valley in those days was like going to church in a bad part of town. Climbers went there knowing about the gods and of their patron saints—Herbert, Frost, Roper, Pratt, and Kor—but it was the renegade that everyone wanted to emulate. Bridwell. Outsiders were happy to engage in the rumor-mongering and self-justification of life on the lower rungs of the social ladder. Tales of Bridwellian misconduct, arrogance, and daring were favorite topics around dinner. Deprecated and envied, Bridwell was Dean of Camp 4, and Lord of all he surveyed.

John Long arrived in Yosemite in 1971 with Bridwell in mind. Brash and muscular, toting an impressive resume and carrying a chip on his shoulder the size of the Columbia boulder, Long pulled in and headed straight for the rescue site.

"I went to Yosemite dead set on proving something," says Long. "I wanted to be part of the cutting-edge group. I wanted to climb with the best climbers in the world, to push the world standard. That meant climbing with Bridwell."

Two hours after arriving he got his wish. "Bridwell took me up the left side of Rixon's and that was kind of an eye opener. But I felt like he was totally open to me," says Long. "I felt extremely comfortable with him immediately."

The relationship was to be a profitable one. With the changing of the guard, many of Bridwell's old partners had either left the Valley or scaled back their climbing. With Long and a number of others in tow, Bridwell again picked up the pace, training and climbing harder than ever. Soon the rescue site and its environs teemed with talented young climbers—John Bachar, Ron Kauk, Werner Braun, Mike Graham, John Yablonski, and many others. Wild and unfettered, they took to the rock like iguanas during the day and happily indulged themselves in the raucous parties and loose living of Camp 4 by night. There was no longer any philosophical agenda to getting stoned. It was recreation, pure and simple. One more way of expanding the high that was life in Yosemite.

"There were neighbors, love affairs, slums, parties, gymnasiums, loonies, territorial disputes, degeneration, and inspiration," Kevin Worral, a frequent partner of Bridwell's, says of those days. There was the Mountain Bar for scrounging drinks, the fireplace lounge for sitting out storms, and, if you were quick enough, free showers or a plate of purloined leftovers at Curry Village. "There was just nothing like it," says Billy Westbay. "There was this incredible energy. Everybody feeding off each other. It was an untouchable growth period."

As the energy increased so did the output. Bridwell's 1973 article for *Mountain* magazine entitled "Brave New World" stoked the fires even higher. Extolling the techniques and standards of Valley climbing, Bridwell's words excited climbers from around the world to come to Yosemite and test themselves in its granite crucible. With visitors from Japan, Italy, France, Korea, England, and Spain all elbowing their way onto the walls, a hybrid of new ideas and bold one-upmanship infused the Valley.

"Everything in the 1970s was open-ended," says John Long. "All of us believed Bridwell's credo that anything was possible."

EBs, tape, chalk, tincture of Benzoin, and nuts accelerated the pace of change. It was as if a veil had fallen. As if everything was up for grabs. The possibilities were mind-boggling and nobody understood them better than "the man." Playing minister and mayor, New Age Sacherer and old-age Ahab to this motley parliament of Ishmaelites, Bridwell set out to push the envelope. Where walls were concerned, the more he climbed the more he saw what was out there. And how vulnerable it was. Like the generation before him, Bridwell understood that any place on Yosemite's undulant granite was reachable if one was willing to spend enough time with drill in hand. An example needed to be set of what could be achieved by minimizing bolts and maximizing the adventure. Finding the line to best express that credo was the challenge.

Likewise, 5.11s were now routine. As harder and harder climbs went up, they were almost immediately surpassed. Conversations focused only on pushing into the next realm of possibility. Dale Bard, Mark Chapman, Kevin Worrall, George Myers, Billy Westbay, Ray Jardine, Rick Reider, and Bev Johnson joined the chase along with the likes of Jim Erikson, Art Higbee, Henry Barber, and Jim Donini. Close behind was an even bigger rogue's gallery of misfits and mutants, all of them pushing and probing at the next inconceivable first.

"We just fed off each other, and that allowed us to achieve more than if we were on our own," says Billy Westbay. "We were able to discover more of what we could really do . . . because we could dream big dreams."

No one dreamed bigger than Bridwell. Always stirred to his best performances by competition, Bridwell now set out to set the highest possible standard. Over a two-week period in the summer of 1975 he climbed the Nose in a day (VI 5.10, A2) and put up the Pacific Ocean Wall (VI 5.9, A5)—routes that placed him alone atop the world of technical rock climbing.

"The Nose was great," says Westbay, his partner on both routes. "Our goal was to get back to the Lodge for last call. And when we walked in everybody was so stoked. We couldn't buy a beer."

The P.O. Wall was another matter. "It was really intimidating up there," Westbay laughs. "We were pretty freaked." And with good reason, for Bridwell and company were nailing into a realm of technicality and commitment that had never before been explored. Coaching and prodding his team through pitch after pitch of desperately hard nailing, Bridwell seemed to know just how hard to push. At mid-height on the seemingly blank wall, when one member of the team insisted on going down, the Bird gave in. "Go ahead," he said, nodding toward the gaping void below them. "You can take two ropes and go." He didn't, of course, and four days later the team completed the hardest big-wall route on the planet and put high-end Yosemite wall climbing out of the reach of mortals.

"The Pacific Ocean Wall probably changed me more than any other route," Bridwell would say later. "After that, I knew that no matter how bad things looked I could still do it." Quiet, pragmatic, and focused, Bridwell's skill on hard aid has left a lasting impression on everybody who has climbed with him. Nobody has ever mastered great difficulty with less showmanship. "You could never tell where the hard bit was by watching Bridwell," says Westbay. "He just kept at it, never seeming to push it but never seeming to slow down, either. Just really clean and steady."

Now into his mid-thirties and with fifteen years of hard climbing behind him, Bridwell could have walked away after the P.O. Wall and still have been remembered as one of the great rock climbers of his era. Nothing could have been further from his mind. Routes in the mid- to late 1970s like El Cap's Mirage (VI 5.11, A4), Half Dome's Bushido (VI 5.10, A5) and Zenith (VI 5.10, A5), and Mount Watkin's Bob Locke Memorial Buttress (VI 5.11, A4) upped the ante even further.

The Sea of Dreams (VI 5.9, A5), completed in 1978 with Dale Bard and Dave Dingleman, was perhaps the touchstone of the period. This seemingly featureless line linked an intricate network of shallow seams, expanding flakes, and hookable edges. Equipped with multi-RURP belays and including an if-you-fall-you-die pitch, the Sea of Dreams remains a highly respected undertaking and presaged the extreme seriousness of today's hardest aid lines.

Clearly, Bridwell was at the top of his form. No one before or since has owned a place and time in quite the same fashion as he ruled the granite walls of Yosemite National Park. Nobody expected that he was already in the process of transforming himself into one of the world's foremost alpinists.

"I thought you could make money with a slide show of big walls," Bridwell explains, "but the real market seemed to be for alpine climbs. I'd always harbored an alpine desire but California climbers were considered rock jocks. Guys from Colorado and Washington were the ones that went on expeditions."

Recognizing his lack of mountaineering skills, Bridwell had quietly set out to fill the holes in his resume. He dove in at the deep end. In the summer of 1974 he drove to Canada to attempt the then unclimbed Emperor Face on Mount Robson. Turned back by a recalcitrant car, he instead soloed Washington's Mount Shuksan before returning to the Valley. After the fabulous summer of 1975, he headed for Patagonia.

To anyone else, the unclimbed east face of Cerro Torre might have seemed something of a stretch for a Valley boy who barely knew how to strap on his crampons. In Bridwell's mind, it was the next logical step. The majority of the route was a rock climb, and he was the fastest bigwall rock climber on the planet. The ice at the top he would figure out. Unfortunately, his attempt with Kim Carrigan was cut short when the Australian was deported from Bolivia with visa problems. Bridwell didn't get back until the winter of 1979, when he again arrived with the east face of Cerro Torre in mind, but switched his attentions to that tower's Compressor Route after a Christmas Eve encounter with a young American named Steve Brewer. Using borrowed equipment and climbing alpine-style, the two notched the route in just under two days—a shockingly fast time on a route that many believed could only be climbed siege style. Their ascent sent ripples of shock throughout the international climbing community.

Like the P.O. Wall, Cerro Torre also held revelations. Exhausted and pressing their descent into a storm, Bridwell fell from a rappel stance and plummeted through space. "It took a long, long time," he says of his 150-foot tumble. "I was waiting, wondering why nothing was happening, watching the rock go by. It was very quiet. I was very clear. You have this capacity to separate your physical body from consciousness, and while I was aware that I was falling I was also very, very calm."

Regrets, secrets, judgments, and the certainty that there was still "plenty of time" passed through his mind. With only three turns of 1-inch webbing around his waist for a harness, the impact Bridwell experienced upon hitting the end of the 9-millimeter haul line snapped his ribs like carrot sticks but saved his life.

It was not to be his last brush with the macabre. Over the next several years each big climb seemed to come equipped with its own unique horrors. A winter ascent of the Moose's Tooth in Alaska with Mugs Stump resulted in a do-or-die rappel from high on the route. He climbed the Shroud on the Grand Jorasse outside Chamonix, France, only to find out that his early mentor Frank Sacherer had been killed by lightning on the same route a year earlier. Returning to Patagonia he dodged storms and falling rock to put up several new routes. He climbed Pumori in winter, traveled to China and Nepal, and nearly died from an intestinal worm contracted during the first coast-to-coast traverse of Borneo with Rick Ridgeway and John Long.

While sponsorships occasionally helped support Bridwell's climbing habit, the majority of his financing came from hard work. In addition to ski patrolling and YOSAR, he toiled on oil rigs, guided, and took whatever odd jobs he could string together. Bridwell's wife, Peggy, whom he had married in 1976, presented the Bird with a son, Layton, in 1979. Bridwell was a proud and doting father. This "magical child" provided new incentive for generating income. Leveraging his climbing skill, Bridwell found work in Hollywood as a rigger and technical advisor, wrote books, and published articles. He also made frequent trips back to the Valley. In the early 1980s he established a string of noteworthy routes including Half Dome's The Big Chill (VI 5.10, A4), Shadows (VI 5.9, A4+) on El Cap, and, one of his all time favorites, Zenyatta Mondatta (VI 5.7, A5), an El Cap horror show that he describes as a mini-Sea of Dreams and "no place for those with a faint heart."

"When I arrived on the scene in the mid-1980s Bridwell was pretty much considered the father of modern aid climbing," confirms Pete Takeda. "Bridwell is in a class alone. A lot of other people have done more routes, but Bridwell was the one who crossed the line. He went after these rotten, expanding features by using heads and hooks and riveting and stuff like that. The things that everybody else was trying to stay away from."

But despite his high profile and sterling resume, the Bird's stubborn unwillingness to accept limitations gnawed at him. As a second generation of friends drifted away into marriages and careers, he kept at it, constantly searching for new climbs, new partners, new directions.

"We climb onward," Royal Robbins once wrote, reflecting on his ascent of El Cap's North American Wall. "Searching for adventure, searching for ourselves, searching for situations which would call forth our total resources." Climbing has always held those overtones for Bridwell, too. Every summit for him was laced with a sense of incompleteness; every insight braided with a mixture of ambition and alarm; every dream a path stretching out through the graveyards of lost friends and forfeited ambitions.

By the late 1980s Bridwell was beginning to feel the toll of time. Though he was climbing as well as ever, he was a father and for the first time in his life had to scramble for income. He rigged for commercials and a series of made-for-television movies. He did more guiding and became a special trainer for the U.S. Navy Seals. He gave lectures and designed equipment. As always though, he climbed. In 1992, at age fifty, he climbed the Eiger's North Face and was cranking solid 5.12.

>   >   >

I can see Bridwell right now sitting at the table of his modest home in Palm Desert, California. The window open, a cigarette hanging between his lips. There is a cup of black coffee in his hand. A steno pad covered with notes lies by his right elbow. A breeze sweeps down off the San Jacintos and rattles the paper like bones.

To say Jim Bridwell's life experience has been rich is one thing. To say it has been charmed is another. Despite a career that has been blessedly free of personal injury, Bridwell has seen his share of death. Stump, Madsen, and Baldwin all died in climbing accidents. Bridwell's mother died while he was in Patagonia. Guiding in the Tetons, he watched a client fall to his death. The murmur over that one was particularly ugly. Accusations were made; lawsuits filed. The Bird's self-promulgated reputation as a wild man hurt him. "We are," as he has said, "our own creations."

Such self-absorption extracts a price. Bridwell has been called the Chuck Yaeger of serious climbing: someone who was prominent in his time, who gave more than he took, who was peerless as a performer. Americans, however, are prone to taking pleasure in the demise of their idols, "it takes a lot of 'atta boys' to overcome one fuck-up," Bridwell sighs. And the likelihood is that he will be as well remembered for his wild bouts of drinking as for the days and nights he spent chasing the wildest dreams of a generation across the vertical landscape of El Capitan.

No one is more to blame for the misunderstanding than Bridwell. In these days of media intrusiveness and voyeurism he has never made a point of tending very carefully to his image. "Climbing is not that important," he says in his own defense. "It's the camaraderie, it's overcoming elements in myself that matters. The thing that I have enjoyed about it most is that there is no superficiality. The idea is to set a goal and do the best job you can. What are the seven to ten days you spend on a wall compared to life? The values people talk about are imaginary. It's all an illusion. You make yourself up as you go along. You are a viewpoint, a set of beliefs, that's all. People take themselves seriously because they want to be separate. But if you are still conscious when all is said and done you'll be laughing."

"People trash each other," he sighs. "My gut feeling is that you should judge others the way you judge yourself. I've set high goals for myself and I've always been willing to suffer the consequences if I didn't get there. It's not how good you are, it's your vision, what you contributed. I gave what I had."

⋗   ⋗   ⋗

You may be surprised to learn that Jim Bridwell believes in God. He thinks the shit is about to hit the fan. "The world can't go on this way very much longer," he says. "What will happen, I don't know, but it won't be good." He believes that psychedelic drugs were an absolutely positive force in his life, but he doesn't do them anymore. ("They don't make good drugs these days," he complains.)

Bridwell regrets never having had any money. He is sorry that he hasn't spent more time at home. He would very much like to find the funding for another trip to the Himalaya. So it goes.

"To really understand Jim Bridwell," says John Long, "you'd have to go back and climb what he did, when he did it." Both tasks have merit; neither is likely. "I guess," Bridwell replies, "that makes me an enigma."

Not really. Like all of us, Jim Bridwell wants it both ways. He wants people to see him for who he is in the full light of everything he has accomplished. He wants to be respected. He wants to do more big climbs. He wants the past to be seen for what it was and not for the myths and misinformation that cloy at him. He wants to be half as much appreciated in his own country as he has been abroad. He wants most to be remembered for the good he has done, and that might be an impossible request from someone who has lived his life like a climb—minimal gear, maximum commitment—throwing everything he had at every moment. "Americans are tough on their heroes," says John Long. "The things that made him so good as a climber make him a pretty easy target for people who don't really know him. I know it bothers him, but his answer has always been to go put up another route. To let his climbing speak for him."

"LES BANS"

FROM
Mountaineering Holiday in *The Six Alpine/Himalayan
    Climbing Books*
BY FRANK SMYTHE

FOR MUCH OF HIS SHORT LIFE, FRANK SMYTHE WAS AT THE CENTER of the contemporary climbing world. The decades between the world wars saw a flurry of exploration and climbing activity in both the Alps and in the Himalaya, and Smythe led the way on both fronts. Sometimes by himself, sometimes in the company of other notable climbers, such as T. Graham Brown, G. O. Dyhrenfurth, or Eric Shipton, Smythe pioneered important new approaches and routes in the Alps and in the Himalaya, including early attempts on Mount Everest.

Smythe clearly loved mountains, and despite what seems a rather frail physical constitution, he climbed some of the most demanding terrain, in terms of difficulty and altitude, of his day. His new routes in the Alps during the late 1920s—two separate lines up the Brenva Face on Mount Blanc, the Sentinelle Rouge and Route Major—remain classic climbs today.

But it was in the Himalaya where Smythe truly hit his stride. His performance on Everest during three expeditions in the late 1930s, where he climbed high above Camp 6, might rightfully be called the best high-altitude effort of the decade. In addition to his well-known attempts on the world's highest peak, Smythe pioneered what would become the eventual route to the summit of Kangchenjunga and he also climbed 25,447-foot Kamet, the highest peak ever climbed at the time.

Smythe eventually became the archetype of the professional climber, one of the first alpinists to make a living doing what he loved. But he eschewed guiding, the conventional career approach, and turned instead to writing.

Smythe proved adept at taking the reader along on his adventures. His accounts have the timbre of reality, from the discomforts (there were many) to the uplifting joy he experienced. He tells his tales with relish, but without the self-aggrandizement that characterized mountain writing of the day. His obvious humility struck a chord in his readers, and his modest approach endeared him to his audience. If his stories reflect an Englishman's innate sense of superiority, a conceit that seems dated now, those foibles can be overlooked when placed within the context of his time.

"Les Bans" recounts a trip to the Alps in 1939, a climber's holiday, bittersweet for its description of those last peaceful climbing days before the horror of the Second World War. The trip ends up with a bold climb of Mount

Blanc's Innominata Ridge with four German climbers, but it begins with an admittedly out-of-shape Smythe struggling up the 12,000-foot summit, Les Bans, in the company of his friend Jim Gavin. The narrative picks up with the pair's arrival (by train) at a lodging in the Daupine district of France, near the mountains. As their first morning breaks, Smythe is worrying over his persistent bad luck with weather.

"Les Bans" was originally published in *Mountaineering Holiday*, Smythe's last book, and it is now in *Frank Smythe: The Six Alpine Himalayan Climbing Books*, on pages 821–831.

We awoke next morning to hear a peal of thunder and a patter of hail. Our suspicions of the previous evening had not proved unfounded. Slate-colored clouds were oiling up from the west and crackling concussions of thunder reverberated amongst the peaks.

In the matter of alpine weather, I consider myself a Jonah and I remarked as much to Jim, with a sort of gloomy satisfaction. His reply was: "Well, I'm usually lucky, so perhaps we shall cancel each other out." I could only hope that what he said was true, for I had come to look upon my ill luck with alpine weather as proverbial and inevitable. What usually happens is that I arrive in the Alps at a time when everyone is complaining of the drought. On the evening of my arrival, dark clouds gather and on all sides I hear people say, "At last we shall have some rain." It is true, there is rain, and snow, and every kind of climatic unpleasantness, continuing without intermission for the next two or three weeks. In disgust I return to England, with the idea of finishing my holiday in North Wales or the Lake District. I arrive back to find that there has been a drought ever since I left. Headlines decorate the newspapers—farmers, it is said, are frantic and prayers for rain are being said in the churches. A day or so later I arrive at Seathwaite or some such normally wet place in the hills, to find every marsh and stream dried up. It has not rained for over two months the inhabitants tell me with a gloomy despair. "Don't worry, it will now I've come," I answer. They look at me unbelieving and incredulous, but sure enough that self-same night rain begins to fall and continues to fall without intermission for the remainder of my holiday. Soon after returning home I receive postcards from friends still in the Alps, the Lake District, or North Wales. "Why on earth did you go back to England?" enquire the former. "The weather has been marvelous since you left." "What a pity your holiday came to an end!" write the latter. "We are having perfect weather."

It was, therefore, with feelings of surprise and amazement that I noticed a distinct improvement in the weather toward midday. The thunderclouds receded with baffled growls, the sun broke through, and a rainbow arched itself prettily across the valley. Was it possible that my Jonah had met its match in Jim? At all events it had received a temporary setback, and I agreed enthusiastically with Jim's suggestion that we should set off immediately toward the Pilatte Hut with the idea of climbing Les Bans, a peak of 12,040 feet, on the morrow. I even went so far as to suggest in my turn that, instead of spending the night in the crowded hut, we should sleep in the open, taking with us our bivouac tent and sleeping bags for the purpose, a proposal to which he acquiesced with enthusiasm.

The weather had almost completely cleared when, shortly after lunch, we set out from La Bérarde, and only an occasional drift of warm rain added its pearls to the herbage as we trudged up the valley.

Now that our mountaineering holiday had properly begun, my first reaction was not, I fear, that of *joie de vivre* and unbounding energy; but a loathing for my rucksack which seemed unconscionably heavy; furthermore, as I labored up the path, I seemed to melt all over like an ice cream on a summer's day. In three words, I was out of training. Let me express at once my unbounded admiration for those persons who are always in training, who skip, run, and jump before breakfast, who plunge themselves in ice cold water, who cut out this and that in the matter of food and drink, who stride over miles and miles and miles of the countryside every weekend, passing every public house with an air of insufferable self-denial and virtue, who twist and writhe their stomach muscles and add knobbly inches to their biceps. I do none of these things, I am much too lazy; therefore, for the first day or two of an alpine holiday, I am out of training and a peak of 12,000 feet and a walk of not more than twelve hours is as much as I can comfortably manage. Jim, being in the army and incidentally twelve years younger than me, was, of course, in training. He had suggested Les Bans as our first expedition and had obtained details from a climbing friend, who described the ascent as an excellent little training climb. All the same, Les Bans is 12,040 feet high and is described by Baedeker as "very difficult; descent nearly as long," and I began to wonder what schemes were afoot for the mortification of my untrained flesh.

The worst of being out of training is that there is a lack of coordination between mind and muscle. The untrained one proceeds uphill in fits and starts, not with that slow, deliberate, rhythmical output of energy and movement that is the sure sign of good training. The feet are not put down exactly where it is intended they should be, and a really stony slog is productive of many unshed tears. So it was on this occasion; the path seemed exceptionally stony and rough; my rucksack grew steadily heavier, and through eyes smarting with salty sweat, I watched Jim enviously as he strode uphill with never a drop of moisture on his brow, serenely unconscious of his laboring companion.

An hour later the path debouched on to the Alp de Carrelet. The weather had almost completely cleared now, and only the thinnest of thin blue showers was being wafted by the warm west wind across the precipices of the Ailefroide. Is there a nobler view in Dauphiné than that from the Alp de Carrelet? Imagine a meadow of brilliant green, all the more brilliant by contrast with the savage surrounding precipices, dotted with small featherlike pines, which unite to sweep up a hillside in a full-fledged forest. Beyond this gentle foreground is a background of precipice, a huge, rust-colored curtain 6,000 feet in height, mellow and remote in the afternoon sun, crested by a thin ribbon of silvery, wind-turned snow.

On the Alp de Carrelet there is a hut at which climbers spend the night before undertaking one of the numerous expeditions in the locality. Experience of the Alps had taught us to associate good viewpoints with refreshments, and a few minutes later we were seated in the hut, a rough stone dwelling resembling a hop picker's hut, drinking light French beer at the moderate sum of three francs a bottle. A number of tourists were doing much the same thing. Most were possessors of ice axes. The ice ax has taken the place of the walking stick and alpenstock with the modern tourist. It is true that it is neither so useful as a walking stick, nor so impressive as an alpenstock with a spiral of place-names and heights engraved on it, but it confers on its owner a certain distinction and separates him from that other kind of tourist who does little walking, and thus does not need even an ice ax. From an ice ax to a pair of crampons is another step, and though the latter may never be used, except perhaps as a substitute for socks over the boots on the slippery ice of a glacier, their ferocious appearance is worth something to their intrepid owner and they are distinctly useful when placed points outwards on the back of a rucksack in a customs or passport queue. A length of rope completes the equipment. I wish I knew how to coil a rope as neatly and as beautifully as the tourist does. I wish, too, that I could get the same thrill out of mere possession and exhibition, but ever since a rude fellow called out to me on the first occasion that I carried a rope, "Goin' to 'ang yourself, guv'nor?" I have sedulously sought to conceal this damning evidence of mental instability. Far be it from me to gibe at these proud possessors of ice axes, crampons, and ropes, even though they do no more than walk up to a hut, spend the following day admiring the view, and walk down again, for I know full well that I, too, went through the stage of owning but not using the tools of mountaineering.

We continued on our way greatly refreshed. After proceeding for a short distance, we came to a point where the path divided. Both branches appeared to continue up the valley, so we took the right hand one, which contours along the mountainside to the west of the stream. I am glad we did so because we entered upon some of the most flowerful slopes I have ever seen in the Alps, indeed I do not recollect seeing elsewhere in that range so varied and concentrated a number of rare and lovely species.

It was now late in the afternoon and the shadows were gathering in the valley. There was no further doubt as to the weather's immediate intentions; the storm clouds had all dissolved and we were assured of a fine day for our climb.

Presently we reached the limit of burnable vegetation and cast around for a bivouac site. After scrambling for some time over the steep hillside we found an overhanging boulder, the size of a cottage, which formed a shallow cave, twenty yards from a tumbling stream arched over with an immense drift of avalanche snow. I could see that Jim's professional zeal was aroused by sundry inequalities in the ground, so leaving him to engineer a comfortable platform, I went in search of fuel.

It was the first time I had ever bivouacked at a moderate altitude in the Alps, and I was reminded of camping in similar situations in the Himalayas. I returned with an armful of juniper to find that my companion had excavated and leveled a sleeping place. Water was not so easy to get. We had to crawl under the vaulted avalanche snow in order to reach the stream, an uncomfortable process, as the packed snow above weighed many tons.

At length all was ready for a meal. Before leaving England, we had weighed the pros and cons of a pocket "Primus" but had decided against it on the score of weight. Instead, we had provided ourselves with a methylated cooker of a type which has a burner consisting of a number of holes round a central orifice, into which the methylated is poured. The scheme is that having three-quarters filled the orifice, the methylated is lit; this heats the burner until presently the spirit vaporizes and jets of flame emerge from the holes. It is a simple contrivance and reasonably efficient, except in a wind; then it is the very devil. On this occasion there was no wind, and we vowed that the tea we brewed was perfect.

There is no doubt that mountaineering, or for that matter any hard exercise in the open air, makes a man appreciate his food and drink, and the most ordinary tea acquires a bouquet and fragrance undreamt of in civilization.

Tea was followed by soup. In the matter of soup, I am not only knowledgeable, I am expert. Once, when staying at a hut, I made a soup that contained sixteen ingredients. My climbing companion who partook of it said that it was unique, but a little later after looking at me for some time without saying a word, tersely remarked that it was a beautiful night outside and went out to look at it. I was only too glad to follow him.

On this occasion I was circumscribed in the matter of ingredients, and the soup consisted merely of a packet or two of "Maggi" powders. But for all that it proved excellent, and we vowed that our bivouac was superior in comfort to any hut.

Our supper eaten, we lit our juniper fire, and lolling back in our cave smoked our pipes. The evening was supremely calm. On high, the crest of the Ailefroide was pink, against a sky of deepening blue, and at the head of the valley beyond the serene curve of the Pilatte Glacier stood Les Bans, a graceful mountain built up of sweeping ridges, aglow in the declining sun. As we watched, peaceably puffing at our pipes, the golden tide ebbed heavenwards. As the dusk gathered the light breezes died away and the smoke of our fire stood up with scarcely a quiver. There was no sound save for the constant percussion of the glacier torrent. It seemed scarcely credible that little more than forty-eight hours ago we were in the maelstrom of London. In retrospect civilization seemed strangely futile and purposeless. I remembered the remark of a Himalayan native. He said: "We have heard of your wonderful machines that go very quickly through the air and across the earth. But tell me, does it make a man happier to go from one place to another quicker than we go on a pony?"

The mental reactions consequent upon spending one day in London and the next day in the High Alps are curious. It would be difficult, to begin with, to imagine a more abrupt change of scene. Then it is undoubtedly true that during the first few days of his holiday, the mountaineer tends to be obsessed by the time factor, the predominant factor of civilized life. A great many mountaineers never escape from time, and that this is so is proved by a slavish adhesion to it when making or subsequently recording a climb. A glance at any climbing publication will prove the truth of this assertion. There is, of course, a certain technical interest about "times" in mountaineering. Furthermore, some attention to time is necessary for reasons of convenience and, on occasion, safety, but I have never been able to understand the type of mind that cannot escape from time on a mountain, and that must needs climb pocket book and pencil in hand noting the time at which such and such an object is reached. For me, perhaps the greatest enjoyment in mountaineering lies in escaping from my normal enslavement to time. The fact that I may have crossed the bergschrund at 3:15 A.M., reached the ridge at 6:25, traversed the first gendarme at 7:10, and gained the summit at 9:42 is of little or no interest, nor does it interest me to know the time of someone else on the same route. I suspect that this abhorrence of watch-in-hand climbing is due to the fact that I enjoy the scenery of mountains as much as I like climbing mountains. I am, however, bound to admit that were the world made up of people like myself, it would be an impracticable sort of affair, and from a material standpoint decidedly primitive. It would rub along in a happy-go-lucky mañana manner; but it would at least be contented, happy, and without wars, for no one can fight a war nowadays who is not a slave to time.

In the present instance time as an associate and reflection of human activity no longer mattered. It was measured only by the deepening dusk and the kindling stars. There was no time in the constant note of the glacier torrent, nor was time measured by a multitude of trivial thoughts. We were content to meditate, to allow ourselves to assimilate, without effort, the beauty and peace of eventide.

Meanwhile our fire flamed and crackled merrily, and as daylight waned, lit up our cave with its ruddy glow. The fragrant smell of the burning juniper transported us back to the early days of alpine climbing, the days of Edward Whymper, Leslie Stephen, John Ball, and A.W. Moore. Perhaps the pioneers shared our campfire. It needed little imagination to picture ourselves bivouacking, not for a popular expedition, but an unclimbed peak, thrilled with the subtle joy that comes to a man on the eve of new adventure into the unknown, the prospect of setting foot where no human foot has trodden before.

The fire died down and the moon rose. The crags high above us shone against the stars, then slowly the pale radiance crept valley-wards. It brought with it a chilling feeling, a promise of frost, and we made haste to get into our sleeping bags while still warm. There was no occasion to employ the tent, which was intended only for an emergency, and we used it as a coverlet.

Jim had engineered a wide platform, and we lay side by side in perfect comfort. Presently I heard him breathing deeply and regularly and knew he slept, but it was a long time before I followed suit. I did not even want to sleep; I was content to gaze upwards at the stars and the brilliant orb of the moon sailing its precise course through the heavens. Gradually, with increasing sleepiness, there came to me a feeling of unreality as I contemplated the mysteries of space; the mountains seemed to shrink and recede and the roll of the glacier torrent was resolved into celestial music . . .

We both awoke later, in my case a trifle chilly as I had the outside berth, and the earth beneath me was damp. It was midnight or thereabouts and much of the romance had vanished from the proceedings. Jim presently went off to sleep again, but I lay awake for the remainder of the night. I have had many sleepless nights in the mountains, particularly on Everest, and very long some of them seemed. The present night was no exception and, as I lay awake with a cold spine and stiff shoulder blades, the world no longer appeared so beautiful as it had done when my stomach was warm and well filled. There is a sordid fact connected with all human activity: it is that aesthetic enjoyment is dependent on a warm and well nourished body, and that failing this condition the loveliest mountain views may be contemplated with a cold loathing. This was a case in point; I longed for dawn and activity, and thought wistfully of those civilized comforts that I had affected to despise.

Dawn came at last; the faintest paling of the sky behind the moon-bathed cliffs of the Ailefroide. In happier circumstances I should not have noticed it, but now I roused my blissfully slumbering companion.

"It's getting light," I told him.

He received this intelligence with an incredulous grunt, gave a snort and a heave, and settled down once more to slumber.

But I had had enough of bivouacking and went off to get water. After a tricky scramble in the dark under the snow arch I filled the saucepan, only to slip on the way back and upset it. By the time it had been refilled the remarks I had to make about breakfasting in the dark, with particular reference to saucepans, had effectively roused Jim into a show of activity.

Hot tea was good; it was more than good, indeed beyond the range of laudatory adjectives. It put life into our cold stiffened limbs and rekindled the damped fires of optimism and enthusiasm.

By the time we had finished our breakfast it was light enough to see, so packing our rucksacks we set off for Les Bans, having cached our bivouac equipment under a boulder.

The moon showed shrunken and pale as we trudged up the stony path toward the Pilatte Hut, and ahead the crest of our peak shone with the first cold pallor of day. We both felt in that stupid, drowsy state peculiar to the early hours of the morning, when vitality is at its lowest. Many writers have enlarged on the excitement of an early start in the Alps, I have been guilty of this myself, but years of indiscretion, if I may put it thus, now compel me to state emphatically that not only is there nothing exciting or romantic about it, but that it is a thoroughly disagreeable proceeding which I associate with a stomach that complains bitterly for not being allowed to complete its normal digestive processes in peace, and a certain mental state best described as fed-up-ness with everyone and everything.

However, it will be inferred that if mountaineering happiness is primarily a matter of efficient circulation and unimpaired digestion, then there is nothing like a good brisk walk for setting things right. So it proved in the present instance; an unqualified gastronomical gloom presently disappeared and was superseded by intelligent interest and even mild enthusiasm.

An hour after leaving our bivouac we came to the Pilatte Hut. Outside it was stationed a solitary tourist of doleful demeanor who growled a surly "bon jour, Messieurs," which greeting we returned with, what to him must have seemed, a hateful heartiness.

Purely as a matter of interest and inquisitiveness we opened the door of the hut and glanced inside. At least Jim did while I peered over his shoulder. Next instant he staggered back, pulling back toward the door as he did so. I have never been in a submarine unable to rise from the bed of the sea with the air becoming fouler every minute, but I should imagine that the experience would closely resemble a night spent in the Pilatte Hut during the holiday season. Our feelings were summed up by Jim, who turned to me and said in a voice vibrant with emotion, "Thank God we bivouacked, Frank."

A few minutes later we trod the frozen surface of the Pilatte Glacier. We were still in cold shadow, but we could see the sun shining on the upper seracs of the glacier, which were silhouetted against the blue sky in all manner of strange poses. We could also see another party evidently bound, like us, for Les Bans.

Tramping uphill over board-hard snow through motionless frosty air was a pleasant preliminary to the more serious work of the day. The glacier was larger and more complicated than we had suspected, but tracks of previous parties obviated the need for routefinding, and we mounted in that preoccupied yet negative frame of mind which I always associate with long and uninteresting ascents on easy snow.

Higher up, the glacier was considerably broken and the ice scenery varied and beautiful, broken walls of gleaming ice alternating with widely rifted crevasses. We had to zigzag through the latter, crossing numerous well-frozen snow bridges, and pass beneath a tottery wall of ice some eighty feet in height, which appeared ready to crumple up and fall at any moment.

Presently we came out of shadow into brilliant sunlight and plumped ourselves down in the snow for another meal; it was several hours since we had left our bivouac and the inner man had long since passed from active resentment into a dull despair and from dull despair into renewed resentment.

Second breakfast, as all mountaineers know, is a solemn and time-hallowed rite. It marks a transition stage in the day's work, a ceremony differentiating the cold hours of dawn from the exciting prospects of a day's mountaineering.

I forget what we ate, but I believe sardines, raisins, and chocolate were on the menu; and I can never eat the first named without thinking of a friend of mine whose favorite mountaineering diet is sardines and honey, spread together on bread and butter.

Our halt span out into a full half-hour. As we sunned ourselves we noticed with an interest that verged upon incredulity living creatures emerging from the Pilatte Hut some 2,000 feet or more beneath us, and remarked that the peaks of Dauphiné, with the exception of the glacier-clad mountains we were climbing, were fully as stony and precipitous as we had anticipated.

Continuing on our way, we made some more zigzags through the intricacies of the glacier, and arrived an hour later at the foot of an ice slope which ended in the East Ridge of Les Bans. At its foot this slope was rifted by a formidable bergschrund separating it from the Pilatte Glacier on which we stood. The rift was bridged by a tongue of snow at one place, but its upper lip was some fifteen feet high and vertical if not overhanging. The party ahead of us had crossed the snow bridge, scaled the lip, and cut steps up the ice slope. There seemed, therefore, every reason for us to do likewise and profit by the steps they had cut. But to my shame I must record that not only did we not do this, but that we avoided their route altogether and climbed up by an easier way. I, not Jim, was responsible for this decision. I crossed the snowbridge and tried to climb the ice lip, and because it was steep and strenuous work, and because I was hopelessly out of training, I returned to Jim and declared myself in favor of an easier route if such existed. I have not the slightest doubt that Jim could have romped up the ice lip, but he unselfishly agreed with me that we could get up more easily on the left. Our "slink round," as I termed it later, meant traversing horizontally until we were almost beneath the Col de Pilatte, crossing the bergschrund at an easier place, climbing some rocks and snow to the col, and doubling back along the ridge from the latter to the final rocks of Les Bans. In the course of this entirely unnecessary maneuver we at least had the satisfaction of treading classic ground, for the bergschrund we crossed was that associated with a dramatic episode during the first passage of the Col de Pilatte by Edward Whymper's party in 1864. The bergschrund was more formidable then and the party, who had crossed the pass in the reverse direction, had to jump down fifteen or sixteen feet, and forward at the same time some seven or eight feet, alighting on a narrow ridge of ice. The first three made the leap successfully. Then came the turn of Whymper's friend Jean Reynaud. The episode is best described in Whymper's own words:

> *He came to the edge and made declarations. I do not believe that he was a whit more reluctant to pass the place than we others, but he was infinitely more demonstrative—in a word, he was French. He wrung his hands. "Oh, what a diable of a place!" "It is nothing, Reynaud," I said "it is nothing." "Jump," cried the others, "jump." But he turned round, as far as one can do such a thing in an ice step, and covered his face with his hands, ejaculating, "Upon my word, it is not possible. No! No!! No!!! It is not possible."*
>
> *How he came over I scarcely know. We saw a toe—it seemed to belong to Moore; we saw Reynaud a flying body, coming down as if taking a header into water—with arms and legs all abroad, his leg of mutton flying in the air, his baton escaped from his grasp; and then we heard a thud as if a bundle of carpets had been pitched out of a window.*

No such excitement befell us, and a little later we found ourselves on the sharp snow crest separating the Col de Pilatte from the rocks of Les Bans. The party ahead of us had climbed the mountain and were descending, and we paused to watch them. There were three of them, one, the middlemost man on the rope, being both bulky and clumsy, so much so that we watched almost anxiously. Largely because of him, the party was moving slowly, and the loose rocks they knocked down more than deterred us from attempting the climb until they were safely off the mountain. Seen *en face* the rocks appeared well nigh vertical, but the lie to their steepness and difficulty was given by the climbing method employed by the party we were watching, particularly that of the fat man, a method destructive to the seat of the trousers. It was not an inspiring spectacle and it became positively alarming when the fat man's feet shot from under him on a patch of ice and he subsided with a jolt on some rocks. However, as I told myself, who were we to criticize? I, at least, should put up an equally undignified performance on this, my first expedition of the season.

They were down at last, and after exchanging greetings, and seeing that they were out of range of any stones we might knock down, we moved along the ridge to the rocks and began to ascend.

The climb proved an excellent first expedition of the season, and the rocks, though steep in places, were neither too difficult nor too sensational and were excellent in promoting that harmony of mind and muscle which is the hallmark of skill and practice in mountaineering.

Unhappily, the pleasure of the ascent was marred by severe altitude headaches. I have suffered from these headaches before, both in the Alps and Himalayas, and they always result from a climb to an elevation in excess of 10,000 feet the first day. I do not know if they are peculiar to mountaineers because, while many members of Everest expeditions have been prostrated by them on arrival at Thangu bungalow in Sikkim, which is situated at a height of only 11,000 feet, tourists frequently visit the bungalow without similar ill effects. If there is a worse form of headache I do not know it. It begins at the base of the skull and drives knives of pain through the head to the eyes. Every movement, every jar of the foot on the ground, is agony, and when vomiting supervenes it does little or nothing to alleviate the pain. My only consolation was that Jim complained of a similar headache. This sounds a selfish statement, but there are few human beings, however Christian or humane, who do not derive a vicarious satisfaction from knowing that their ills are shared by a companion. Therefore while I said "Bad luck" to Jim, when he complained of his headache, I was secretly glad that I was not the only one to suffer.

Had it not been for our headaches, we should have enjoyed better than we did the scramble to the summit. Fortunately memory has the inestimable advantage of eliminating physical sensation and promoting to the fore, often in false perspective, latent mental and spiritual enjoyment. Thus I remember the climb as interesting, the weather as perfect, and the views as extensive and beautiful. Memory tells me that the rocks were pleasant to handle, that they were soaked with sun, and seemed almost to breathe warmth as we climbed up them. What memory does not tell me is that at the time I had a bursting head, and that I swore to myself over and over again that come what might never would I climb a peak as high as Les Bans the first day of a mountaineering holiday.

Moving for the most part both together we progressed rapidly, at least Jim did, while I labored in the rear, a prey to my lack of training which transformed an easy and pleasant rock climb into a sweating, puffing, unharmonious labor.

My head was feeling like a Mills bomb that has just had its trigger released when, of a sudden, rocks no longer loomed above, and we trod with dramatic unexpectedness the level summit of Les Bans.

Headachy and sick we sank down on sun-warmed slabs of schistose. "That's that," said Jim, with the air of one to whom the climb has seemed unexpectedly and disappointingly short. "Thank heavens!" I replied fervently.

A few minutes' rest improved our malaise, and we were able to take stock of the view. The Dauphiné Alps certainly confirmed our first impressions of wildness and grandeur. What we saw was not fantastic and bizarre like the Dolomites, nor serene and well ordered like the principal ranges of the Alps, but something in between. There were glaciers to be seen, in particular the Pilatte Glacier that curved away at our feet, but these were incidental to the main theme, which was an intricate jumble of savage rock peaks, not peaks with sweeping ridges and faces like those on the main watershed of the Alps, but mountains whose principal characteristics are steepness and complexity. To an orthodox mountaineer the view from Les Bans is depressing rather than elevating. It is uneasy and somehow incomplete. It is neutral in color; there are no green alps and smiling pasturelands such as the mountaineer gazes upon from the heights of the Oberland or Mont Blanc; there are no gentle and gracious forms, no shining snowfields and remote wind-fashioned snow edges. Order and methodicity is lacking and, instead, there is a vast untidy mess of rocky mountains and narrow tortuous valleys. The Dauphiné massif is a by-product, a collection of shattered peaks arranged anyhow, not in supreme disregard for ordinary laws like the Dolomites, but rather as an untidy afterthought to the Alps. It is as though Nature had said, "Well, there are the Alps, they look all right, but there's a vacant space here, and I've a lot of stuff left over, not much snow and ice but any amount of rock; I'll plonk it down here and make the best job I can with it."

But already I can sense my mountaineering friends writhing inwardly. To say such things about Dauphiné! Look at the Meije, the Écrins, they say; graceful mountains, splendid climbs; this fellow, confound him, is only writing to annoy—deliberate contentiousness! Therefore, let me hasten to add that the Dauphiné Alps grow on the mountaineer. I have recorded here faithfully my first reactions to these mountains, but later, only a little later, I came to like Dauphiné better. A conventional mountaineer requires some time to accustom himself to the unconventional, and unconventional from an architectural standpoint Dauphiné certainly is. During my few days in this country I came to learn the charm of its stony valleys, where little flowers peep out in unexpected places, and the untamed splendor of its peaks and precipices. I learned that it is a range of unsuspected views and odd and delightful corners, as many of both in a mile as in any other mountain country I know. Then there is the spell of the unknown. In point of fact there is nothing unknown about the peaks of Dauphiné, though there are many new routes to be made up them, but the early reputation of inaccessibility gained by this labyrinth of ridges, gorges, and valleys has never been quite dispelled. It is accurately and meticulously mapped, but the mountaineer feels that to him personally it is *terra incognita,* and that he must explore it: in the course of his explorations he will experience much the same feelings that the pioneers experienced who first worked their way from valley to valley over the intricate ridges. Such then is the charm of this strange country, and if the charm is at first not apparent it becomes perceptible with increasing knowledge and experience.

Apart from general impressions, what did we see from the summit of Les Bans? First and foremost our gaze sought out the Meije, 13,065 feet which, except in the matter of height—Barre des Écrins, 13,450, is the highest summit in Dauphiné—is the undisputed monarch of the district. It also enjoys the distinction of being the last great alpine peak to have been climbed and this not so much on account of its forbidding appearance as the sheer difficulty of the climbing. The Meije is unmistakable from any direction, a square-built mass with a long summit ridge bristling with towers, with one conical-shaped point, the Grand Pic, at the westernmost end, to complete the resemblance to a Norman fortress. Les Écrins was not seen to advantage because of the interposing mass of the Ailefroide. Les Rouies, 11,775 feet, and the Pic d'Olan, 11,740, are the highest peaks to the west, the latter a beautiful wall-sided mountain renowned among rock climbers.

Yet we were little concerned with topographical details. For one thing we were too headachy and tired; for another the sun blazed down with lambent intensity, and there was not a breath of wind to temper its heat. It is not often that the mountaineer finds himself frizzling on an alpine summit 12,000 feet high, and Jim, feeling that he had done all that was required of him in the matter of the view and topographical identification, settled himself back to a boulder with his handkerchief over his face and fell fast asleep. I would have followed his example had it not occurred to me that if I did so we might both of us continue to sleep for hours and be benighted in consequence. Therefore I contented myself with a doze.

In this way over an hour passed. It is a curious experience dozing or sleeping on a mountaintop. The mountaineer, half drugged by the sunlight, rouses himself by slow degrees. He sees before him peak, range, and valley shining and unsubstantial like a vision, so much so that it is difficult to separate reality from unreality, and it requires a conscious mental effort to face up to the hard fact that a long, toilsome, and difficult descent has to be negotiated. Sleeping on a mountaintop is not always a safe luxury, and I can recollect more than one occasion when I have set off down a difficult climb, yawning and drowsy and an incomplete master of myself for the first minute or two. It is in such moments of physical and mental inertia that accidents may occur.

The descent proved easy, and we rattled down the rocks. Our headaches were finally dissipated by the loss of height, and we both felt in good fettle by the time the ridge was regained. There we decided to descend the ice slope we had avoided on the way up. It was easier than expected, though the vertical lip of the bergschrund needed delicate balance. Jim went first, and after asking for plenty of slack rope, jumped the last ten feet or so down and across the rift, alighting gracefully on a snow ridge forming the lower lip, whence he skidded off down the slope below for a yard or two before coming to a halt in the soft snow of the glacier. I followed, and if my performance was not so dramatic as that of Reynaud's seventy-five years before me, I felt equally ridiculous as I sailed through the air, to alight with an undignified thump, and shoot down pell-mell to my laughing companion.

Thenceforwards we ploughed and glissaded rapidly down the sun-softened snow of the Pilatte Glacier. The seracs and the crevasses were behind, or so we thought, and we were on smooth unbroken snow when of a sudden down went my feet into a concealed crevasse. It was not a wide crevasse, but wide enough for a lissom mountaineer, and I had a momentary vision of somber bottle-green depths before I struggled out. The rope was by no means taut, and Jim told me afterwards that he was over the same trap. It was a lesson to us both; nothing could have seemed more innocent than the snow slopes we were on when the incident occurred, and we apostrophized ourselves as fools.

The shadows were lengthening as we passed the Pilatte Hut, and scampered down slopes of scree and snow to our bivouac place. We retrieved our equipment and strolled down the flowerful slopes to the Alp de Carrelet, where we quenched our thirst with beer.

Forgotten were our headaches and fatigue as we lolled contentedly outside the Carrelet Hut in the late afternoon sun. Life was very good; the clock had moved on a few hours; another mountain memory had been gained. In any dark or evil hours that might lie ahead we could return in spirit to a star-filled night by a juniper fire, sun-warmed rocks and the meadows of the Alp de Carrelet. Such memories endure.

So we lingered a while on the Alp de Carrelet. The sun slipped lower and lower in a cloudless sky and cool shadows gathered in the valley. Peak and precipice stood immobile in a silent air. Only the stream continued its litany and birds twittered in the hushed pine forest. At such moments earthy man is aware of something greater than his earthiness.

Dusk was falling as we walked down the path to La Berardé.

"EDUCATION IN VERTICALITY: A SHORT COMEDY OR FARCE IN FOUR SCENES"

FROM
A Fine Kind of Madness
By Guy and Laura Waterman

FOLLOWING THEIR MARRIAGE IN 1973, GUY AND LAURA WATERMAN moved to a remote Vermont cabin where they created a wilderness home in which they wrote books about their simplified lifestyle and their beloved New England mountains. Their homestead was a mile from the road, and lacked even the basic comforts of plumbing or electricity (but it did have a Steinway grand piano, carried up piece by piece). Their way of living was a statement in itself.

The Watermans were avid mountaineers who had climbed all forty-eight peaks in New Hampshire that are 4,000 feet or higher, many of them in winter. In February 2000, Guy Waterman, was to make his final ascent. He climbed to the top of 5,249-foot Mount Lafayette, in the White Mountains in northern New Hampshire, and sat down to die in the predictably brutal winter conditions and sub-zero temperatures. He had notified friends of his intentions by letter, and his body was retrieved days later. Guy was sixty-seven years old at the time of his suicide, and his last book—*A Fine Kind of Madness*—was about to be published.

Waterman's death ended an extraordinary life; from jazz musician to presidential speechwriter, Waterman had been successful at multiple professions before he retreated to the New England wilderness. The reason for his suicide may never be known, but he was said to be despondent over his inability to protect the beloved mountains in which he lived.

The Watermans wrote five books during the quarter century they were together. *Backwoods Ethics, Forest and Crag, Yankee Rock and Ice, Wilderness Ethics,* and *A Fine Kind of Madness.* The Watermans's commentary was a mixture of practical advice based on their years of experience, condemnation of those who failed to measure up to their high ethical standards (such as hikers who use cell phones in the wilderness), and humorous observations about the hardship of the life they chose.

The following piece was written in 1981 by Guy, because, as he put it, "We wished to write vividly about the hardest climbs done in recent years, but our own abilities, or rather the limits of those abilities, prevented our exploring them on our own." So in the company of a friend, Mike Young, who was a superb technical ice climber, Guy Waterman ventured onto the steep ice climbs of Lake Willoughby, Vermont, so that he could get an authentic taste of life at the sharp end.

The story can be found in *A Fine Kind of Madness,* on pages 68–72.

[Authors' note: When writing our history of technical rock and ice climbing, we faced one severe handicap. We wished to write vividly about the hardest climbs done in recent years, but our own abilities, or rather the limits of those abilities, prevented our exploring them on our own. Still, when it came to describing the most extreme ice routes in the northeastern United States, we felt that at least one of us should have personally experienced the exotic pleasures of climbing them. Fortunately, a young man named Mike Young, a superb ice climber and mountaineer, had become a close personal friend—not because we joined him on his hard routes, but for other reasons. In the interest of our research, Mike agreed to take one of us up one of the infamous climbs at Lake Willoughby in northern Vermont, locale of the longest and steepest ice in all of New England. Guy nominated Laura for this honor; Laura nominated Guy. Eventually one of us was condemned—that is, chosen. Heading off on that morning, Guy tried to keep in mind the value of direct involvement as a key to vivid writing. "At least we're not working on a history of capital punishment," he thought. The ensuing events, we decided, lent themselves less to the high drama usually associated with high-level climbing than to some sort of low farce.]

THE DATE: February 7, 1981.

THE SCENE: Lake Willoughby, Vermont, which lies roughly three million miles north of anywhere warm.

DRAMATIS PERSONAE: (1) Mike Young, an ice climber of considerable attainments; (2) Guy Waterman, of considerably fewer attainments, if indeed any at all.

SCENE I.

The two climbers are roping up at the base of more than three hundred feet of almost dead-vertical hard-frozen water ice. Wind whistles mournfully through the leafless trees in the woods below. Spindrift races fitfully across the cold surface of the ice.

WATERMAN (throwing out the rope, while looking up fearfully at the towering ramparts of frost): Say, Mike, does anybody actually fall on this stuff? I mean, do these ice screws really hold a dead-vertical drop like you could take on this?

YOUNG (abstractedly, while lacing on crampons): Oh, sure, the modern ice screw is really quite reliable. People fall a lot. No problem.

(A few minutes pass in silence, the two climbers busy with their preparations.)

WATERMAN (lacing on crampons, but evidently the idea has occurred that Young weighs approximately fifty-one pounds more than Waterman, and will be leading, of course): Uh, Mike . . . do you ever fall?

YOUNG (absorbed with sorting hardware): Huh? Oh, fall? Me? Yes. Funny thing, actually. Every season I seem to take two leader falls. Never more than two. No matter how much I climb, or how little, I always seem to manage to take two falls, and only two. Every winter. Isn't that funny?

WATERMAN (hastily): Yes, yes, funny . . .

(A few more minutes pass in silence.)

WATERMAN (a bit more softly): Uh, say, Mike . . . have you taken any falls this winter?

YOUNG (to the point): One.

WATERMAN (barely audible): Oh.

Curtain.

SCENE 2.

The second pitch. Young has executed a flawless lead of the second pitch and is now belaying at a point two-thirds of the way up the ice. Waterman is attempting to follow. Starts to fall. Actually, let's skip this scene. If you like, we could tell you about the first pitch, which went very smoothly.

Curtain (quick!).

SCENE 3.

Top of the second pitch, and showing the ice a bit above that point as well. Both climbers have tied in here. Waterman is wearily handing the rack to Young, who seems unwearied in spite of the strenuous weightlifting he has just completed, having hauled a weight scarcely fifty-one pounds lighter than his own body weight up most of the second pitch.

YOUNG (with enthusiasm that Waterman finds hard to take): Wasn't that a great pitch, though?

WATERMAN (smiling weakly): Yep, wonderful!

YOUNG (gesturing upward): This next part's a whole lot easier. You won't have any trouble. It's really nice climbing. You'll love it.

WATERMAN: Yeah, wonderful!

(Waterman puts Young on belay. Young leads up about ten feet.)

YOUNG: This is lousy ice. It doesn't take the tools well at all. (Pause.) I don't think it would take ice screws either. Just flakes off.

(A further pause. Young has moved up another five feet.)

YOUNG (falling): Falling!

Curtain.

SCENE 4.

Top of the second pitch, but showing also the ice a bit below, rather than above the belay point. Young now appears approximately thirty-five feet below the spot where he appeared at the end of the previous scene. He is in a horizontal position, face up, not significantly touching the ice, swaying gently in the air, rather like a piece of scaffolding against the side of a sheer glass skyscraper. The rope, taut as a piano wire, runs from his harness up to the waist of Waterman, who is holding on for dear life.

YOUNG (shaking his head slowly): Two.

Curtain.

"EARLY ALPS: THE WILD YEARS"

FROM
The Burgess Book of Lies
BY ADRIAN AND ALAN BURGESS

THE BURGESS BROTHERS ARE ICONS OF MODERN CLIMBING. THE notorious bad boys of mountaineering, identical twins Adrian and Alan Burgess long ago established themselves as players in the international climbing scene. Their outrageous acts have become legendary, but not more so than their climbing moxie. These Yorkshire lads are equally famous for what they have climbed as for the raucous behavior they exhibited getting there and back again.

The brothers have an extensive climbing record in both the Alps and the Himalaya. They climbed together on Everest, Manaslu, and K2. Both climbed Dhaulagiri and Annapurna IV, the latter a rare Himalayan success in winter. They even attempted a winter ascent of Everest with Joe Tasker. But it was in the Alps where these famous siblings lived through some of their scariest close calls and, by dint of youthful ignorance, had some of their boldest successes.

Alan, who authored the following chapter, clearly relishes the unfettered life he and Adrian lived in those formative years as climbers, from 1968 to 1972. To support their passion, they taught school near Snowdonia, Scotland, where they climbed every weekend, and scrimped and saved mightily throughout the school year to fund summers in the Alps.

"I wrote the chapter 'The Wild Years' while hanging out on a beach in Thailand in 1987," Al Burgess told me. "I had just returned from an expedition in Nepal. I wrote it longhand in an old notebook, and it was edited a number of years later, by myself and by my twin brother, Adrian, shortly before being published.

"The idea was to describe the lifestyles and the colorful people who made up the elite of British alpinism from 1966 to 1972, and to show how single-mindedness and ambition overrode the poverty and lack of equipment that the climbers suffered. It was a melting pot of characters who would move onto other climbs around the globe in the following twenty years. There is a certain nostalgia for the lost innocence of such commitment."

"Early Alps: the Wild Years" is in *The Burgess Book of Lies*, on pages 37–65.

After the alpine season of 1966, school could never be the same. Sitting in a hot, stuffy classroom and struggling with economic geography and the nuances of Shakespeare, it was too easy to stare through a misted window and dissolve . . . to reappear high on a Dolomite wall or an icy north face. The future was as far ahead as the next weekend, and lunchtimes were spent thumbing through climbing guidebooks. Invariably, Monday mornings found us with hands grazed and torn from a viciously steep gritstone crack, forearms and shoulders aching from the latest "extreme."

The secure prospect of another year in school did not conceal doubts about the future. We both were gravitating toward a teacher-training course in physical education, especially if we were accepted at Chester College of Education, only a couple of hours drive from the climbing in Snowdonia.

Life was acceptable, each weekend's climbing balancing five days of academic boredom. We had few school friends; they lacked the color and experience of our older climbing companions. We had not discovered the delights of female distraction, so we single-mindedly pursued our rock-climbing passion, to the detriment of homework and examinations. It was not surprising that we were less than perfect students.

We scraped through our examinations and were accepted into Chester College. That summer we took jobs as climbing instructors at an outdoor-education establishment in north Yorkshire. Working at Bewerly Park gave us enough funds to buy a small van, and it introduced us to a sport that would take on more significance later: Girls!

Loaded with the basic academic materials for our college course and an unreasonable amount of climbing hardware, we arrived at the steps of the somewhat conservative Chester College. We quickly established our priorities by seeking out fellow climbers from the college mountaineering club.

The academic year passed slowly, but we developed an interest in gymnastics and physiology; both disciplines appeared helpful in climbing. We socialized very little with most of our fellow students, whose interests were more in the direction of soccer, rugby, and cricket. With one or two close climbing friends, we'd leave soon after lectures on a Friday afternoon and drive to Snowdonia, the Lake District, or Derbyshire. We traveled in our small van, camped out regardless of bad weather, and cooked all our meals over a small kerosene stove. We attempted climbs even if hampered by heavy rain, and we were never satisfied unless challenged to the edge of our ability.

One incident demonstrates our single-minded attitude toward our sport. We were in the Llanberis Pass of Snowdonia, the rain was lashing at the crags, and no other people were out climbing. Three of us sat huddled in our steamy van: engine silent, wind buffeting, rain splatting against the windshield. Above, dominating the road, Dinas Cromlech soared to the clouds: malevolent and black. Splitting the sheer rock walls was a corner, like an open book cleft in two. Climbers knew it as Cenotaph Corner, and it had a reputation for steep, sustained difficulty. We had climbed it previously in dry conditions and knew it to be well protected and easily within our capabilities.

Given those weather conditions today, we would go for a run or head for the pub. But in those days we needed to be heroes, to take sword and lance in hand and ride forward into danger to slay the mythic dragon—which was within ourselves. To wait for another day was unthinkable. With the dragon ever-present, action—hard and immediate—was the only solution. So we climbed the loose scree below the crag, no longer seeing it as just another rock climb but as a voyage into a living legend. By challenging the very flesh of that inert cleft, we could partake of the myth ourselves.

After a rope-length of easier climbing, we crouched below the corner, already soaked to the skin through our canvas jackets. The corner ran vertically over our heads, and a torrent of water sluiced down the narrow fissure. I agreed to give it the first try. Tying onto two thick hawsers of nylon and carrying a selection of machine nuts, drilled out and threaded onto nylon-rope slings, I started up the rock. I worked my way slowly upwards, straddling the corner, and by fixing protection every six feet or so, I knew I would come to no real harm even if I should slip from the slimy green holds. Aid shouted encouragement through the wind, as I looked down between spread-eagled legs, with water streaming down my arms and back. The holds were sometimes sharp, square-cut and secure and, in places, offered space for three fingertips, while others were sloping or narrow cracks where two fingers were inserted vertically and twisted cruelly for support.

At 100 feet, I approached the crux of the climb. I was shaking hard with cold, and my fingers were slowly losing all feeling. A decision had to be made quickly: to continue up or to escape down. Suddenly the situation was taken out of my hands. My corduroy pants, rain-saturated and heavy, slid down around my knees! I kicked them free. Aid lowered me down, and we retreated to the climbers' cafe in Llanberis village. The climb was not completed, but the dragon, if not completely slain, had been driven away for that day.

⋗   ⋗   ⋗

As summer approached, we were drawn to the guidebooks of Mont Blanc and the Alps. We had saved hard from our college grants, sometimes at the expense of course textbooks, and we would be traveling as cheaply as possible. Amos, a climbing friend from Huddersfield, would join us. He was a big man, a few years older than us. He played rugby and climbed only in the summertime, when he went to the Alps. He had a robust, rather vulgar sense of humor and great physical strength. He became our self-appointed mentor for the summer. His death a few years later, while he was descending the Matterhorn, came as a great shock to us. He had seemed indestructible.

Driving down the long, empty roads of France, with the van loaded with English tinned food, we laughed at Amos's wild stories and spoke of outrageous climbing plans. I'm sure Amos thought us quite naive.

"After a training climb, to get fit, we could do the Walker Spur or the North Face of the Dru," Aid asserted. "They'll be quite long, but I don't reckon they're that 'ard, especially if they're dry."

"Which route d'ya think first then?" I asked. Amos remained silent.

"Oh, somat short but technical, like South Face o' Midi," said Aid. "Gets us 'igh enough, but can be done in a day."

"That'd cost us a *télépherique* ticket," I replied. "Mebbe a route on L'M'd be cheaper, cuz we could walk t' bottom o' route."

"It's not 'igh enough, though," countered Aid. "We want t' get up t' 13,000 feet t' get fit."

Amos cautiously suggested: "Well, lads, if we took a week's food up to a hut, we could do a few shorter routes and see what the weather's up to."

He didn't want to squash our enthusiasm but probably felt it better to see how we climbed together and what we were capable of.

We drove directly to Chamonix, and went to the Biolay campsite in the woods behind the town, the traditional place for British alpinists. There were already many tents, vans, and plastic cook shelters scattered throughout the forest. We set up our two tents alongside a Czechoslovakian group. In the steady alpine mist and rain, the campsite was a dank, dripping place. Water had to be carried from the railway station fifteen minutes away. There were no toilet facilities, except the sheltered woods, and it took a brave man to wander there barefoot or at night.

The climbers of the Biolay were a hard-bitten crew, more resembling a band of brigands resting between forays than the elite of British alpinism. Any crime was defensible if it provided an opportunity for the next hard climb. The Biolay bunch raided supermarkets, looted wine from the back of hotels, and jumped the rack-and-pinion railway that led up to the peaks. Local vegetable gardens rarely grew to maturity.

In the evenings most climbers drifted down to the Bar National to sip a glass of *vin ordinaire* or split a bottle of Alsace beer and discuss the weather and the next climb. The bar owner, Maurice, was a half-blind ex-colonel in the French army, who had a special affection for the British climbing characters who frequented his bar year after year. He understood well enough what a lawless bunch they were, but over the years he had come to appreciate their passion for hard climbing. He had known many who did not return.

Men with scraped fists and sunburned faces spoke of epic ascents and stormy retreats from mountains with names that lingered fearfully on the tongues of these alpine veterans. Legends of British climbing sat hunched over half-empty bottles of "Old Guides," while novices whispered their names and were careful not to stumble against their chairs. Names like Freney Pillar and the Droites Direct caused conversation to hush respectfully as these mythological hardmen spoke in tense, understated dialect.

"Aye, lad," eavesdroppers heard, "there was a rock the size of a minivan . . . just missed us . . . cut the rope . . . wha' wi' no stove we 'ad to eat snow . . . ah, not that bad . . . "

Aid and I listened in wonder, little thinking that we might already be as strong as those characters, only younger and less experienced.

         ➤   ➤   ➤

We had heard of a climb on the Grand Capucin, an 1,800-foot smooth granite pillar. When Walter Bonatti first climbed it by its overhanging East Face, his ascent was considered a breakthrough in boldness and technique. Today there are many hard technical free-climbs on the pillar. Climbers arrive from the nearby Torino hut, equipped with lightweight rock slippers and sophisticated protection equipment. They carry tiny day packs, climb quickly, and rarely need to spend the night out. In 1968, alpinists climbed in mountain boots and frequently carried bivouac equipment, which caused them to move more slowly and therefore use the equipment they were carrying. Climbers now avoid storms, but in those days, we often had to sit them out. Finishing a climb while enveloped in swirling snow and howling wind was all part of the game.

We reached the foot of the pillar by taking a cable car to 13,000 feet and then traversing glaciers and snowfields through thigh-deep snow. A steep snow-gully ran for 400 feet to the start of the steep rock. While we traversed slabs to a low rock cave, an unnerving boom echoed around the mountain walls, and an avalanche crashed down the gully, the debris spewing far out onto the glacier. We stared numbly at one another, an unspoken understanding of a near miss.

It was already midafternoon and beginning to snow lightly, so we dug the snow out of the cave, settled into down jackets, and made tea on our small stove. Later that afternoon, a couple of Italian climbers arrived and moved past to minuscule ledges above, securing their lead position for the next day.

In those days before the advent of Gore-Tex and fiber fleeces, bivouacs were times for reflection and often suffering. We used lightweight down jackets to the waist and a short down-filled sleeping bag—a so-called "elephant's foot"—from feet to waist. If one was lucky, it didn't leave too large a cold spot around the midriff. We laid a large nylon bag on the snow to sleep on, and if it snowed, we pulled the bag over our heads. Sleeping in this "Zardsky" sac was a mixture of claustrophobic nightmares and partial suffocation. To light a gasoline stove and cook in the damn thing was like cooking dinner around a diesel truck's exhaust pipe. The condensation soaked our gear and froze into a crackling suit of armor. Our boots, wet from the deep slog across the glacier, became like frozen logs.

Nights began by lingering and ended with a slow, dragging breaking of dawn. One story I always felt sympathy with dealt with a couple of alpinists crouching and shivering in their bivouac as they waited out the night. Stoically suffering the tremors that tormented their shaking bodies, they waited for the pale light of dawn. The sky flickered on the horizon, and a faint beam of light streaked the distant peaks. Their hopes soared as the flickering swelled into light—and the moon rose. It was still six hours to daybreak!

That morning on the Capucin was not too bad as frigid awakenings go. At least we were on an east face, and the sun struck us early. We munched on chocolate bars and drank hot tea, savoring each warming mouthful, before uncoiling our rope and preparing to climb.

The first few hundred feet were up vertical shallow corners and cracks, not too difficult but unnerving with our clumsy frozen boots and numbed fingers. There is nothing quite like the exquisite pain experienced as one hangs from a piton, gasping clouds of frosty breath while cold, swollen fingers fill with hot blood, bringing nauseous waves of rising vomit, slowly ebbing to hands glowing with a steady throb of heat. Truly the agony and the ecstasy!

The sun rose, the rock steepened, and the ground crept farther away below our heels. We attached rope slings to the fixed pitons as the face leaned outward. At one small stance that was the size and shape of a broken dinner plate, I was attached to a single four-inch blade of steel alloy. It had been driven into a vertical crack above my head, and like a romantic lover with a beautiful woman, I gave it 100 percent of my hope and trust. I tied myself to it and ran the rope, clipped through its eye with a steel snap-link, downward into the abyss where my brother was swarming through a series of overhanging flakes. A muffled cry and then a throaty curse swept upward as the rope went taut and then surged down like an angry reptile. I grabbed at the rope. It stopped. The piton held. A crash from the glacier and the smell of sulfur confirmed Aid's comment:

"I pulled up on a block the size of a minivan! The bloody thing came off! Lucky it didn't cut the rope!"

"Ya OK?"

"Could be worse. Could be down there!" He glanced backward over his shoulder.

"D'ya fancy leading the next pitch?" I was shaking now, after the surge of adrenaline.

"Give us a break, man. I'm a bit shook up. Couldn't you do it?"

"Lucky this peg held, eh? Should get easier higher up." Optimism said more in hope than fact.

It was almost dark when we pulled onto a sloping rock terrace almost on the top of the pillar. Mouths parched and hands torn by the rough granite, we prepared for another vigil, only this time a warm glow of achievement and muscular fatigue flowed through us. The challenge of the ascent had been faced and won. Danger was virtually over. Tomorrow was another day.

I lounged in a half-dream—comfortable, soft. Too warm, suspiciously warm.

"Aid. It's snowing."

"Yeah." Muffled. Unconcerned.

"No wind, though. Suppose it's OK"

"Yeah."

Can't do anything about it anyway. Why worry?

⚓   ⚓   ⚓

Calm, gentle grayness: a watery dawn with snowflakes the size of thumbnails did not inspire fear. We only had to find the anchor points to rappel from, and the weather would clear as we got lower. We pulled on our oiled cloth jackets over eiderdown jackets—and looked like replicas of the Michelin Man. We prepared to climb.

The easy slabs of yesterday gave us tiptoe balances, and gloves scraped for incut flakes. We climbed up the final slabs.

This peak was a free-standing 1,800-foot rock pinnacle, which was joined to the main mountain mass at a narrow col. We were atop the huge pinnacle, and the mountain soared behind us.

To get to the only way down, we had to find the 300-foot vertical drop that hit the narrow col, which had steep gullies on each side of it. It was absolutely crucial to be correct in making the two rappels down onto the notch. If you missed the col, the vertical drop became at least a thousand feet on each side. It was vital to be able to see exactly what we were rappelling onto.

As we traversed around the summit ledges, we found old pitons and old slings that looked like rappel slings. We caught up with the two Italian guys who had passed us the day before and who had bivouacked on the summit. They were looking for the same slings and were as confused as we were about the route.

In those days, we didn't have anything like figure eight descenders [a double-loop alloy device used to provide friction and absorb heat during a rappel]. We just had simple rappelling rope that we wore over our shoulders and wrapped round our body. We got the two 250-foot ropes tied together, threw them down the face into the mist, and started to rappel down. It was a boiling sea of mist, and snowflakes the size of quarters were falling.

I rappelled down 150 feet and came to a small ledge and a rock-spike about the size of a man's fist. I put some half-inch nylon tape behind it, clipped myself onto it, and shouted to Adrian: "OK, come on down."

He came down, and then the two Italians followed him. We pulled the rappel ropes down behind us, which meant that all four of us were now hanging on this tiny ledge. Down below, it dropped vertically and overhanging. But we were confident because the guidebook said it was one long rappel. We should easily reach the notch, the col, within the next 150 feet.

I threw our climbing ropes down again. It was fortunate, as it turned out, that I also took the Italians' ropes as an additional safety rope. As Adrian pays out the rope—which was around his waist and he was belayed [secured by a rope] to the rock-spike—I go into the mist.

I'm hanging free, not touching the rock. I've got on a pack that weighs more than twenty pounds and it's pulling me over backwards. I've got on thick woolen gloves, the rope's icy, and I'm sliding down and down, thinking that sometime soon I must reach the notch.

Then I look down. The wind has blown away some of the cloud below me, and I can see the place where I should be. The notch is 150 feet over to one side!

Where I'm rappelling is down an overhanging rock wall. There's no way I can reach a ledge. This means I have to get back up the rope. Aid is standing on the ledge, belaying me around his waist. I'm hanging about fifty feet down, twisting and spinning, feet not touching rock.

I think: Holy shit! I better get back up! I'm in the wrong place!

I was scared, because we didn't have jumars or anything for getting back up the rope in those days. [A jumar is a device that slides easily up a rope and locks when downward pressure is applied.]

I think: What am I gonna do here?

I'm hanging on and I'm spinning around. And I'm tired! With my thick woolen gloves and ice on the rope, I'm having to keep a tight grasp on the rope to stop slipping farther down. What I've got is an aid sling—étrier they call it—around my shoulders. So I unclip this thing and put the carabiner over the knot in the safety rope.

Quickly I shout up to Adrian: "Hang onto the rope! Hold the safety rope!"

The wind's blowing my words away. I'm getting really tired. So I put my foot into the sling, stand up, and transfer my weight off of the rappel rope and onto the safety rope. That pulls Aid off the ledge and turns him upside down and leaves him hanging on the belay. When that happens, he lets me go, lets the rope slip as I suddenly put all my weight onto it. And I go horizontal—spinning, falling.

I think: This is it!

I'm falling, spinning!

It lasts only a split-second, of course, because Adrian holds me just before I drop off the end of the rappel rope. There I am, literally hanging on the edge. And I'm so tired.

I think: I'm dead, gone!

I see the whole gully below me and clouds swirling around and snowing. I'm turned upside down, still hanging free. I'm spinning around on the end of the rope.

The Italians helped Aid back up on the ledge and, thank goodness, they'd grabbed the end of the safety rope and blocked it directly over the rock-spike.

So then, I've got a problem. I'm hanging there, and I have to get back up a 150 feet of overhanging rock. I didn't have any pressure slings or anything like that for getting back up the rope. By this time, Adrian obviously knew what was happening and realized I wasn't on a ledge.

All of them were paying close attention to what was going on. I had all the rope attached to me. If I lost the rope, *they* weren't going anywhere!

So then I thought: O.K, pull! I'll try to go hand over hand up the double rappel rope with these thick icy gloves, and Adrian can block me with the safely rope as I pull myself up. So I start doing that. Well, if you've ever tried to pull yourself hand over hand up a gymnasium rope, which is the width of your ankle, then sometime try to do it on a rope that's the thickness of your thumb, and do it wearing a rucksack and thick woolen gloves and with ice on the rope.

I make ten feet up the rope and I'm shot! I can't pull up any more! So I rock forwards with my feet in the etrier-sling on the safety rope and just hang there. I'm only attached by a waist belt, and I'm trying to keep in balance without strangling myself on that belt. (I didn't have a full harness then, like we have nowadays.)

So I'm hanging on the end of a rope, hunched over it so that my weight is taken partially on my feet. The rope is taut. It feels like a steel cable. I'm not pulling up any more. I'm too tired.

Then suddenly the rope just keeps coming up six inches at a time. I'm gradually being pulled up the overhanging rock. I imagine the three of them have some system of pulling me, and they're starting to bring me up. I start to get closer to the edge of the overhang. Then I get my feet back onto rock, so I can again start to take some of the weight onto my feet.

Then another twenty feet higher and I look up and I'm almost back at the ledge. I see Adrian's face. It's bright red! He's leaning over and pulling on the rope with his bare hands. He's pulling and straining, and every time he pulls, the two Italians block the safety rope behind the rock-spike. So it was Adrian alone who pulled me back up!

Well, can you imagine how I felt when I arrived on this tiny ledge that now seemed the size of a football field? I'm exhausted. We kind of hung there to get our bearings.

All I can say is: "Well, guys, it's not down there! It's across to our right!"

We're in the middle of these rock slabs. We have to get across feet to the right of these slabs and then make another rappel to the point where we want to be. By this time, I was out of it and too tired, so it was someone else's turn to make decisions. We know where we should be, but how are we going to do it?

The Italians led off across with their safety rope and their climbing rope. Adrian followed and I came across last. From that point on, it was easy. It was a straightforward rappel down to the little notch col.

In another couple of hours, we were rappelling down a 50- or 60-degree snow gully, where a lot of the weight could be taken on our feet. Two or three hours later, we were back on the glacier.

I was feeling: "Wow! I'm really lucky to be alive!"

➤   ➤   ➤

In 1968, during our second alpine season, the climbers we met were mainly British or French, but there were also Czechoslovakians, Dutch, Poles, and occasionally a few Americans. The most important fact about the campsites in the forests behind Chamonix is that they were free. The people there were not wealthy—mostly young climbers trying to make a few hundred dollars last the whole alpine season from June through August.

If you were in these woods behind Chamonix from the middle to the end of June, you'd see vans with British registration plates creeping up into the woods. You'd see many vans. There were Austin minivans and Morris One-Thousand vans—not flashy cars: no Porsches!—and old Ford transit vans like Econolines, all loaded to the gills with English tinned food, climbing equipment, and old tents.

The vans carried itinerant climbers. Some of them had real jobs and were there on two weeks' holiday, but most of them were people who had at least a month, many of them taking three months. A lot were unemployed. They'd stashed their vans full of food from England. They understood English food and were distrustful of French food and French culture. With little money, they'd show up and live for free in the woods.

Chamonix is not the driest place in the world. Camping there in the forest, even in the summertime, can be a very wet experience. The amount of climbing you can do there is relative to how well you can read the weather. Storms come blasting in off the Atlantic and hit the Mont Blanc massif, so timing when to do the climbs is dependent on the weather. That's all the conversation around the campsite: "When is the weather going to come good? How many days is it going to last?"

The small tents at the campsites were barely sufficient to survive in. So within their first two or three days, people went down into Chamonix or the villages just south of Chamonix to look for big sheets of plastic at construction sites. With this plastic, they'd build lean-tos and put together shelters to act as kitchens for the whole season: temporary shelters for the summer. People slept in tents but hung out under these plastic shelters. With little money to spend, they couldn't hang out all day in the Chamonix bars, where it was nice and warm and dry. They'd go from plastic shelter to plastic shelter, drinking tea and talking about climbs with friends.

＞   ＞   ＞

When nighttime came, the scams started. They mainly involved getting food. Someone might know of an ice-cream machine that would be unattended after midnight, and a substantial quantity of ice cream could be released from it. Someone else might know where red-wine crates were stashed out in back of a hotel. A guard dog was there, and you had to get past the dog without waking it up.

In Chamonix, there was an outdoor glass-fronted rotisserie where a dozen whole chickens would be turning on the spit. You could see the chickens turning slowly, roasting and smelling delicious. One time the sight and smell were just too much for a character known as Daniel Boone. He whipped open the glass door of the rotisserie and grabbed half a dozen spitted chickens—in broad daylight and right in front of the shop owner—and ran off down the street. He just assumed that no one would pursue him. And no one did. So people didn't starve.

French bread is always very fresh, so every morning people would go down to the pastry shops, the patisseries, to get French bread. French *patisseries* have shelves in the front window that overlooks the sidewalk, and these shelves are filled with wonderful-smelling *gateaux*—big cakes. We could never afford those, not even one slice.

The scam was to work in pairs. There was a big fat lady in one of the stores. One person—the decoy—would go in and ask to buy a loaf of bread, a *pan longue*. As the lady put the *pan longue* on the countertop, the decoy would put out the money but "accidentally" flip one of the francs so that it fell on the floor behind the counter. This fat lady was not very mobile and a little slow, and she'd wearily bend over to pick up the franc. At which point, the accomplice—the fox—would sneak into the shop, rip a *gateau* from the window shelf and be away before the fat woman straightened up. So she gained one franc and lost forty! Then the climbers would go to a cafe and share the loot, this treasured *gateau*.

At the Bar National, where we were allowed to eat the *gateau* (because that was where we'd bring our own food sometimes), Maurice, the owner, came over to our table one day. A lady was sitting next to us and buying us coffee because we'd got the *gateau*. Maurice said, in French: "Oh, nice *gateau*." And the lady said: "It's their birthday." And Maurice said: "Yes, every day is their birthday!"

Outside Chamonix, directly above the village, is a beautiful needle-sharp spike called the Aiguille de Dru (Aiguille is French for needle). It has a North Face that's 3,000 feet high, with a classic mixed rock-and-ice climb that was within our abilities. The Aiguille de Dru is an historical mountain, because each generation attempts to put up a climb that makes a statement for that generation. As techniques and equipment improved, the climbing grew harder and harder. No climber could sit in one of Chamonix's outdoor cafes and look up at the granite spire of the Aiguille de Dru without dreaming of climbing it.

The North Face is one of earliest, and yet most classical, ways of climbing the peak. You can see halfway up the ice field, and with your naked eye, you can trace the line of the North Face, winding its way from the lower cracked granite slabs through the barriers of icy chimneys and gullys to the fine old, steep, cracked upper buttresses. The North Face was a wonder. We decided to try it.

Normally it took people more than one day to climb the North Face. In those days with the equipment we had, if you climbed it in one day, you'd usually bivouac very close to the summit on easier ground. The next day, you'd traverse round and rappel down the other side of the mountain, down a much easier descent route. The idea was to try to climb the peak quickly so that, if the weather changed during the nighttime, you wouldn't be caught in the steep technical difficulties of the upper part of the climb. You'd have them behind you.

And that's more or less what happened to us.

>   >   >

Part of the journey to the foot of the climb involved a steep glacial moraine. To get up to there, you could wind up 2,500 feet of steep trail through a pine forest, which took probably two or three hours. If you had the money, you could buy a ticket on a rack-and-pinion railway. Unfortunately, that cost a good deal of francs and was beyond the pocket of most of the young climbers.

However, we had another method. After the railway leaves the station in Chamonix, there's a brief time before it enters a tunnel into the mountain. It slowly works its way out of the station and up into the forest. We'd hide behind trees in the forest, with packs on our backs and all ready to go. As the train came past, and before it had time to build much speed, we'd quickly spring out of the forest, leap toward the track, jump and grab one of the train handles, and hang on. Then before the train could go into the tunnel and sweep us off, we'd whip open the door and dive inside. We had to do all this without being seen, so while the conductor was in the front of the train checking tickets, we'd jump on the back.

For this particular climb, we hid in the forest and successfully leaped onto the train and got a free ride up to the head of the railway. From the station, it was another three or four hours crossing the glacier, and then a steep climb up a tenuous lateral moraine up to a bivouac on some big boulders at the foot of the North Face. As Adrian and I approached this bivouac, we saw that a number of other people—mainly French and German climbers—were also bivouacking at the foot of the face, intending to do the same climb that we'd planned for the following day.

In those days, there was a certain animosity and competitiveness toward some of the other climbers, because by most standards, British climbers were technically very competent and yet had little big-mountain alpine experience. The French climbers had lots of mountain experience, having the Alps in their own backyard, but then they were technically fairly incompetent. (This is definitely not true today.) The last thing we wanted was to get stuck behind some slower-moving groups of French or German climbers.

We planned to leave before them in the dark, by head-torch. That way, we'd get ahead of them. We intended to get up about three in the morning, but we overslept. By the time we were ready and had made tea in the morning, we saw a stream of head-torches, French and German, leading up to the foot of the face. Maybe half a dozen parties were ahead of us. We were at the back of the queue!

Fumbling around and rushing up the trail, crossing the bergschrund [the void between a rock face and the top of a glacier] at the foot of the face, we began to solo and climb up toward the first series of icy rocks. We realized now that we might have to bivouac on the face if these climbers in front of us started to go really slowly. Somehow we had to work a system of passing them. In the Alps, there's a kind of protocol: you ask for permission to pass. But if it's a rock-climbing pitch—if a guy's got his hands in a hand-jam crack— it's pretty difficult for you to get your hands in right alongside and climb round him. So passing is done on the ledges, when they're belaying.

On some of the easier rocks lower down, we had a system worked out. Adrian would lead off up and get in front of some of the people. Then we'd have two or three parties between Adrian and me. But everyone would start to climb again, and I couldn't come up behind him. So we'd still be behind the whole group.

We somehow had to rush past them all, all at one time. But for us to pass, we needed them to stop. So on the next pitch, I ran out as much rope as I possibly could and passed the whole group again. I kept on moving and started to bring the rope in for Adrian to climb. But Adrian found that the other leaders were also starting to climb, and he couldn't get round them. So he decided what he would do to give him a few minutes respite. Out of sight round a corner of rock, he tied a big overhand knot in all of their ropes. The knot then jammed up in their carabiners, and there was confusion—in French and German—between the leader and his second: "What's happening? Give me more rope! The rope's jammed!" By the time they discovered the overhand knot in their ropes, Adrian had managed to pass. We were in front of all of them!

Looming overhead was the first of the steeper technical pitches. It looked as though there had been some recent rockfall in the region. Adrian led off up this very loose section and anchored on about a hundred feet up. Some slack loops in the rope hooked over a rock pinnacle, and when Adrian pulled, it dislodged. A pinnacle the size of a medium-sized cow started to fall outwards. I threw myself into the back of a chimney crack. The huge boulder bounced past, cut our climbing rope and exploded straight over the heads of all the other climbers. All the way down you could hear the crash of rock: *Achtung! Achtung!*—just passing the German group. *Attention! Attention!*—just passing the French group. Finally, a huge crash and the smell of sulfur as the boulder ground itself into the rocks at the foot of the face. Then silence.

Following that, there were shouts up. Obviously they wondered what had happened. They didn't know if we'd knocked that rock off or if it had fallen naturally. One of our climbing ropes had been cut (we had two of them; we were climbing in double ropes). I quickly climbed up to join Adrian and we held a discussion. Should we continue or not? With one rope, we could certainly climb up. That was not going to be a problem. But the second rope being cut would cause a problem on some of the long rappels of the descent route. And if the weather changed and we had to come back down this same North Face route, we would need the ability of long rappels that two ropes provide.

The exploding boulders had probably cut some of the other people's ropes below us. They, too, were having many discussions. We decided to continue, but the rest of the groups, obviously shaken by this experience and not wanting to have it repeated, decided either that it was too dangerous to continue or they didn't have any rope. They all began to descend. So now there were just the two of us on the North Face.

The climbing was magnificent. One of us would lead five or six rope-lengths, then we'd switch and the other would lead. The feeling of climbing quickly and confidently, racing rope-length after rope-length up the face, was exhilarating. We made a commitment to go using one rope, the possible afternoon rainstorms were accepted, and we were racing for the top. Later that afternoon we emerged on the rocky summit: a climber's dream peak.

                    ➤   ➤   ➤

This is a story of a Scotsman. At some point, he'd made the big mistake of taking too literally the idea of living on the cheap. On the way back from the bar at about one in the morning, we'd all seen the bakers working early, pounding dough and mixing up the bread, with hot ovens steaming.

One night the Scotsman sees this pile of bread at the bakery. Everybody's working, and it's dark. And he's drunk. So he collects huge armfuls of bread and fills his pack up. Somebody must have seen him. He staggers back to the campsite, about half a mile up the valley. He puts the bread in his tent, punches up his sleeping bag, collapses, and passes out.

Next morning he's awakened by a tapping on his tent and shouts: "Monsieur! Monsieur! Monsieur!" So he looks out of the tent and says: "Ay, what's up, Jimmy?"

"This is the police," comes the answer. "We understand that someone in this campsite stole bread from the baker's shop last night."

And this Scotsman says: "I dunno what you're talkin' about. What bread?"

And there he was—lying in the middle of all the bread!

So they carted him away. He had to go down to the police station and get himself photographed.

                    ➤   ➤   ➤

The technique the police used with some of these miscreants was to take the shopkeepers down to the police station to see if they could recognize photographs of the various individuals. Sometimes the police would bring shopkeepers to the campsite and walk them around to see if they could identify anyone.

One day a black van showed up at the campsite. Out jumped all these gendarmes, some armed with submachine guns. They spread out all around the campsite, creating a barrier so that no one could escape. Then an officer came into the center of the campsite and said: "OK, we'd like to take photgraphs of everyone." Everyone was, of course, "completely innocent," so they could barely refuse.

Outside our plastic shelter in this camp, we had a beautiful white plastic table with a Cinzano umbrella and a series of chairs that we had "liberated" from outside a cafe. Our area was next to that of some rather well known establishment-types of the British climbing scene.

The cops lined us all up. It was like a group photograph at a wedding. They were going take this big shot. Just the baddest people suddenly had to get up to the bathroom or somewhere. We were trying to shade our faces, hide our faces. A lot of sweaty foreheads were being wiped at the moment the shutter was about to click.

The establishment-types just thought it was a real hoot because, of course, they *were* innocent!

⸎   ⸎   ⸎

The Biolay campsite was a little too close to town for many of the residents of Chamonix. The poor guy down by the railway station who grew lettuces and radishes—well, his lettuces never survived. On the way back from the bar at night, everybody would just pick a lettuce. *Salade Anglaise!*

So the French tried to move us out of Biolay. They did that easily—just by trying to charge money. (It was, you see, illegal to camp there.) Everybody moved about three miles out of town up the valley toward Argentiere; we went into a field the size of a football field next to the river. It was owned by Monsieur Snell, who also owned the local climbing shop in town. I think the police agreed to it. They wanted all the thugs in the same area!

Finally, the Chamonix police decided to get the climbers removed. The townspeople were sick of being marauded by these English guys, so the cops found a reason to remove us: lack of sanitary toilet facilities. There was only an old toilet hanging over a torrential glacial river. There was a walkway out to the toilet, which was just a hole in the bottom of the toilet shed. The whole thing was held together and secured by a cable from the roof of the shed back into a tree.

We wanted to take responsibility, establish the campsite and rebuild the toilet. We went around and actually raised some money for the project. But first of all, we had to tear the old thing down. As a lady was entering the toilet for the final time before it was going to be reconstructed, we decided that this was the appropriate time for demolition. Half a dozen of us swung on the supporting cable, and the toilet rocked like a taxi with a burst tire, careening backwards and forwards across the river. Eventually it actually jumped off the foundation and flooded inside. The girl came shrieking and screaming and leaping outside.

The toilet was rebuilt, and people managed to stay on that campsite for a few more years. It satisfied the police—the hygiene and so on. . . .

➤   ➤   ➤

Later in 1970, I ended up with a real job. While Adrian was still freelancing, doing a number of jobs and sometimes guiding for the army, I had a job at a mountain school in North Wales, Snowdonia. This gave me enough financial security to buy a big red motorbike: a Norton 750cc Commando. It would do 120 miles an hour and compensated me for missing climbing.

Meanwhile, Adrian had gone to the Alps that winter with Bob Shaw, a stocky black-curly-haired Derbyshire guy. Aid had also gone out to the Alps earlier than I could in the summer. I could only get six weeks off in the summer of '71, but Aid had gone out again for a full three-month season. I was in Wales when I got a postcard from Aid that said something like this: "Just done the second ascent of the Red Pillar of Brouillard."

It was first climbed thirteen years before by a top Italian alpinist, Walter Bonatti. It's a 2,000-foot red-granite pillar set in one of the most remote regions of Mont Blanc. It was a real coup just to repeat the route. But to put up a direct, harder, rock-climbing style to it! You can imagine how I felt. That's where I wanted to be. And what was I doing? Walking schoolchildren around the Welsh hills in the rain!

But at least I did have a motorbike, and I was doing a lot of rock climbing on the weekends. On the bottom floor of the old residential school, I had a room that saw . . . a number of visitors—I was living my kicks some other way. But come summer, I intended to meet Adrian and Bob out in Courmayeur on the south side of Mont Blanc and join up with them to do some climbing. I'd also agreed to meet the peerless Dan Boone.

To help pay for gas to the Alps, I was to give an ex-girlfriend from Chester (I'll call her Susan) a ride out on the back of the motorbike. The time to leave came. On a motorbike, you don't have much room for equipment. So I put one pack on my back, one on my chest and one on the back of Susan, and off we went. I drove nonstop to Chamonix, then went through the Mont Blanc tunnel and met Adrian in Val Ferret, a beautiful valley of flowers and trees—and no people, not like France.

After I arrived, we had to decide which climbs to do. We made a couple of attempts on some unclimbed sides of the Grandes Jorasses. Adrian and I eventually climbed the Pointe Gugliermina, and Bob Shaw soloed it just behind us. It was a fun climb, even though technically it was graded fairly extreme. It went very straightforwardly, and we climbed it in a day. Then we looked for something else to do. Because the weather was bad around the whole Mont Blanc area, Adrian and Bob went off to the Swiss Alps to do some rock climbing, and I went with Dan Boone to the Italian Dolomites.

▸   ▸   ▸

Dan and I took the Norton 750 across the northern Italian plains to the Dolomites. In those days, you didn't have to wear a helmet, and I remember doing 90–100 miles an hour, chasing Italian cars. And then we were winding up these steep passes in the Dolomites, some of them with more than fifty tight U-turns.

Dan had climbed a lot in the western Alps, and he was a very accomplished rock climber. He'd had a couple of epics, retreating while his friends had got frostbitten. He'd had another on the Central Pillar of Frêney, which at the time was a climb we'd not done; it's similar to the Pillar of Brouillard. Dan had a major retreat on it the previous year and only just escaped with his life.

He refused to climb in rock-climbing shoes. He would only climb in double-boots. He had a pair of big leather double-boots for gymnastic rock climbing in the Dolomites! I realized this was going to be a problem. So we decided we had to find him a pair of boots in Cortina d'Ampezzo, a major center in the Dolomites. I wouldn't buy him boots, and Dan thought he didn't have the money.

I didn't want to be involved in any hit-and-run thievery, so outside the store I told Dan that if he was going to steal climbing shoes, I was not going to go in with him. I'd wait outside. So Dan disappeared into a store that sold leather goods as well as shoes. When I saw him about half an hour later, he was smiling broadly.

"OK, Dan, got yourself some boots?" I said. I wasn't going to ask anything about how he got them or how much he paid.

He smiled and said: "No, I didn't get any boots but, hey, I got this great pair of leather trousers!"

As we walked past the front of the shop, I saw that the plaster model in the shop window was no longer wearing trousers!

Eventually Dan did find a pair of shoes, and we climbed the South Pillar of Marmolata, a 2,500-foot pillar rated Grade 6. We managed to climb it in a day. It was first climbed sometime in the late twenties or early thirties. It's known because at the top it has a big icy couloir, a gully with overhangs. A number of people had died when they couldn't get around those icy overhangs. We climbed it very quickly.

All I can say about Dolomite climbing is that it is incredibly steep, but the climbing is not desperately hard. By American standards now, if you're climbing 5.9 or 5.10, you can do all kinds of impressive climbs in the Dolomites where you get into overhanging rock situations that you would never get on any other kind of rock.

Returning to Courmayeur, we had one small epic as we were coming out of the mountains and negotiating about fifty hairpin turns. At one point, the motorbike suddenly lurched across the road. I thought I'd just blown out the back tire. I pulled over and found out what had happened: Dan had fallen asleep on the back of the motorbike and rocked all his weight over to one side. If you do that on a motorbike, it changes the steering.

When we drove back into the campsite to meet up with Adrian and Bob,

I thought that traveling with Dan Boone had been like traveling with a time bomb. You never quite knew when it was going to go off.

>   >   >

The alpine season of 1972 was probably the best season we'd had. It brought us some recognition as British alpinists. There were about twenty British climbers doing top-standard climbs, and our climbs were as good as any being done by them.

At the same time, equipment was improving. Technical ice-climbing equipment made at least a small step forward. Curved ice tools were available, so you didn't have to cut steps going up ice faces. Crampons were the same as they'd always been, but hand tools—the things that connected your hands to, say, 70-degree ice—were better. In the old days, we had to cut steps with the ice ax and then put our toes in them and thus create a staircase of holes to climb up. With these new curved ice tools, you could hit them into the ice and pull on them. They were a major reason we managed to do some of the ice climbs we did in 1972.

By that time, a pattern was forming of what a three- or four-month alpine season consisted of. We would be rock climbing in England in the spring. Then we'd go directly to the eastern Alps—the Kaisergebirge or the Dolomites, where the summer season started earlier. The climbs there were not as serious in terms of objective danger—glaciers, rockfall, and storms—and they were usually one-day rock climbs. And yet they were technically difficult: steep, overhanging, sustained rock climbs. It was a great place to train, to get into the swing for doing longer climbs. In England in the spring, the longest climbs were only a few hundred feet long. But then we could go to the eastern Alps— the limestone Alps—and train on longer climbs. After that, we could move over to the Swiss region.

In 1972, that's exactly what we did. We started out in the Kaisergebirge of Austria and did some great Grade 6 rock climbs. Then we moved to the Swiss Alps, to the Lauterbrunnen Valley. It was famous for the Lauterbrunnen North Face: a series of big north-face ice climbs. In June, the conditions were good. You had good snow cover, and if you were lucky, maybe you'd find that these long, hard ice climbs had all the loose rocks frozen into them. You could just kick steps of snow. As it happens, it never works out completely like that, but that was something we always hoped for.

In June, Adrian and I camped in the Lauterbrunnen Valley at a place called Stechelberg. First, we wanted to do a training climb. We chose the Ebnefluh, which is a 2,000-foot snow-ice slope. The climb started from the Rottal hut, which was 5,000 feet above the valley. We carried big packs up to this hut of the Swiss Alpine Club. There was no warden there, but there were beds and blankets and a little wood-burning stove. We took our own stove—sometimes gas, sometimes kerosene—and cooked our own food. As we were approaching the hut, we saw footprints in the snow and two other people way up ahead of us. We wondered who they were and thought maybe they were going to do the same climb as ourselves. From a distance, I could see that one of the guys had an ice ax on the back of his pack. It looked steeply curved. That meant a technical ice climber, somebody who probably was going to do a hard climb, somebody who knew that conditions in the early season could be good.

When we caught these people up, we found out they were Rab Carrington and Alan Rouse. So we all hung out together in the hut. We didn't really know them that well then. We were kind of acquaintances. They were going to try a new climb on the North Face of the Gletscherwand (it means "glacier wall" in German). Later that season they actually did the climb, but this time they were just trying it.

The next morning we all left at the same time, around three in the morning. We climbed the Ebnefluh with a couple of other climbers: an American named Gary and a young French-speaking Swiss boy named Marcel.

At the top of the Ebnefluh, where most people traverse out to the right and climb snow and ice around the corner, there was a big, steep, green headwall, probably 75 degrees. It was a wild pitch to climb, with the whole wall below us. But we decided to try to climb it.

Adrian led the first pitch. It was 150 feet of green ice. He used the new curved Chouinard ice tools. He'd cut a small notch above his head, about three inches wide and three inches long. Then using the ice tool, he'd crampon up until his foot was in the notch. This meant he actually got to rest in a little foothold once every eight feet. That was the technique we used on really steep ice.

That season I didn't have a good pair of climbing boots. At a party a couple of years before, Adrian had burned down the apartment in Chester, and my French technical-climbing boots had gone up in smoke. So I bought a pair of boots for five pounds and had an extra pair of steel shanks put in them, but they still were not good technical-climbing boots. I had a hard time on the steep ice, because my calf muscles had to make up for the rigid boot and the rigid crampons that people now use. I never get calf strain nowadays, but in those days it was a major problem.

After finishing the Ebnefluh climb, we came down to a hut, which had a summer quarters and winter quarters. There was no warden there. We spent the first night in the winter quarters, which were dark, dingy, and cold. Then we found that with a piece of bent wire and a little ingenuity, we could enter the warm atmosphere of the summer quarters, which had *kirsch* and considerable amounts of Swiss food. We thought this was a good place to rest up, rather than going straight down to the valley.

We searched the hut, looking mainly for food and beverages. We found the hut warden's revolver: a Luger or something. It wasn't loaded, but I hid it in case the warden should suddenly show up uninvited and head for his pistol and kick us out at gunpoint.

It was early in the season, and snow almost covered the hut. When you approached the hut, you actually walked on its corrugated iron roof. The second night we spent there, I heard the clank! clank! clank! of crampons walking on the corrugated iron. And I thought: Oh, oh! The warden! As it was the beginning of the season, it would have been natural for him to come and check his hut.

What would we say to a Swiss warden? We were basically living free in his private hut. Actually, we'd already arranged what we would do, but I don't think we seriously believed it ever was going to be necessary. I stood behind the door at the entranceway with a snow shovel. I stepped out like a cricketeer about to hit a homerun.

Then I saw that the person coming toward me was Rab Carrington! Rab's eyes grew to the size of ashtrays, as he saw I was about to plant him with a shovel. We welcomed Rab and Alan Rouse inside and took them into the luxury interior of our establishment. We stayed there a couple of nights before we all descended together.

           ➤   ➤   ➤

We went back into the valley and camped at Stechelberg. By this time we were friends with Rab and Al. We got to know them in the hut and during the walk down. The British guidebook said that the area's hardest climb—pure ice climbing—was the Direct on the Face of the Gletscherwand. We really wanted to do that climb. It was a dangerous route, because you climbed for at least half of it under big ice cliffs, and occasionally a big chunk of ice would break off. One of the safe ways of doing this climb was to move quickly. This meant you needed good conditions and equipment you could move quickly on. It was the new curved ice-climbing gear that enabled us to do that. If we'd had to cut steps up all the way, it would have taken too long. The guidebook said it took two days. We climbed it in eighteen hours.

We started out by head-torch and climbed up the lower sections. The middle section was steep ice, about 80 degrees. The boots I had—those things I'd bought for five pounds—were bending, and they got wet. Adrian had lightweight double-leather boots. When we pulled up just below the top of the face, we bivouacked in the lower lip of the crevasse. We didn't have sleeping bags. We sat on the ice, using our packs for insulation. It was a cold night.

In the morning, my boots were frozen hard. I took a vasodilator pill that makes the blood rush to your feet and hands. I stuffed my feet into the frozen-solid boots, and the blood pulsing around in my feet eventually thawed the boots out. That morning, we climbed the face and were really happy. We had about 500 feet of snow slopes, with quite deep snow—knee-deep snow at about 45 degrees—up to the summit ridge.

We descended down to one of the Swiss railway stations, called the Jungfraujoch. It was the end of the rack-and-pinion railway that ran up inside the north face of the Eiger and up to the Jungfrau col. We got down there about midafternoon.

Adrian pulled out his guide *carnet*—his little book with his photo in it—and I had his guide badge stuck on my jacket. I went in first to try to buy a ticket at the guide discount rate all the way back down to Grindelwald. The ticket seller refused me. He asked for the *carnet*, the book. I said I'd left it down in the valley because I got it wet. He still wouldn't give me a discount price, so I had to pay full price. Then Adrian came in with his *carnet* and bought himself a discount ticket. What we didn't know is that the ticket-seller had figured out immediately that we were using one guide's *carnet*, and he radioed to the station ahead where the train came out of the tunnel on the Eiger.

I went in the station there to try to buy the second half of the ticket to Grindelwald, and that's when we realized that the guy had phoned through with his warning. So Adrian got to ride down for about two or three dollars, but the ticket seller was going to charge me something like fifty dollars.

Adrian got on the train, and I became vindictive about all this. I ran down the trail and put big rocks between the rails, so that the driver would have to keep stopping and climbing out to remove them. That would slow him down a lot. So Adrian wasn't down much faster than I was.

⋗   ⋗   ⋗

Then we moved to Chamonix and set up camp in Snell's Field. It was like going home, because we felt confident about that area by now. We were already fit, having done a couple of good climbs. Like successful alpinists in the '70s, we'd got the rock-climbing skills; we'd got the new ice-climbing tools and some practice using them; and we were starting to get better weather forecasting in Chamonix. That was crucial, because there are so many different kinds of climbs, depending on what the weather is. Some of them are purely ice climbs; you climb mainly at night and finish by six in the morning. Some are rock climbs, very long, serious climbs that require an overnight bivouac. And some are rock climbs that you can do in a day.

The improvement in weather forecasting in '72 meant that we could plan much better. The weather forecast would say: "Tomorrow there will be afternoon thunderstorms." Then we knew what kind of a climb to look for. We knew for some of them that we had to get up to the hut by night. You could leave the hut at midnight, do an ice climb by torchlight, be up over the summit by midday, and be back down before the storm hit in the afternoon.

Or you could choose a short rock climb, so you'd be up and over the top before the storm came. Ice climbs were generally done better at the end of June and in July. In August, when the thunderstorms built up more, the ice climbs were drier and you got falling rocks.

We chose to do the West Face of the Petites Jorasses as one of the first climbs we did when we got to Chamonix. It used to be considered a full day's rock climb; many people spent a bivouac on it. But we thought that by carrying little equipment and climbing quickly, we could probably do the thing between six and eight hours. Which is exactly what we did.

Five or six years before, people considered this a major climb, but we were now looking at it as a less serious climb. It was a 2,500-foot rock climb, which started up a huge inside-corner dihedral, climbed over a series of roofs with a few pitons, up a diagonal crack, and then up the final slabs. If you got caught on the upper slabs in the afternoon thunderstorms, we'd heard rumors that it would totally ice up. We knew some very good climbers who'd been turned back because of ice on those upper slabs. We climbed it in about seven hours, so that wasn't a problem. After we finished the climb, there were a few rappels down on the Italian side of the pillar, and we were back in the hut just as the afternoon thunderstorm started.

We did our next climb—the 2,500-foot North Face of Aiguille de Leschaux—in a similar way. It consisted of a big ice slope on the lower part of the face and mixed climbing in the middle part; we could do all of that in the dark. At the top there was steep rock. By starting in the dark and by traveling super-light, we managed to reach the top of the face in half a day, and we were back in the hut by the time that afternoon's thunderstorm hit. In climbing the ice face, we hadn't noticed the bergschrund because it was pretty well snowed over, so when we thought we were at the bottom of the ice face, we actually were halfway up the face.

We had a list of climbs ready to go, depending on what the weather looked like. If it looked as though there were going to be two or three days of great weather, we did have other climbs: the bigger challenges like the Frêney Pillar, the North Face of the Droites. That's the kinds of climbs we were hoping to do.

We were not the only people who were doing hard climbs in Chamonix.

There was a small-knit group of good climbers, and some of them were very colorful.

Peter Minks, a Liverpuddlian, was two years older than us. He was a plumber-electrician. He was an excellent climber who was waiting to solo the North Face of the Grandes Jorasses; he was also waiting to do the Frêney Pillar. And there were Cliff Phillips, a wiry little guy from Wales who was soloing hard rock climbs, and Eric Jones, a tall, broad Welshman who was later to solo the North Faces of the Eiger, the Walker Spur, and the Grandes Jorrases.

I hate lists of the top climbs. But if I was asked to say what those climbs were, I would have said the Frênay Pillar, the North Face of the Droites, the Walker Spur, the Direct on the West Face of the Dru, the Eckpfeiler Buttress on Mont Blanc, the Brouillard Pillars.

Peter Minks soloed the Walker Spur brilliantly in a day. At the same time, Rouse and Carrington, who were also climbing the Walker Spur, were bivouacked on a ledge just below the top.

In those days, if the weather was good enough to do a big climb, there would always be more than one party on it. There were some Japanese guys bivouacked above Alan and Rab. As the two of them were melting snow, they heard WHOOOSH! and looked up—it was a falling Japanese body! One of the Japanese had slipped higher up and come falling down. Rab said: "A wee Nip in the air!" A hard-core Scotsman!

"NECK AND NECK WITH REINHOLD"

FROM
Spirits of the Air in *The Kurt Diemberger Omnibus*
BY KURT DIEMBERGER

KURT DIEMBERGER HAS ENJOYED ONE OF THE LONGEST CLIMBING careers in the Himalaya. After making the first ascents of two 8000-meter peaks, Broad Peak and Dhaulagiri, in 1957 and 1960, he climbed three more in the late 1970s: Everest, Makalu, and Gasherbrum II.

In 1974, Diemberger and Reinhold Messner were tied in the quest for 8000-meter peaks; Diemberger had "his two," while Messner had climbed two as well, Nanga Parbat and Manaslu. The pair decided to try to climb Makalu together in an attempt to record their third 8000-meter summit, but the plans suddenly went awry when Diemberger, as he put it, was "ex-vited" from the expedition.

With that snub, the seeds were planted for a rivalry with Messner. Diemberger went on to surprise many in the climbing community by reaching the summits of three more 8000-meter peaks in a span of just fifteen months. At the conclusion of that effort, in 1979, Diemberger once again was tied with Messner and conceivably could have been in competition with him in a strange new game that was brewing: who would be the first person to climb all fourteen of the world's highest peaks? Both Messner and Diemberger each had five to their credit as of 1979.

Although Diemberger "lacked the passion" for the race to climb all the 8000-meter peaks, he clearly felt a sense of competition with Messner, who was coming on strong in the late 1970s. The friction between the two was exacerbated when, in 1979, Messner picked Diemberger's climbing partner on Makalu, Hermann Warth, to accompany him to K2, not Diemberger, despite his better climbing record. Diemberger attributes this move to Messner's strategy to come out ahead in the race for the highest peaks.

It's against this backdrop that Diemberger chronicles his account of this strange competition in "Neck and Neck with Reinhold," which comes from his third book, *Spirits of the Air.* The story is reprinted in *The Kurt Diemberger Omnibus,* on pages 688–702.

K urtl, our third eight-thousander, let's do it together!" said Reinhold Messner at the Trento mountaineering film festival, always a good place to catch up with old friends. That was before the 1974 summer season. Wolfi Nairz was there as well, the Tyrolean climber and expedition leader. We were discussing an attempt on Makalu's South Face, which—if it succeeded—would mean a third eight-thousander each for Reinhold and me. The two of us had recently given a marathon joint lecture—organized by Charlie of Innsbruck—entitled "Four Eight-Thousanders" (Reinhold's two and my two).

That had proved very interesting, if long. I was convinced that with the exception of some experts, by the end of the evening nobody in the hall could have stood a further ascent, wanting, then, only to get home "by fair means!" I think the lecture had lasted four hours. (The British have more endurance in these matters: at the mountaineering conference in Buxton in 1976, I delivered a six-hour nonstop slide and film lecture on my own, the longest so far in my career. It was, by the way, a very exciting meeting. At that time Cesare Maestri had just climbed the extremely difficult South American granite tower of Cerro Torre placing bolts with a compressed-air drill. He was there in Buxton as well and, not surprisingly, stimulated a really animated discussion.)

In Trento, before the mountain summer of 1974, it certainly looked as if Reinhold and I would be climbing the South Face of Makalu together ("together," or one after the other . . . that would remain to be seen), but then one morning soon afterwards I received an official letter (and one could feel from its tone how hard it had been for Wolfi Nairz to write); it was an "ex-vitation" (or whatever is the best word to describe a revoked invitation). Somebody on the expedition (or several) clearly did not want my presence. For me—who already saw the shining Makalu so close—this was a black day. It does not help very much now to go on about my thoughts then—the fact was it left me with very little time to wrestle the tiller . . . but I succeeded: I became instead a member of Gerhard Lenser's Lhotse expedition, which from the beginning was beset with bad luck and difficulties.

A big Spanish expedition held the permit for Everest, and did not want to share its climbing route with anyone—and the standard approach for the highest mountain of the world is essentially the same as that for its satellite, the 8511-meter-high Lhotse. (Only a saddle separates the two peaks.) This was a rich and influential expedition: the battery firm Tximist in Navarra was picking up the tab. Our protestations that we could peacefully coexist on the route were dismissed by the prestige-conscious Spanish, who feared a one-sided success. In the end, the Ministry of Tourism in Kathmandu told us: you have the permit for Lhotse, fine, but try the mountain from another side!

Hell, what kind of concession was that! Two years before, Gerhard Lenser had deposited in Lukla all the equipment suitable for a normal ascent of the eight-thousander.

. . . Or indeed, no less useful even for the South Face.

None of us, however, felt ready to venture on to this deadly face. Avalanches, avalanches, avalanches . . . a Russian roulette. And so we came to the decision to try the Great Ridge: one of the greatest traverses in the Himalaya—not attempted hitherto, though perhaps possible—the Lhotse Ridge starting from the Barun Glacier. Given good weather, we reckoned we stood a real chance of getting over the two virgin 7000-meter peaks, Shartse (7502 m) and Peak 38 (7589 m), at least as far as Lhotse Shar (8383 m) . . . It filled us with renewed enthusiasm: such a wonderful route and—if it succeeded—a fantastic achievement! So we told ourselves.

We felt a little like pioneers for the future—even if we succeeded only in taking the first tentative steps toward what would doubtless be the ultimate, and far-distant challenge of this great ridge . . . You could project the line farther, from Lhotse over to Everest, and from there down into Tibet to give you the greatest 8000-meter traverse in history. And including three seven-thousanders into the bargain. Such a feat would certainly need multifaceted military-style organization, working on a number of different levels. Music for the future . . .

➤   ➤   ➤

Our dream of doing the great Lhotse Ridge came true only in part—we experienced one of the worst premonsoon periods ever in Nepal. Scarcely any expedition was able to realize its high-flying project. The Spanish had to go home without Everest (which we wasted no tears over!), and Reinhold Messner was rebuffed on Makalu. I didn't reach Lhotse or Lhotse Shar. Neither Messner nor I got his "third."

But one mountain success did bless our expedition: Shartse—the first of the two virgin seven-thousanders on the ridge, the eastern corner of the Everest massif (Shar = east, Tse = corner, summit). It was the highest first ascent that season in Nepal and proved extremely dangerous as well as much more difficult than I had thought. What I carried home from this expedition were friendships and the memory of storms and sickness. Extracts from my diary:

"If it goes on like this, we'll use up all our tents," moans Gerhard Lenser. Never before has he experienced such a series of bad luck:

In Camp 2 on a day of tempest there came a sudden retort, like a shot, and a wonderful Jamet Tent ripped open along its full length . . . a stray gust had found its way in through the entrance, which happened to be open.

In Camp 3 wind-borne drift crushed everything, broke all the poles, and tore the tent. So often before, we had carefully collapsed it when we left, but this time, for some reason, did not.

In Camp 4 devils were on the loose. A cornice collapse destroyed the camp, burying it under tons of snow and ice. It was good luck only that nobody was there when it happened.

In Camp 5 the Schwabian, Hermann Warth, and his companion Nawang Tenzing were buried during the night by a snow slide. Even though they extricated themselves, they had terrible hours till morning. All the tent poles were broken by the force of the impact. "Many danger," smiles the strong little Tibetan, whenever the conversation comes back to that night. "Camp 5, no die." Perhaps we can repair the tent for a further summit attempt.

Only in Base Camp were no tents broken. A bad sandstorm had flattened them all—but it was not disastrous.

"In all truth, it was the most terrible season for weather," complained Gerhard Lenser, and he should know if anyone does. He is more at home in Nepal than in Europe, so often does he go over there. It was no exaggeration: how many thunderstorms had we seen that set the whole night sky aglow over Makalu with continuous lightning-flicker, lasting hours at a time—a breathtaking firework display around that black silhouette. Around us on Shartse, fantastic snow shapes formed, magically created by this extraordinary winter: nuns' hats, on the ridge, all white and starched, fresh from the laundry, and forty meters high.

There was a giant snowdrop, and from Lhotse Shar you could see it clearly—floating like an angel with spread wings.

Farther down on our wild ridge, the wind played another of its jokes: a snowman was wringing his hands.

I railed at cruel fate because I was sick: was that the fault of the weather, or the big cornice that fell on my head at 6300 meters? "My right lung feels like a sandbag, I am breathing mostly through the left side. But I don't have any fever. Nevertheless, it stabs so much . . . " I wrote. As it turned out, I had a broken rib, but that certainly was not the only thing. Even so, on May 23, 1974, Hermann Warth and I stood on the summit of the 7000-meter peak, "our" Shartse, the first mountain on that mighty Lhotse Ridge. Our faces were bedecked with icicles. We looked more like monsters than men and Hermann had two of his fingertips frostbitten during the summit climb.

This difficult mountain is only the "first obstacle" on the Lhotse Ridge— we were happy that we had at least managed to bag that.

What else had this expedition given us? So much. The fact that four years later Hermann Warth, Nawang Tenzing and I were able to stand on Makalu is in no small part thanks to our epic on Shartse (I can't call it anything else), which left us such friends. Day after day we had pitted ourselves against an unkind destiny, that simply didn't want us to win through—against tempests and cornices. We had to endure so much. But we also experienced wonderful moments during this wild adventure. Sometimes, when toward evening the clouds were rising, that giant granite monolith with the name of Mahakala—a dark godhead—burnt like a sacrificial fire in the sky. Then we would urge each other to the entrance of the tent and look up through the icy silence of the evening till the light went out.

. . . Makalu . . . Mahakala . . .

At such moments this mountain is the most secretive place in the world.

⋗   ⋗   ⋗

One day before we got back to Tumlingtar—into the wide valley of the Arun River—as we were ambling along the path through the bramble bushes, stopping from time to time to pick a couple of the sweet, yellow fruits which are so full of taste, and when once again I was asking myself why in Nepal the blackberries are yellow, along comes the postman.

Mail from home! We bury our heads in the letters and read and read. At the same time I am still half-thinking about the blackberries because I know that Teresa, my wife, is coming for her first visit to Nepal, to wander with me, and she is crazy about blackberries. I will lead her into a great yellow bramble-heaven.

There, it is written: she has obtained her visa. In ten days she arrives! I open the next letter. Whoaa . . . What's this? I have been engaged to make a film in Greenland—in two weeks' time.

Oh, oh! Poor Teresa . . .

When will we finally wander through Nepal?

(We did succeed—many years later!)

"ICE CAPADES"

FROM
Sherman Exposed
BY JOHN SHERMAN

JOHN SHERMAN SAYS THAT HE TOOK UP THE WRITING OF "LOVABLY vulgar satire" because, as he put it, "I hoped to get climbers to take themselves less seriously." (A benefit, he adds, was providing his editors with a "juicy target for outraged readers to go off on in the letters column.")

Long a fixture at *Climbing* magazine, Sherman said that "Climbing should be fun, and I want my writing to be fun." His frequent columns and occasional books have given Sherman a rare stature among writing climbers, and made him uncontested king of the low ground when it comes to climbing humor, or what passes for it.

Perhaps best known as a climber for his bouldering abilities, Sherman isn't afraid to try other disciplines. And that provides the basis for "Ice Capades," a story in which he describes his first foray into ice climbing. But he makes the point that since he wasn't writing at the time he made his first hard boulder moves, or first long free climbs, or first big walls, this story represents a departure of sorts: "This is the only piece I've written that explores the awe and innocence of a rookie pushing his limits."

Like other good comedy, this story, while amusing, touches on historically important people—Jeff Lowe, Andy Embick, Carl Tobin, Chuck Comstock, John Weiland — and routes—Keystone Greensteps, Bridalveil Falls, Wowie Zowie— in a milieu—Valdez—that is worthy of historical note. Beneath the veneer of overt humor, the piece is a surprisingly lyrical account of climbing in Keystone, proof that Sherman can be more than a funny man, when he sets his mind to it. And like much of Sherman's writing, it makes an authentic contribution to the record of climbing at the same time it's making its reader laugh.

The story, which first appeared in *Climbing* magazine, tells the story of Sherman's visit to one of the epicenters of the ice climbing world: Keystone Canyon, Valdez, Alaska. Keystone by now is well-known to be ice-climbing heaven, with everything from low-angled smears to "650-foot monster lines."

Written in 1995, the piece was reprinted in a collection of John Sherman's writing, *Sherman Exposed*, on pages 166–177.

[Author's note: The innocent, easily excited phase of a climbing career is too short, but by dabbling in several disciplines one can experience it several times. I wasn't writing at the time of my first hard boulder problems, first long free climbs, or first big walls, so this is the only piece I've written that explores the awe and innocence of a rookie pushing his limits. Should I be daft enough to attempt an 8000-meter peak, then I might write another. As for ice climbing, the innocence is gone, but the awe remains.]

was damn near choking to keep the vomit down. Sheets of rain washed across the black ice in front of me and it was dark. My hands clenched into a death grip as my neck slowly lithified. Marginally attached to this world, I waited for the accident, reaching a state of fear and angst Marc Twight would be proud of. Problem is, I had yet to step out of the car.

One's first drive into Keystone Canyon is supposed to be memorable. More than once, the reaction of an ice climber glorying in the splendor of Keystone's frozen waterfalls has been likened to a rock climber first beholding the walls of Yosemite Valley. My thoughts, however, lay not with the crystalline promises flashing us from the shadows beside the road, but with the slips and drifts of the Aerostar and dark red dreams of the Jaws of Life. Fifty-mile-per-hour flashbacks of four-lane near-death donuts fueled my mental meltdown, drawn out to agonizing lengths by our fifteen-mile-per-hour descent down Thompson Pass. I couldn't handle the adrenaline jolts each parting with the pavement produced, so I disengaged the wheel from my grip and let Rob Raker drive. Huge mistake. Ignoring the abominable road conditions he doubled my speed. Not that he would know, because half the time he was turned around looking for us in the dark of the backseat to make a point, both hands off the wheel gesturing like Dick Vitale. My pleas that he grip the wheel and decelerate were for naught; the only thing that could slow him down was when he thought he glimpsed big ice next to the road.

My mind a mass of sledgehammered Gummi worms, we reached Valdez around 11 P.M. and descended on Andy Embick's house. Andy, one of Valdez's ice pioneers, greeted us at the door, a glass of Macallans scooped in his left hand and a thin smile breaking a half-inch above his Abe Lincoln/C. Everett Koop beard. A bearskin hung on the wall to his right and the semblance was not lost. Embick is stocky, thick-limbed, and powerful-looking. Perhaps his ursine physique has helped him sneak up on the bruins he has shot. He quickly made us at home, showing off the guest quarters and sauna in the basement, the drying room upstairs, and running through a few quick house rules.

The next day dawned in the upper-30s, but at least it had stopped raining. We headed up to Keystone Canyon, the center of Valdez ice climbing. Size-wise, Keystone Canyon more closely mimics Eldorado Canyon than Yosemite Valley. The guidebook lists more than five dozen ice formations in the canyon, from 50-foot low-angle smears to thick, fat, 650-foot monster lines. Contrary to most ice climbing areas, Keystone's approaches are measured in yards, not miles. It almost seems unsportsmanlike to walk a hundred yards, mostly downhill, to get to some of America's best ice climbs. Die-hard ice jocks will want to visit when the Lowe River is breached, and one must wade its icy currents to reach the climbs on the east side of the canyon.

Horsetail Falls is the most climbed route in Valdez so we felt obliged to hop on it. It is 260 feet long, if you don't count the hundred feet of horizontal snow leading from the parking lot to the base. From a narrow cleft at the top, it spreads out in a wide, low-angle apron of ice forming a shell over a plentiful flow beneath. Rob and Annette Bunge cruised up the steeper ground on the left side, while Bruce Hunter, tired of waiting for me to emerge from behind my camera, soloed the right side in about fifteen minutes, or roughly double the seven-minute record time.

Horsetail Falls behind us, we set our sights on Hung Jury, a ten-minute stroll down the road and across the river. We took advantage of the still day to hop on this notoriously windy climb. On most days, the wind at Hung Jury blows so hard it carries ice chunks *up* the wall. It also causes the ice to form arches up to 30 feet wide that resemble multiple band shells hanging from the flow. These arches, called "bells," "parachutes," or "umbrellas" by the locals, lend a beautifully spooky architecture to the climb. Usually one can weave one's way through the bells, staying on solid ice, but not always. Two years ago local heavies John Weiland and Brian Teale were on Hung Jury, positioned inside one of the bells near the base to escape the wind. Warm conditions followed by a flash freeze had made the ice brittle, so when Weiland placed a tool in an icicle, the vibrations caused a different icicle twenty feet away to collapse. All hell broke loose, raucous and white, as huge blocks of ice fell out of the ceiling and walls of the bell. They exploded against each other and rained on Weiland and Teale. One chunk smashed into Weiland's foot, crushing bones and ripping the heel off his boot. Meanwhile, another block hammered Teale, smashing his scapula before tossing him off his feet and pasting him into a wall. He could feel the quick snapping of his ribs as they caved in, puncturing his lung. Pinned under the block, Teale shoved it off immediately, stood up then collapsed, realizing he couldn't make it down the short hill to the river and road. Weiland had to crawl down to get help.

The previous night's rain left a two- to four-inch stream flowing over the ice encasing the Lowe. Donning crampons gave just enough clearance to keep our boots from leaking. Having heard the story of the falling bell, and wary of above-freezing conditions, Bruce, Annette, and I postholed up the snow well right of the fall line. In a hurry to wait for us, Rob trusted his luck and blasted straight up through the line of fire. The climb was wet, but more fun than a barrel of monkeys on acid.

That night and the nights to come we got a chance to know Andy Embick better. Embick, through his scores of first ascents, his authorship of the *Blue Ice and Black Gold* guide to Valdez ice, and his spawning of the annual Valdez Ice Festival, has done more to popularize ice climbing in the Valdez area than anyone else. A doctor, Embick moved to Valdez in 1979. The Alaska pipeline, which terminates in Valdez, was completed the year before and the oil boom fostered a Wild West atmosphere. At the time there were only two other ice climbers in Valdez, John Weiland and Bob Pudwill, and Weiland was in temporary retirement from the sport. Hence, Embick took to introducing non-climbers to the sport. He offered ice climbing and other outdoor activities as a healthy alternative to the other winter recreation to be found in Valdez, such as marathon swilling sessions at the Pipeline Club or the Acres. And even if it wasn't really that safe, Andy was there to stitch them up. Of the dozen or two tyros he took out, half a dozen stuck with the sport, some climbing up to grade V ice before they ever touched a rock climb. Eventually, the ice climbers who stayed in Valdez after the pipeline construction days found themselves getting older, getting married, and repopulating. Embick blames "kids and other near-death experiences" for the current decline of the local climbing scene. Nevertheless, it may be the kids he delivered who will be the future of Valdez ice. Embick himself rarely ice climbs these days, concentrating more on kayaking, hunting, and biathlons.

I had heard wild stories about Embick, the most outrageous being when, while lecturing at a black-tie American Alpine Club affair, he started disrobing to point out his muscles to the aghast audience. I'd also read his *Blue Ice and Black Gold*, in which the about-the-author blurb runs two full pages. I was expecting a raving egomaniac, but the Andy Embick I met did not live up to this reputation. I'm not saying he was humble, but he told just as many stories about others as about himself and his personal stories are sprinkled with self-deprecating humor that may escape some of his detractors. Besides being an accomplished storyteller, he is full of good advice; for example, rubbing purple ski wax on ax handles for better grip with neoprene gloves. And one thing even his detractors grant him is that he is generous to a fault. He has had up to forty ice climbers crashing in his house at one time. He gives them free use of the sauna, access to the kitchen, use of tools and a workbench, and so on. All he asks in return is that they obey the posted house rules and help shovel snow off the driveway and roof. All winter strangers wander in and out of his house. When his wife Kathy asks her daughters, "Who's that downstairs?" they say, "It's just ice climbers." I couldn't help suspecting that if Andy is as smart as his fellow Rhodes Scholars, his generosity toward climbing bums will be tempered in about ten years . . . when his daughters reach their teens.

The Big Two had to come next: Bridalveil Falls and Keystone Greensteps. These 650-foot twins dominate Keystone Canyon. One-hundred-yard downhill approaches, pitch after pitch of aquamarine ice, minimal avalanche danger—the thought of my editors OD'ing on Ex-Lax couldn't have cheered me more.

I'd dreamed of Greensteps since I'd started swinging tools a few winters ago. I was antsy, so I grabbed the first lead. Warm temperatures had softened the ice so one swing would sink a pick two inches; the only limit to your speed was how fast you could clean your tools and how often you wanted to hang out and screw in pro. Having led only a dozen pitches of ice before, I was intent on each move and anxiously drove the picks in deeper than necessary. My world was a ten-foot diameter patch of ice in front of me. The steep walls beside me, the exposure below me, the majesty of the rent in the earth I was climbing out of—I was oblivious to it all. Swing swing, kick kick, my focus and rhythm produced a strange monotony. Had I been more relaxed, I could have reveled in the surroundings. Had I been more gripped, I could have basked in my fear. As it was, the one thing that separated human from automaton was the cool macerating squish of leather gloves on skin. I had a spare pair for the next pitch, but I knew Embick was right again—neoprene gloves were the way to go at these warm temps.

The first ascent of Greensteps (Jeff Lowe, John Weiland, 1976) was a three-day affair, complete with a brandy-warmed bivy in an ice cave. Today, even ice rookies such as myself can manage the route in a day, especially with 100-meter ropes. The four steps of ice break up as to allow the route to be done in two 100-meter pitches. This melts down the psychological barrier to a puddle you can hop over. Nevertheless, 100-meter ropes have their disadvantages. First, even with a dozen screws, you have to run it out over thirty feet between placements if you want to have any left for the belay. After twisting in the anchors at the first belay, I hadn't so much as a snowflake left on my gear sling. Secondly, despite the one-swing hero ice, it seemed like I could have shaved twice before Bruce arrived at the belay. He was motoring; it just takes awhile to climb that far. He then led the next 300 feet so I had a few more hours to hop and stamp on my belay pad in the snow. Lastly, the degree a rope tangles does not rise linearly with rope length; it increases exponentially. Coiling them is wasted effort, it's best to just stuff them in a pack (leaving the ends out), let the leader take the end on top, and feed the rope out of the pack as he or she goes. When the pack's empty, the second tosses the camera, thermos, etc., in and follows. Stuff the rope back in the pack at the end of the climb.

Bruce stopped at a fat fir tree thirty feet shy of the lip. Many parties rap from this tree, but we felt compelled to pull over the top. Between us and the top, however, was twenty feet of decreasingly coherent ice, then the alder zone.

To withstand avalanches that pluck out more rigid trees, alders have evolved with thin, whippy trunks and branches rarely more than a few inches in diameter. The branches point downhill, so to tie them off it's best to lash prussiks around them. By avoiding a nasty bushwhack traverse over to Bruce's belay, I had saved time but hadn't collected the cordage from him. When I reached a bunch of alder branches poking out through a 10-foot snowbank atop the climb, I had no way to sling them. Virgin alder climber that I was, I figured I'd just reef up on the branches and be on top in no time. When I pulled on the branches, however, I wouldn't move up, they'd move down. It was like working out on a lat pull machine instead of a pull-up bar. I felt none too secure bouncing around on the limbs with no pro. I dug back to get to the branches where they thickened. Here they were less flimsy, but I was creating an overhang of snow above me. The snow wouldn't support my weight and it looked like it might take hours to dig my way through to the summit. Finally I clued in that if I didn't sweep the snow away, but punched it into the cliff face, that I could create platforms that, if I mashed my shins against them, would just support my weight. Ordinarily, I enjoy being on the steep part of the learning curve, getting better each time out on the ice. This time was scary. It's best to learn such techniques on the dull end. Notwithstanding, it was a necessary lesson used many times in the next two weeks.

The next day Bridalveil beckoned. Like Greensteps, it is tiered, and like Greensteps, the first ascent (Carl Tobin, Clif Moore, and Jim Jennings, 1977) was a multiday affair. Carl Tobin described it thusly in *Climbing* (November–December 1980): "Having never seen the falls, and not possessing any knowledge of the climbing history of the area, the three of us set off from Fairbanks in mid-December, determined to "fast lane" our way up Bridalveil. However, it took three days of hungover, drugged climbing to grope our way up the route. The long vertical section of the fourth pitch weighed constantly on our thoughts.

"None of us quite understood the intricacies of protecting a long vertical section. Extreme winds slowed us down (100 km/hr is not unusual in Valdez). We started at noon on the first two days (we experienced trouble controlling our drinking). And it was necessary to rap down in the dark each day at 4 P.M. (Happy Hour began at 5).

"None of us had seen ice like Bridalveil's. My Banff experiences had not taught me how to protect long vertical sections. We could not figure out a method Chouinard would approve of, and so, on the final day, starting at the predawn time of 8 A.M., we decided to do it our way, unprotected. At our experience level there was a good freakin' to be had by all."

I hadn't seen ice like Bridalveil's either. Following Bruce's lead, I reached the second tier. It was the smoothest sheet of ice that size I'd seen, like a vertical hockey rink freshly Zambonied. The warm, wet ice had already healed from Rob and Annette's ascent the day before. Bruce's efforts had strafed the wall with tiny star cracks rising to the left. The other flaws were no bigger than door dings, the former pickholes, mere navels in the ice. It was glorious to be on such a splendid wall, such a world-class climb, and not have it all pigeonholed like the classics in Colorado.

While Keystone Greensteps had been of consistent difficulty for its entire length, Bridalveil was more varied, the harder sections being harder than on Greensteps, and the easy sections being easier. Slabby romps bridged the gaps between pillars and afforded me the opportunity to look around and trip on what a tremendous position I was in. A good freakin' was had when I reached the top of the Killer Pillar pitch. I'd followed weaknesses from right to left, tracing a steep half spiral up the ice. When the angle relented, a hole in the ice greeted me that a sports car could drop through. From powder blue to aqua to navy and indigo then black, the gullet descended. A Jonahesque bait fish view if there ever was one. The shell of ice was glowing and Bridalveil Falls poured down the gap between the gently ribbed ice and the chunky black rock. The thought of busting through was inescapable. Could a person climb back out against the deluge, or would the climber drown or freeze to death first?

Many parties rap from above Killer Pillar, as the route eases considerably at that point, but again we felt obliged to top out. This meant another posthole session to get to the descent gully, but at least we knew not to try the "direct line" we had the day before. Instead we hiked straight uphill to the road beneath which the Alaska Pipeline is buried, then traversed this west to the avalanche chute descent. One doesn't get near-virgin ice for free.

Modern gear and 100-meter ropes have brought Bridalveil and Greensteps down to a level doable by a fairly fit and moderately experienced ice climber such as myself. Not so the Keystone Wall. Just left of the big two, this 80-degree diamond-shaped face lies less than a shortstop's throw to first from the highway. The foreshortening caused by viewing it from the base of the narrow canyon causes it to look small, but it is nearly as tall as Longs Peak's Diamond. Flat laid slabs of stone form a face broken by thin dihedrals, ledges, and roofs. A paisley motif of moss blebs and verglas stains decorate the slabs.

Up to the mid-1980s, Valdez ice climbing was focused on the prominent flows and pillars. Then in 1987 Steve Garvey broke new ground with his ascent of Sans Amis on the Keystone Wall. Everyone we talked to agreed that Garvey is currently the hard ice guru of the area. On Sans Amis, he climbed long sections of ice no more than an inch thick. His best protection consisted of snargs pounded in the bigger "moss clouds." On the upper pitch, he surmounted multiple roofs involving leaning off tools levered in beneath the overhangs, then scratching up the thin smears above the lips until he could get his feet back on the wall. Thus started the assault on the not-so-prominent lines: the ephemeral drips, the thin pro-less smears, the mixed nightmares, the strings of frozen moss clods. Despite assurances that frozen moss, being a fibrous composite material, was bomber compared to a similar-sized chunk of frozen water, I had no intention of dulling my tools and/or punching into the snow at the base of Keystone Wall. When we were there, however, several Alaskans were vying for new lines on the Keystone Wall, including Teale, Paul Turecki, and Chuck Comstock.

It seems every Alaskan ice climber has a Chuck Comstock story to tell. I first met Chuck in the Bridalveil parking lot with Brian Teale. Teale knew I was there on *Climbing*'s behest, and I assumed Chuck knew it too. Comstock came trudging up the embankment to the parking lot, shoulder-length dreadlocks dripping from a ratty old wool cap and framing a long, thick bushel of red beard. He was attired à la army surplus and his skin looked bleached. I wasn't climbing that day and dressed in forest green canvas pants and an orange jacket. He gave me the once-over then asked, "Are them those fancy fashion pants?"

I was taken aback. Here I was, torso a $400 glowing Gore-Tex ember, and he's flipping me shit about my pants.

"Them's cotton?"

Comstock seemed leery of people, or was it just reporters? Either way, the ploy worked. I was so uncomfortable I wasn't about to ask him for stories. Besides, I had plenty fed to me by others already.

Comstock, an Iowa farm boy, arrived in Valdez as a Coast Guardsman and never left. Prior to his arrival he had no climbing experience but soon became, to use Embick's words, a "neophyte member of a loosely bound group of bored, eager, and ignorant Valdez ice climbers." Comstock's propensity to get into dangerous predicaments was the stuff of legends. I'd seen a hairball series of photos of him escaping off a multiton fractured ice pillar just in time to watch it collapse and burst on the ground. When I asked Brian Teale if Comstock liked taking unnecessary risks, he said, "I don't know about that. He just doesn't like to go do stuff and have an ordinary time. Chuck likes to have epics." Embick and others had recounted many of these epics, both on the ice and off. Every time, Comstock gets in deep shit then pulls through. Paul Turecki claims Comstock "has some kind of guardian angel looking out for him." Brian Teale provided the proof.

One night, Comstock was soloing Bridalveil Falls. "Chuck takes pride in having shit for gear," Teale told us. As usual, Comstock was climbing without a third tool. Part way up he broke a tool. For most climbers this would mean curtains, but Comstock kept going with a single ax. Sure enough, salvation arrived twenty-five feet later when Comstock found a tool left by a Navy SEAL who backed off the route earlier that day.

While we were in Valdez, Embick never missed a chance to tell us how fat Wowie Zowie was this winter. One only has to take his spotting scope, one of his many toys, a few yards from his front door to confirm this. First done by Tobin and Embick, Wowie Zowie was the big-name climb of the early 1980s with a reputation for steepness, unprotectability, and poor consolidation. On the first ascent, Tobin climbed around the backside of the pillar, hacked a window through thin ice to the front, then crawled through the window and onto the over-hanging pillar above. The pro was miserable in bubbly Swiss cheese ice, and twice Tobin slipped, catching himself on just a single tool.

Wowie Zowie is still taken seriously. When Boulder big names Kevin Cooney and Michael Gilbert visited Valdez in '93 they churned up the standard classics in short order. Throughout, they allegedly refused to swill any booze until Wowie Zowie was in their coup bag. And indeed they came back singing of its praises and its horrors, though one wonders if an ascent done after a week of sobriety can be considered to be in good style.

A rest day was due, so we slapped boards on and headed up Mineral Creek to view Wowie Zowie up close. We skied up the deep and broad V-shaped canyon. Crack, rumble—avalanches serenaded us in stereo from both sides. We could smell the snapped alder branches on the close ones. In the course of a few hours we witnessed thirty to forty slides including one right over Wowie Zowie, and two barreling down the gully a hundred feet left of it. We also slapped a few mosquitoes.

Certain climbs are so visually striking that one redefines their level of acceptable risk. Standing beneath Wowie Zowie brought that scary feeling of excitement. Huge fangs of ice coalesce to form the most striking pillar of ice I have seen. On the dark overhanging walls on either side hang dozens of white bayonets, casting an evil, gothic look about the climb.

I wanted Wowie Zowie. I psyched myself up, telling myself I was good enough to lead it, and if not, at worst I would leave a tool to back off. Every now and then the thought would seep in, "What if the ice is too shitty to get back off gear in?" I didn't have an answer for that other than downclimb and pray. It was in rare shape, thick and plump, and I spied a groove creasing the notorious final pillar. All this fueled delusions of grandeur. If only I could talk my partners out of it, I could lead this thing. Work up the weakness, stay cool, find the rests. Crack. Another avalanche cascaded down the gully 100 feet left of it. Okay. Find a good warm-up pillar to test yourself on, then come back when the avalanche danger has settled and the temp drops below freezing.

Had the stock market dropped as fast as the temperature in Valdez, they would be calling for a wet cleanup on Wall Street. One day it was all soft and drippy and Horsetail Falls looked like Madonna's jeans (1986). Two days later it was fully frozen. We had ducked the avalanche danger by climbing in Bear Canyon and Hole in the Wall Canyon. More great ice, but without the sporadic traffic noises of Keystone Canyon. Hole in the Wall is particularly pretty, a deep, winding gash in the bedrock, with a small stream bubbling through it. At places the canyon walls are but thirty feet apart, and rise more than 200 feet.

By the time avalanche danger had subsided, conditions were so frigid that huge pillars had sprouted vertical fracture lines and otherwise easy climbs shed placements on large-pizza-sized dinner plates. We were spared our appointment with Wowie Zowie, at least for this year. We also missed out on avalanche-prone Sheep Creek, where some of the really long climbs lurked. The canyons around Valdez are well developed, but the potential for new routes elsewhere in southeast Alaska boggles the mind. In most cases, long ski-ins or snowmachine approaches will be required. Steve Davis tried to combine the two, having one person drive the snowmachine (called snowmobiles in the lower 48) while the other person is towed along on skis behind the vehicle. As it would be ridiculously pumping to hang onto the tow rope for the nine-mile approach, Davis attached himself to the rope with a fifi hook. The skidoo took off and Davis's heel popped out of one of his Ramer bindings. The roar of the engine drowned out his cries, so he was flying along behind the snowmachine on one ski. Finally he crashed, and still bound to the rope, got towed behind the rig. The cowboy-behind-the-horse stunt went on until the driver thought his engine was starting to run rough. He stopped, only to look back and see the human sea anchor behind.

To cap off our trip, we decided to hit the beaches near Homer. Jim Sweeney, a garrulous and lively character from Anchorage, had given us the hard sell on this area he did much to develop. He jokingly put down the big ice in Valdez to pump up the Homer climbs. Furthermore, he billed the town of Homer as "Berkeley of Alaska," and coaxed us with tales of the wild nightlife there. His cheap tactics worked. We drove back to Anchorage, then headed south down the Seward Highway. Ordinarily, dozens of roadside ice climbs would have presented themselves to us along the Seward, but scant groundwater flow and high temperatures conspired against us. There wasn't even enough ice to do the stand-atop-the-car-to-reach-the-bottom-of-the-flow trick to get started.

Homer was pretty sedate when we visited. No tear gas, nobody offering us acid, none of that stuff I grew up with in Berkeley. In fact it pretty much lived up to its self-proclaimed moniker "The Halibut Capital of Alaska." There were no nose rings (we only saw one in our two-week stay in Alaska) and the militant feminazis must have flown south for the winter. The only hint of Berkeley we saw was the blatant lesbian couple at Neon Coyote restaurant. At least Sweeney was right about the ice climbing. Though no taller than 120 feet, the routes at Ninilchik (one of several seaside areas near Homer) were wild.

Approaching the routes involved a mile-long stroll along the beach south of a small fishing hamlet. Depending on when waves last washed over the sand, it ranged from frozen hard as concrete to a crusty slush prone to foot-deep postholing. Under the former conditions I found donning the spikes to be a favorable alternative to cratering on one's ass. The end of the beach gave way to near-vertical cliffs dropping into the tidal flats. Every thirty yards or so, a floe of ice would adorn the wall. The ice was impregnated with sediment from the soft mudstone. One drip would be gray, the next one brown, the one next to it snot yellow. At high tide waves would lick away at the base of the routes, so several were devoid of ice for the first four or five feet. The fatter floes looked simple, but the subzero cold made them exciting. Repeatedly, I'd get gripped as a dinner plate flashed within inches of a neighboring tool placement. The wind was so stiff it gave me instant ice cream headaches and blew my tools off trajectory in mid-swing. I had to stem out with my right foot to keep the gale from barn-dooring me off. Unless I kept them constantly twisting, screws would freeze tight in mid-placement. Add frequent stops to warm numb hands and the going was slow. Eventually I got in my token Ninilchik lead, set it up as a toprope, and lowered back down.

Slow going is no big deal on most one-pitch climbs, but not so when the tide is coming in. Rob went up to clean the pitch. Between my extended sojourn on the sharp end, and his difficulty getting out the screws, we had chewed up a fair bit of clock. Waves of Slurpee consistency were marching up the beach. One or two of these splashing into you could cost you some appendages. Bruce and I moved the packs away, hanging them on tools sunk into the soft, icy stone. The waves were thirty feet away, then twenty, then ten when Rob stepped over the lip and I gratefully abandoned the belay and immediate vicinity. Rob got himself down and somehow deftly managed to retrieve the rope without it blowing into the soup.

The actual climbs at Ninilchik were not as impressive as the surroundings. Large driftwood snags draped in icicles adorned the beach as did hundreds of icebergs from twelve-pack to jukebox size. In the water a school of seals played king of the ice floe while the sun set over the snow-clad volcanoes across Cook Inlet. It was hard to leave, so we trucked over to an attractive little smear above the high-tide line. Bruce was bouldering around on the thirty-foot vertical formation when brittle ice and bottoming crampon placements convinced him to climb down. Midway up was a basketball-sized rest knob that snapped when Bruce stuck it with his ax. Bruce hung on but the knob didn't. It hit the snow slope at the base, and instead of tumbling straight down, it followed the path of our footprints and plowed right into my pack, breaking my sunglasses and powdering the filter on my camera lens. I was choked. Rob stepped up and gave the block a righteous kick that didn't faze the block, but broke his crampon. Bad juju was in the air. It was time to go home.

"GREEN CARD"

FROM
Postcards from the Ledge
BY GREG CHILD

ANY CLIMBER WITH A RECORD OF ASCENTS AS LONG AS GREG Child's, particularly one that includes Everest, K2, Trango Tower, and peaks in remote regions of Central Asia, is going to be a veteran international traveler. A certain jaded sensibility comes with the territory after so many years of journeys that start with transoceanic flights and end with yak trains and lines of porters. It sounds like fun, and it is, but the experience can also be wearing. Child appropriately quotes writer Paul Theroux on the subject: "Travel is only glamorous in retrospect." And to that, Child adds that travel in the Third World has the almost certain potential to "fray the nerves."

Child's travel began when, after years of climbing as a teenager in his native Australia, he finally made a pilgrimage to Yosemite. Big wall climbs such as Aurora and Lost in America made a strong impression on the young Australian. "As soon as I could afford it, I bought a ticket to Yosemite. It remains a special place for me," Child said. "It was a life, or a lifestyle, that revolved around climbing. In retrospect, it was a very rich life there, and an era that will never come again."

That first journey would lead to many others, to the Himalaya, the Karakoram, and remote Arctic regions. But eventually, Child made his home in the United States, a fact that figures in his story "Green Card." For any climber or traveler who has been stuck somewhere, in Lukla or Katmandu, in Ushuaia or Calafate, or any foreign locale far from home, this story invokes genuine horror.

The setting for "Green Card" is Islamabad, Pakistan, in 1992. Following his climb of Trango Tower, in the Baltoro region of the Karakoram, Child and his climbing companions are more than ready to get home after months of hard physical struggle in the remote region. The predictably chaotic scene at the boarding of his international flight to New York takes on a grim aspect when Child realizes a critical travel document has gone missing. Child knows that he is going nowhere but into a long, dark hole of government bureaucracies (in three countries) and corrupt travel officials, accompanied by the panic of diminishing resources.

"Green Card" can be found in *Postcards from the Ledge*, on pages 61–67.

Travel is glamorous only in retrospect," wrote the globe-trotting storyteller Paul Theroux. His words also apply to that particular breed of lunacy—the Himalayan expedition—where getting to, or home from, a mountain can be harder than the climb.

Take, for example, the summer of 1992, when I got stranded in Islamabad, the capital of Pakistan. It was the end of a successful expedition to Trango Tower in the Karakoram Range, and, like all expeditioners after a sojourn in Asia, my cohorts, Mark Wilford and Rob Slater, and I were desperate to get home.

Expeditioning in the Third World frays the nerves. Two months earlier, we had arrived as polite as choirboys; but now the insufferable heat, bribe-sucking officials, tragic beggars, and the indignity of diarrhea had warped us into three petulant travelers, as diplomatic as Harvey Keitel on a bender. If one more taxi driver attempted to overcharge us, we would tear off his head and make a curry from it.

Which brings us to Islamabad International Airport, where we were trying to elbow our way onto a flight to New York. The scene around us was chaos. The plane was overbooked, and we were trying to fly standby. Scores of wanna-be passengers mobbed the counter, pleading, bullying, trying to pay their way on. It looked like the exodus at the fall of Saigon.

It was then, when checking my travel documents, that I discovered that my Green Card was missing. Carried with my Australian passport, this little laminated card identified me as a U.S. resident-alien and let me enter America freely. Because I owned the Green Card, a U.S. visa had never been stamped in my passport; without the card or a visa, I had nothing to prove that I lived in America, nor any hope of escaping Pakistan.

With only half an hour before departure, I went as crazy as a rat in a coffee can. Ripping into our duffel bags, I scattered pitons, ice axes, sleeping bags, and dirty underpants across the floor. But alas, no Green Card. Instead of flying home, I realized, I was stuck for who-knows-how-long in a city where the idea of nightlife is sipping a 7-Up while trimming one's fingernails and watching geckoes chase bugs across the ceiling.

Misery overcame me. I slumped onto our baggage. Mark and Rob looked on with pity. We had shared great torment to climb Trango Tower, and had we been in the mountains, my friends would have waded rivers or dared avalanches to save me; but I was nuts if I thought they were going to spend one more minute in Islamabad just to keep me company. They skedaddled home.

Back in town that night, I bivouacked on the office floor of my trekking agent. The British mountaineer Doug Scott lay beside me, shaking and moaning from an attack of malaria. In the morning, after Doug staggered feverish onto a flight home, I waved down a taxi.

"Please take me to the American Embassy," I told the driver.

"Yes, no problem," he said. A long ride to the outskirts of town brought us to a shack surrounded by oxen. Behind it, men with hatchets chopped at ox carcasses.

"No. This is a slaughterhouse. Take me to the American Embassy."

I can only imagine that the words "American Embassy" somehow mimicked the Urdu sounds for butcher shop. I repeated my desired destination; then on a piece of paper I sketched a building with Old Glory flying over it. "Ah, yes! American Embassy. No problem!" he exclaimed, and drove off, this time to the embassy, an imposing fortress surrounded by surveillance cameras, rebuilt to repel invaders after a Shiite mob had destroyed it during the Iran hostage crisis. But today the embassy was closed.

"Why closed?" I asked the driver.

"Today holiday. Birthday of Islamic prophet."

I closed my eyes and sighed, the first of many such surrenders I would make that week. That morning I had phoned my wife, Salley, in Seattle and instructed her to ask U.S. immigration authorities at home to reissue my Green Card. But it was Labor Day weekend, and everything was closed there, too.

The next day at the U.S. embassy, I pleaded my case to a two-inch-thick panel of bulletproof glass, behind which sat a secretary. I told her I had lost my Green Card and couldn't go home, and I asked her to do whatever necessary to get me home.

"But you cannot go to America. You don't have a Green Card," the secretary replied.

"I know. That's why I'm here. For help," I said. "Please get me your supervisor."

"He is busy. Come back tomorrow."

I went ballistic. "I'm a taxpayer!" I shouted. "I have a job to get home to, a wife and family to support." Furthermore, I told her, I was penniless and had frostbite from two months in the mountains. Half of this was a lie, but I felt compelled to maximize my pathetic situation to gain her sympathy.

A supervisor appeared. I repeated my story. He then called for his supervisor, and I told her as well. Then they told me they could not give me an official letter to enter the United States; the State Department forbids such letters being issued in Pakistan because they are often forged by terrorists. Worse, I was told that there was no U.S. immigration office in Pakistan, and I would have to go to Delhi or Bangkok to find one.

"Can't you phone the office in Delhi and ask them to help me?" I asked.

"I can't act on your behalf because you are not an American citizen," one supervisor answered.

"Then I'd like to apply for a tourist visa to enter America. You can stamp it in my Australian passport, and I'll be out of here."

"I can't do that because you've told me you have a Green Card, and tourist visas can't be issued to Green Card holders."

Only Kafka could have scripted a Catch-22 as seamlessly confounding as this. I stared into the bulletproof glass my taxes paid for. It wasn't glass, I decided, but a special screen that filtered out logic and compassion—stealth glass, a CIA invention. I knew the person to whom I was talking was a decent human being, if only I could get through to her. Then something tweaked and I started raving about being treated like a second-class citizen and writing letters to congressmen. The surveillance camera zeroed in on me. I imagined marines in the next room pegging me as a security threat and itching to monster me. I got paranoid and left.

Back at my trekking agent's office I phoned U.S. immigration in Delhi. Public holiday. Office closed. So I sent them a fax, which they never answered. When I visited the Indian Embassy to get a visa for going to Delhi, it, too, was closed for the holiday.

Days passed. My cash dwindled. I was forced to move out of the cockroach-infested Flashman's Hotel into something cheaper. I stayed at Flashman's because it was one of the few hotels in this prohibition town where I could obtain a quota of beer, though only after filling out a declaration pledging I was not a Muslim. At night, bottle in front of me, I watched Pakistani TV till I felt as if I'd had a frontal lobotomy. Aside from Islamic soap operas, TV was mostly prayer, with sporadic CNN broadcasts that blacked out at the first hint of women in short skirts, couples dancing, or anything suggesting that men and women ever come within thirty feet of each other. My new hotel room didn't even have TV, let alone plumbing. When I called for washing water, a bellboy brought a bucket of suspicious-smelling brown liquid pumped out of a ditch beside the hotel.

While I rotted in Islamabad, back in Colorado Mark had recovered from the bottle of Pakistani rum he'd poured down his neck on the flight home and was poking around the gear we'd shoveled into duffel bags at Trango base camp. He found a life preserver he'd pilfered from the Pakistan International Airlines 747; then, amongst a pile of miscellany, he saw it: my Green Card. When a fax rolled out of my trekking agent's machine announcing that my Green Card was jetting toward me, special delivery, everyone in the office rejoiced, happy that soon they'd be rid of me.

That is, if I could get on a plane. The flights were booked full for a month. At PIA headquarters I barged into a manager's office and implored him for help. He had heard the sob stories—stranded, broke, ailing mother—a thousand times before. He pretended to hear me out while listening to a cricket match on the radio and was about to give me the bum's rush when I said, "Yes, cricket is truly the finest game. As a matter of fact, I went to school with the son of Sir Donald Bradman (a cricket star of Michael Jordanesque status)." I lied. I hate cricket, and as for Bradman, if he ever had a son, I wouldn't know him if he jumped up out of my soup bowl.

Bullshitting changed everything. The manager handed me a cup of tea and promised to try and get me on a flight. After a lively discussion of cricket, which I faked very well, I rushed to the airport to get my Green Card from customs. Customs was closed, another national holiday.

Two days later I had my Green Card, but my prospects were dim for escaping Islamabad. My cricket-loving friend at PIA had cut off the flow of tea and now gave me the brush-off. But while walking back to my hotel, I passed a travel agent shopfront and entered it on an impulse. I told the ticket agent my problem.

"Would you pay $250 to fly tomorrow?" the woman, Anita, asked.

"Is the Pope Catholic?"

"What?"

"Never mind. It's a deal."

Next morning, Anita and a surly fellow hiding behind Raybans met me at my hotel, took my cash, passport, and airline ticket, and said, "We'll be back in a few minutes." Ten minutes later my friend from PIA phoned. "Good news. You are booked to fly tonight," he said. I put the phone down and marveled at my stupidity: I had just given everything I owned to two people I didn't know, while I got my reservation anyway.

Hours passed with no sign of Anita. I was panicked that I'd miss my flight and began to wonder if I'd been ripped off. Two British climbers had told me that day that they'd been held at gunpoint by policemen outside their hotel and had lost a small fortune. My paranoia redlining, I caught a taxi to Anita's office.

The only person at the office turned out to be the manager, a beefy Pakistani who told me he lived in Texas, where he operated a chain of laundromats in addition to this travel agency. When I explained why I was looking for Anita, he went berserk, screaming that I'd just proved what he had long suspected—Anita was running a black-market ticket agency under his roof.

I began to feel mighty uncomfortable. "I don't want to get anyone in trouble. I thought it was business as usual," I said.

"You can't be blamed. You are just a poor dupe, desperate to get home."

"Right. Furthermore, I'm an idiot."

He thanked me for exposing Anita's nefarious trade and apologized for the corruption eating at his country. "Now you must tell my brother this story," he said, escorting me to a room where a dignified gentleman—obviously the don of this family operation—knelt on a prayer rug, facing a framed photo of Mecca, mouthing a verse from the Koran. I stuttered out my story.

He hammered his fist on the floor. "Fire the bitch!" he roared.

Next I was hustled into a Mercedes with a security guard cradling a sleek, automatic machine pistol in the back seat. Suddenly I wondered if this whole charade wasn't an elaborate plot to take me hostage. Don't laugh. It happens. In 1986 a friend of mine, Michael Thexton, was on a flight taxiing down the runway at Islamabad when terrorists hijacked the plane. When the hijackers' demands weren't met, they grabbed Michael and held a .45 to his head: he was going to be the first to die. Luckily for Michael, Pakistani commandos burst in, and he dived out a door amid grenades and bullets. Afterward, Bryant Gumbel on the "Today Show" asked him why he didn't try to overpower his captor. "Because he had a gun pointed at my head," Michael said very slowly, just so Bryant didn't miss the point.

"Where are we going?" I asked as we screeched through the streets of Islamabad.

"We are gonna nail Anita," the driver says.

Wonderful, I thought, I was about to see a drive-by shooting. Frankly, I couldn't have cared less if Anita was running heroin. I just wanted to be on that flight in four hours, but things had spiraled out of control.

After checking the airport and several other sleazy hangouts, we found Anita waiting at my hotel. Her mouth dropped when she saw her boss. A massive argument followed. Onlookers gaped while our gunman passed the time combing his hair and inspecting his reflection in the car mirror. Everyone kept pointing at me and apologizing on behalf of Pakistan. I felt like an insect, and I shrugged my shoulders at Anita to say, "Sorry," then took my ticket, my documents, and a refund and made a beeline to the airport.

Going through Pakistani immigration, it occurred to me that Anita's gang might avenge themselves on my lousy rat-fink hide by spinning a story to the famously corrupt airport police that I was smuggling drugs. This thought made me break into a guilt-smelling sweat. While an official inspected my documents I tried to look casual, but the more casual I tried to be, the more nervous I appeared. A machine-gun-toting cop frisked me, while another one opened my camera and inspected it closely. He made me remove the batteries, "in case there is a bomb inside." Visions of the movie *Midnight Express* filled my head. I expected to be pulled aside for a full-body search; some gloating sadist would plant a brick of hashish in my pants and then drag me off to a prison and subject me to unspeakable abuses. I gulped with relief when my camera was returned.

As the immigration officer stamped my passport, he noticed that I had been to Pakistan six times.

"Oh, my God," he said, smiling. "You have visited us too many times." "Yes," I replied. "Too many."

"THE GEARFREAK CAPER: A STORY"

FROM
A Fine Kind of Madness
BY GUY AND LAURA WATERMAN

"THE GEARFREAK CAPER" IS A TAKE-OFF ON THE PRIVATE-EYE TALES from the 1950s and was directly inspired by Woody Allen's "The Whore of Mensa," which appeared in *The New Yorker*. Guy and Laura Waterman, who for nearly thirty years lived on a twenty-seven-acre Vermont homestead without electricity or running water, found the modern-day obsession with outdoor equipment at odds with their simpler approach to the wilderness. So Guy set out to lampoon it and was perhaps more successful than he would have believed.

The Watermans met while rock climbing at the Gunks in New Paltz, New York. Of the five books they wrote together, two are considered to be seminal works: *Backwoods Ethics* (1979), a practical guide to low-impact wilderness travel, and the more philosophical *Wilderness Ethics* (1993), a tirade against the crowds and encroachment of the modern world on the fragile wilderness.

The Watermans's commentary is a mixture of practical advice, based on their years of experience in the wilderness and on their homestead, and a condemnation of those who fail to measure up to their high ethical standards (such as hikers who use cell phones in the wilderness). But their writing could be funny as well.

Stories from their final volume, *A Fine Kind of Madness*, including this one, by necessity are colored by the tragic suicide of Guy in 2000. He took his own life by climbing to the summit of one of his beloved mountains in the middle of winter, where deadly conditions and below-zero temperatures quickly killed him.

The original byline, Rex Slim, is Guy's homage of sorts to Rex Stout, who wrote the Nero Wolfe mystery series. Guy sat down to write this satirical piece after reading Allen's story. As Laura put it, "We stand convicted, on all fronts, of the opposite tendencies from those satirized in this tall tale, concocted by Guy shortly after reading Allen's gem."

"The Gearfreak Caper" is in *A Fine Kind of Madness*, on pages 174–182.

BY REX SLIM (WITH APOLOGIES TO WOODY ALLEN)

I n my business you got to be able to spot a meal ticket from a dry hole right off. I was pretty sure Lady Luck had sent me home a winner when this tweedy gent with a pipe comes through the door marked "CLAUDIUS FOX PRIVATE INVESTIGATOR" and walks up to my desk.

He smelled like money. Trouble too. But that's my bag, isn't it?

"Mr. Fox?" he queried.

"That's what the name says on the door," I countered.

His suit was rumpled and not exactly new, but you could tell he didn't get it off the rack at Korvette's. His shirt was expensive and the tie was as conservative as a baked potato. But what caught my eye was the tie clasp: a thin, small, neatly embossed golden dollar sign. I liked that.

"My name's Godfrey Gearfreak. I need help, and I'm willing to pay for it," he started in, me not objecting to that last part.

"I've never dealt with a private detective before, but I don't want this to get to the police. You see," his eyes fell, "I'm being blackmailed."

I'd heard this story before. Only this one turned out to have a new wrinkle.

I motioned him to a chair and drew paper and pencil from under the flask in the desk drawer. "Tell me all about it," I mused in my most understanding tone.

"My wife and I used to go rock climbing together a lot. We met in a Sierra Club beginners' group. We used to go to Yosemite, Taquitz, vacations in the Tetons, Rainier, the Gunks, everywhere together."

"Sounds nice and healthy," I smiled. "What went wrong?"

He plunged in: "The equipment—all the climbing gear. I found it fascinating; she was bored by it. I got all the latest catalogs—Chouinard, REI, North Face, Sierra Designs, EMS, you name it. I grooved on the Mountain Safety Research newsletters. I had to try all the latest hardware, each new belay plate and seat harness, not to mention all the new tent designs, pack frames, sleeping bags, stoves. . . . "

"And your wife didn't like your spending the money?" I put in.

"It's not that. We can afford that kind of money." I liked hearing him say that; it gave me a warm feeling in my wallet.

His voice lowered. "She just never took an interest in the equipment, she still wants to go hiking and climbing on weekends. Clambering around on the rocks is all right, I suppose, but there's so much new gear to try out and read about, I don't want to waste all my free time just out there climbing around.

"Christ, Claudius," he blurted, "who wants to sweat out some lousy 5.7 move when you could be looking at and talking about this hot new foam-back material for cagoules that uses a super K coated nylon taffeta with a .050-inch layer of bonded foam and a lining of thin nylon tricot!"

No question, I had to agree with Gearfreak there.

"Well, I found out there's a place in this town where they'll set you up with a girl who knows all about climbing equipment and will talk with you for an hour about any gear you want to talk about—for a price."

He paused, embarrassed. "Go on," I urged.

"I never wanted to get involved. I'm just looking for a quick, stimulating exchange of ideas on all the latest gear—then I want the girl to leave.

"They've got all kinds of girls—some of them know all the latest tents, some can tell you about ropes and their test strength, some are technical ice-climbing specialists." He sighed a crooked, bitter sigh: "It's really satisfying, Claudius, to spend an evening secluded with a girl who really *understands* how baffles are superior to sewn-through seams and can talk intelligently and sympathetically about proper stitching, who appreciates the difference between goose down and duck down, and who isn't afraid to talk openly about foam as a medium for sleeping bags."

"All sounds great," I commented. "What's the prob?"

"Blackmail! I've been arranging these rendezvous for several months. The price was stiff, but it was worth it. Now they're upping the ante—asking for real money—or they'll tell my wife."

His voice dropped to a whisper: "They've even got a photo of me showing a Sticht belay plate to a young girl in lederhosen."

I was intrigued. I'd heard that the boys down at the Vice Squad were working on some big-time racket involving outdoorsy types, but I also knew they weren't getting anywhere on the case. Maybe this was a lead.

"Tell me what you know about this operation." I hunched over the pad.

He demurred. "But will you help me? Will you take the case?"

I looked again at the thin, small, neatly embossed golden dollar-sign tie clasp. "Seventy-five bucks a day plus expenses. And I don't guarantee results. But I've got some hunches I'd like to play."

He looked assured. I had me a client.

After he left, I also had me a packet of notes on all he knew, including the telephone number for his contact. I was ready to make my first move.

➤   ➤   ➤

Going out to a pay phone so the call could not be traced, I plugged in my dime and dialed the seven delectable digits. A husky voice, like Harlow with bronchitis, answered.

I started off briskly: "I understand a fellow could get a little companionable talk on the advantages and disadvantages of different lightweight stoves at this party."

"I'm totally mystified as to what you're talking about, mister," responded the decidedly unmystified voice.

"I have a hundred here to refresh your memory," I growled.

Madam Husky-Voice was suddenly all business. "Do you want to talk heating capacity or weight and volume, honey?"

"The works," I thought it best not to seem cheap.

"That C-note will get you a nice evening with a girl who knows all the stoves and has tried them out in high winds and at different altitudes. She was one of the first to use the MSR."

"Sounds like my ticket," I opined. I gave her a room number at the Belmont and hung up.

➤   ➤   ➤

An hour later I answered the buzzer at this same room number to see a shapely young sheba who was all Miss Outdoors, from the tip of balaclava right down to the toes of her Civettas. In between she filled out her hiking knickers and L. L. Bean sweater like so many well-packed (but just right) stuff sacks.

Her Kelty bulged with odd shapes and sizes of stoves.

"Hi, I'm Bobbi," she cooed sweetly.

"Baby, I don't know how you got by the house dick," I winced as I pulled her into the room. "Anyone can tell you're an equipment nut."

"A five-spot usually keeps them happy," she smiled confidently. Unshouldering her Kelty, she shot a glance around the room. "Would you like to begin by comparing the heating properties of the Optimus IIIB with the newer MSR?"

I parried, "I've heard the MSR's a fabulous heating machine, but won't simmer on low heat like the Optimus." I had to string her along, see what she'd do, see how far she'd go.

"True," she laughed, a hollow, brittle laugh. "But the weight of that old IIIB never appealed to me. And since you have to carry a fuel bottle anyway . . . "

She started in and kept it up, with just an occasional query or rebuttal from me, for fully an hour. Here she was, probably not old enough to buy a set-up at the local bar, but with all the hardened flippancy of the jaded equipment freak. I was amazed. I mean, I've been around, but this was something new.

When she got through explaining how the adapter valves for the new Rich-Moor stoves accommodated several varieties of fuel, I got up, stretched, and, taking two fifties out of my wallet, stuffed them in the outside pocket of her Kelty.

"Say, you're nice," she grinned suddenly. "Would you like to do it again sometime? Or maybe try something a little different . . . a little unusual?"

"What'd you have in mind?" I countered.

"Well, I have a girlfriend you'd like," she purred. "The two of us could come up and talk about cross-country ski wax for a really divine evening. We could even get into . . . " her voice trailed off, but her lips shaped the word, " . . . bindings." She winked.

"I think we might make a deal," I murmured, bluffing. "I'll call you in a day or so," and I ushered her and her Kelty out the door, familiarly patting her D-rings as she passed.

Pay dirt! I knew I had stumbled right into just the mess the Vice Squad was after. I suppressed a snicker. I knew the lieutenant would be climbing walls (5.9) when he found I had beaten him to the quarry again.

➤   ➤   ➤

Before I took the direct route to my prey, though, I thought I ought to do a little advance nosing around through a third party, a certain shady character of my acquaintance, name of Slightly Roddey, who is willing to give me underworld information on occasion in exchange for my not giving the boys downtown certain information about Slightly Roddey.

Slightly was his usual obnoxious and uncooperative self until reminded of the advantages of being on this side of those Sing Sing walls. Then he sung sung.

"The Vice boys haven't got to first base on this one," Slightly told me over a draft in the Shady Deal Café down on lower Filth Street.

"This operation is really big-time and the cover's held up airtight so far. For fifty bills you can spend a couple of hours with a brunette going over the pros and cons of A-frame tents versus the exoskeleton design, reviewing ventilation condensation, tunnel entrances, mosquito netting, zippers, and cook stove holes.

"For just twenty-five, you can get a set-up with a leggy Swedish broad, lighting lanterns and stoves and testing for beryllium and carbon monoxide.

"If you're into technical climbing, you can climb into and out of every seat harness, chest harness, and leg loop in the book with two cuties who can tell you the fall force each one could absorb and will listen sympathetically to all you want to tell them about different hard hats, even including their energy absorption and lateral rigidity. That would cost you seventy-five bucks."

Slightly paused to order another brew.

"Write down this name: Gloria Rucksack. She's the brains and the muscle behind this one, from what I hear."

"What's her background?" I wheedled.

"She's an equipment nut from way back. You know Jack Stephenson's fancy Warmlite tent?"

"The one with the unique condensation-dispelling properties?" I questioned.

"That's the one. Well, Stephenson doesn't know it, but Gloria Rucksack spent a weekend in the pilot model before he did."

I gulped.

"You know Dirty Harry's new sleeping bags at Alpine Designs?" went on Slightly. "She slept in it the first night the baffles were stitched."

"With or without Dirty Harry?" I quipped.

"You want solid info or witty repartee?" Slightly shot back. "She knows them all—Penberthy, Chouinard, the Whittaker brothers. Anyway, the place you want is a little backpacking supply store on the outskirts of town, Northern Alpine Sports. It's a front, of course. The real operation runs out of the back of the store. You'd probably find Gloria there."

➤   ➤   ➤

An hour later, when I walked into Northern Alpine Sports, a young man in Vibrams asked if he could help me.

"I'd like to see a rucksack," I croaked.

"For what purpose?" he inquired.

"Glory-a only knows," I muttered.

"In that case, go right on back." He knowingly waved me down a long hall that led to a door marked "stockroom employees only." I pushed open the door and gingerly stepped in.

Here indeed was Gloria Rucksack's pleasure palace. The place was a perfect set-up. A huge high-ceilinged room, with windows along one side as tall as your grandmother's giraffe. Only no light showed through the heavy maroon velvet floor-to-ceiling curtains, thickly embroidered with gold. The light was supplied by three glittering silver chandeliers suspended from the ornate ceiling. An Oriental carpet large enough to fly in Farouk and all his concubines buried the floor. Victorian decor all the way.

And girls? Wow! A trio of beauties sat on one outsize sofa, provocatively leafing through the pages of REI catalogs. A gorgeous redhead in crimson knickers, who looked like she'd just been poured into her Whillans seat harness like thick strawberry jam, was sorting hexentrics voluptuously on the floor at one end. Slouched in an armchair near the door, a slender, pretty girl no more that seventeen years old was opening and closing Jumars and Gibbs ascenders.

Within seconds after I entered, a slinky black girl sidled up to me from nowhere, slipping her slim hips in and out of a wraparound pack frame, and breathed huskily, "Would you like to go upstairs and talk about different kinds of back bands?"

"Catch you later at Camp Four, baby," I snapped out of the corner of my mouth. "I got other things on my mind right now."

A honey blond in a leopard-skin 60-40 whispered at me from the other side. "If you're into technical ice, we could have a cozy chat about the test strengths of Salewa tubulars versus wart hogs. And I have a new wrinkle on how to use a Terrordactyl that would tickle you."

Before I could answer, a familiar husky tone from behind me intervened: "Later, Birgit. This one's for me."

Swinging around, I saw before me the queen mama of them all—a statuesque raven-haired Venus who would make anyone forget to button down his supergaiters. Her skirt was like a good tent fly—form-fitted and not too long. And the blouse material was strictly sewn-through.

"You look like you could use a sociable brew in the back room, honey," she purred as she guided me toward a low door near the back, just past a carved-ebony bookcase sporting titles like *Freedom of the Hills, Advanced Rockcraft,* early Chouinard catalogs, and a handsome leather-bound complete set of MSR newsletters.

She slipped a key chain out of her bosom and sorted through the Swiss Army knife, Taylor pocket altimeter, and Dwyer wind meter until she came to a tiny key for the little door. But not before I noticed on that key chain one other little trinket . . . a thin, small, neatly embossed golden dollar sign.

I followed her into a richly appointed little boudoir, and as she walked ahead of me, I said, "Nice little pad you have here, Gloria Rucksack—or should I say . . . Mrs. Gearfreak!"

She wheeled around, sporting a new piece of equipment—a shiny little black revolver that I knew she hadn't picked up at Holubar's. "That's right, Fox, you walked yourself right into the middle of more than you bargained for this time."

"I don't get it, baby," I sauntered, stalling and trying to look calm. "Your old man said he couldn't get you to talk about clevis pins at breakfast."

"That creep?" she snarled. "He doesn't know his rear end from a cook stove hole. What he doesn't know about equipment would fill three Bauer catalogs. Just as soon as I get this operation a little more profitable, it'll be goodbye, Godfrey! And meanwhile, Foxie, you're going to take a little hike of your own—down the middle of the Hudson River in a pair of cement P.A.s."

I thought fast—and acted faster. With one swift karate chop, I separated Miss Gloria-locks from her shiny black plaything, and in another motion I swooped an extra-large down mummy bag over her head. She ripped out her Swiss Army knife and cut her way out, filling the room with more feathers than you'll see at a Northern Goose Hoedown on Hudson Bay. By this time, though, Your Humble Narrator had the revolver and the outing was over.

The rest of the story came out downtown, and today Miss Rucksack—Mrs. Gearfreak—is doing a ten-year bivouac in a really windproof stand-up tent at Sing Sing.

Except for my check from Mr. Godfrey Gearfreak, which arrived in the mail, I neither saw nor heard from him again. But I've been told that he now roams the High Sierra, with no climbing hardware, no tent, and just an old army blanket in which he rolls all his simple belongings, so that he needs no fancy pack. They say he takes no interest in the latest gadgets and gear of the other climbers and hikers he meets on the trail, but simply invites them to join him in looking at the birds and the wildflowers.

"FIT FOR NOTHING"

FROM
Storms of Silence
BY JOE SIMPSON

DISASTER SEEMS TO FOLLOW JOE SIMPSON AROUND. HE'S SUFFERED an extraordinary amount of misfortune in his climbing career, including having had ledges fall out from beneath him, and having been abandoned in a crevasse with two broken legs—basically left for dead—on a Peruvian peak in 1985.

At least the painful material makes for good books. *Touching the Void*, the gripping story of Simpson's self-rescue from the Andean peak Siula Grande is undoubtedly his best-known work. And Simpson's experiences have also given him a twisted perception on climbing and what drives people to do it.

Coincidentally, the accident described in *Touching the Void* figures in this piece as well. After breaking both legs, Simpson was forced to undergo months of rehabilitation in order to regain the use of his limbs. The experience left him addicted to working out to stay fit, even if at the same time he detests having to do it.

Simpson's endorphin-driven desire to stay in shape leads him to a modern gym, where the lycra-clad denizens seem alien and the aerobics class is an absolute physical horror. Just when Simpson thinks he's done with it, he finds out that he's only survived the warm-up as the instructor barks out new orders.

The experience eventually drives Simpson to the refuge of a local YMCA, but his troubles aren't over. The story takes place between his attempt on Nepal's Cho Oyu and his first visit back to Peru since the accident that almost killed him. Simpson learns that the travails of the gym are nothing compared to going back and facing the place of his greatest challenge.

"Fit For Nothing" can be found in the *Storms of Silence*, on pages 219–228.

T he mirrors are everywhere. In every gym and fitness club in the country the mirrors shine back at you. There's no getting round them. They begin to play insidious games with your mind. At first you avoid them, alarmed at the thought of appearing narcissistic, but very quickly you find that they are unavoidable. Someone has gone to great lengths to position them around the room in such a way that whichever way you look there are always at least three images of yourself peering back at you. Unable to escape them, you rush through your training program in faster and faster times, tormented by sweaty contorted postures of yourself, chased by vain demons.

I detest training and all the vanity of body sculpting for its own sake. The tedium of endless leg-raising, swinging chrome dumbbells up and down, squats, thrusts, pounding up rubber-stepped hills, and chasing cartoon boats on the computerized rowing machine drives me to distraction. I seem to do it from a distance, as if looking down from above and questioning why I'm strapping myself into some horrifically complicated gizmos designed to isolate one muscle into spasms of agony. Some of the machines seem better suited to torturing cattle than gaining spurious fitness. I dread waking up in the morning and feeling as if I've been hanging from the ceiling all night on meat hooks thrust through my nipples. Then there is the agonized stagger down to the bathroom on legs so wire-tight and muscle-bound that I feel sure I can hear the sinews shredding, with calf muscles so hard that it feels as if a rivet gun is about to fire bolts out through them. I confess to a nagging suspicion that it's only making me fitter and stronger so that I can train even harder. When eventually I escape the gyms and find myself in the mountains, I don't seem to be any fitter than my companions and a whole set of arcane unusable muscles, honed to the peak of perfection, soon wither and shrivel from lack of use.

Although I loathe training, I am addicted to it. I don't know what it is—some endorphin-flooded fixation about having three days a week in the gym. I never used to train before I broke my legs, never thought about it until months, if not years, of physiotherapy, dire warnings about never climbing again, and the withered stick of a leg after eight months in plaster prompted me to join a local fitness club. By the time the leg had regained its muscle mass I was hopelessly trapped. Oh, I know the importance of it and how quickly my legs will deteriorate if I don't train, but that doesn't mean I should be addicted to it.

I remember the first gym, a slick room of chrome and mirrors and neatly ranked machines of torture. Three of us had somehow wrangled six months free membership and we turned up in tatty shirts and track suit trousers with holes in the knees. A trainer cheerfully put us through a regime that left us nearly weeping on the floor.

"Do you lads fancy some Quando aerobics?" he asked.

"Quando what?" we chorused from a collapsed heap by the buttock-separating device.

"Fit young lads like you," he sneered. "You'll love it. Come on, let's feel the burn."

He handed each of us a pair of plastic coated dumbbells and led us into a small room surrounded by wall to ceiling mirrors and dominated by an enormous pair of stereo speakers.

"Hey, these weigh nothing," I said, hefting the dumb-bell experimentally. "Less than a bag of sugar, I reckon." I grinned confidently. "This will be a doddle."

"Yeah, what are we worried about?" Richard swung the weights nonchalantly over his shoulders. "Nothing to it."

"Have you done this before?" Tom asked as he tested himself with a few stretching exercises. Bending forward from the waist, he was struggling desperately to touch his knees. He had the flexibility of an iron bar.

"Nope, but it can't be that bad," I replied. He said we'd only do forty-five minutes."

Twenty minutes later we were barging drunkenly into each other as we tried to follow the trainer's instructions. Dance music thumped hypnotically from the speakers, and I watched our regimented rhythmic choreography descend into uncoordinated rag-doll spasms. The dumbbells now weighed close to fifty pounds, and our bodies were wracked with burning muscles from holding them continuously in front of us, over our heads, and out to the sides. I could barely see for the sweat flooding into my contact lenses and someone appeared to have removed one of my lungs. I was grateful for the odd painful crack of a wayward dumb-bell in the ear to keep me going.

"Lift those legs higher, pump it, pump it, PUMP it." The man yelled into the microphone curled in front of his mouth. In ragged unison we reeled off to the side, collided with a mirror, and bounced roughly back into line, making pathetic little hopping steps. He was virtually chinning himself with his kneecaps, holding the dumbbells ramrod straight in front of his chest.

"Lift."

The weights arched above his head. There was a loud thump as Richard dropped his and howled as it crushed his foot.

"And out to the side, one, two, three . . . and lift. Get those knees up. Feel that burn."

Burn! I was standing in flames. Tom was resting his dumbbells on his shoulders. In an effort to raise one above my head I twisted to the side and let the left one drop. I lurched out of line like Quasimodo on acid, wondering who the manic, twisted creature in the mirror was. Richard staggered into view clutching one weight in both hands and bending himself almost into the crab position in an effort to get it to stick out in front of him. He sank slowly to his knees.

"And down," the torturer said, lowering his weights. He kept jumping lightly on his toes. He hadn't broken a sweat.

"Okay, slow it down, lads."

Slow it down? We stared at him in horror from our kneeling position on the floor.

"Okay, warm up over. Let's go!" he yelled, making us shrink back in alarm.

"Warm up?" Richard croaked. "Warm up? If I get any hotter my blood will start boiling. Bugger this." He tried to throw his dumbbell to the floor in disgust only to find he had already let go of it. Tom had got to his feet, but didn't have the stretch to lean down and pick up his weights. He bent from the waist and flapped his hands pitifully at his knees.

"Sod it!" I gasped, and leant back to back with Richard on the floor. The music suddenly stopped. The room was filled with the stentorian rasp of our breathing.

"What's up with you guys?" the fitness god inquired.

"Knackered," I whispered.

"Help . . . " Richard added.

"Have you been listening to Walkmans?" the trainer asked, as he shepherded us from the room.

"No, why?"

"Well, you seemed to be dancing to different music, that's all."

It took a couple of weeks before we got over the shock.

"Must have been the Quando bit that did us," Richard speculated optimistically.

"Which bit was that exactly?"

"The dumbbells, I suppose. Why don't we do the normal aerobics class?

I'm sure we can cope with that," Tom suggested. We looked at him balefully.

"You're kidding," I hissed.

"May as well give it a try," Richard said. "After all, it can't be any worse than carrying loads at twenty thousand feet."

"And when did you ever carry a load at twenty thousand feet?" Tom and I chorused at his departing back.

"Why's he so keen?" I asked, amazed by Richard's uncharacteristic lust for pain.

"Have you seen the rest of the class?"

We went over and looked in the mirrored room. Ten gorgeously attired young women were limbering up in two lines facing the mirrors. A fearsome-looking body-fascist was adjusting her throat mike. Richard was enthusiastically bending and stretching at the back. The women sported big hairstyles, makeup, jewelry, tight multicolored body suits, and bodies that would make a professional model weep. This isn't a keep fit class, I thought, if this lot gets any fitter they'll snap.

"He's got a point. I mean aerobics might do us some good," I suggested to Tom, who was already getting into line at the back next to Richard. I shuffled furtively into the room just as the music boomed into life.

"Hey, this isn't bad," I whispered to Tom after thirty minutes. "It's nothing like that Quando stuff."

"Well, there is some distraction from the pain."

"Yeah, I noticed." I executed a few nifty high-faluting kicks and spun round on the instructress's command. Tom was still facing the front, and Richard seemed to be dancing with the side wall.

"Hell, I've seen more fat on a chip," I said as Tom and I spun neatly to face one another while the rest of the class jigged in perfect precision, eyes on the mirrored front. Richard danced with the door.

"And down!" Everyone sank to their knees. "And stretch that pelvis!" I looked sideways across the line. A tangerine-spangled shapely leg whipped back, narrowly missing Tom's face. I lifted my leg up and back copying the contorted kneeling position.

"Oh Jesus! Ouwch!" I yelped as something parted company between my buttocks and my lower back.

"And stretch up!" Miss Lycra Thighbreaker sang cheerfully from the front. My head pressed down on the floor and my left buttock seized up in a tight knot of a cramp. I lowered the leg and writhed on the floor, trying to release the cramp. Glancing sideways, I saw Tom and Richard on their hands and knees staring up and forward, necks outstretched, eyes bulging. Richard was craftily resting his leg on the mirrored wall behind me and I noticed the oddly fascinated stare on his face. A whole row of shapely Lycra buttocks were arrayed in a row in front of him. There was less then a foot between them and Tom's and Richard's faces.

"Well, that's not such a bad exercise. My pelvis could do with a loosening up," I muttered, abandoning my cramped bum and hastily getting to my knees. I assumed the position and stared expectantly forward. To my horror, I was confronted with a pair of hairy testicles hanging from the loose shorts of some hearty rugger-bugger type who had insinuated himself into the class after we had started.

"Yeargg." I pulled my face away from the awful sight to see Tom in spasms of laughter. Richard was miles away.

There is a peculiar contradiction of signals in some of these establishments that I have never been able to resolve. On the one hand, everyone is there to train, to work up a sweat, tone those muscles, and get fit; on the other hand, sometimes it seems more akin to a fashion parade than a no-pain no-gain routine. I know it's rude to stare. Naturally it's politically incorrect to display the slightest attraction for your fellow devotees of agony, but it is also well nigh impossible. If everyone one wore baggy loose-fitting tops and track suit trousers, there wouldn't be much of a problem, but life isn't so easy. The trend of ladies' gym wear makes it hard, so to speak. There seems to be an obsession with leotards, body suits, buttock-splitting Lycra thingies, swim suits worn over swim suits, countless variations of attire that leave absolutely nothing to the imagination.

From a practical point of view, I can't think of anything sweatier and more uncomfortable to wear during training sessions. Performing squats while wearing a cord-thin g-string that threatens to split your cheeks up level with your shoulders looks unspeakably painful. And if you are wearing, say, a black leotard, why then put a skin-tight swim suit on top of it with the legs cut so high that they seem to go up to your armpits? Or pull on what looks like a scarlet pair of bikini bottoms so lacking in material that they merely create a vivid red triangle which for the average man has the effect of a hypnotist swinging a fob-watch?

Some of the leg machines found in the gyms today place the athlete in the most undignified and vulnerable positions imaginable. To wear such luridly revealing clothes and then climb onto a machine that threatens to spread your legs so wide that you're in real danger of having your ankles meet behind your back seems to me absurdly illogical. The more so when some unfortunate male, already plagued by mirrors, happens to look up at the wrong moment and finds himself helplessly transfixed by an overtly sexual vision in red and black who glares back in ferocious condemnation of his lechery.

I'm not sure it is lechery in fact. When the very style of clothing is screaming out "look at this body," and the design makes the legs look twice their length, the buttocks split and lifted, the breasts outlined perfectly in fluorescent color, what are you supposed to look at? Nine times out of ten, looking away simply brings another color-isolated part of a women's body squeezing and thrusting and spreading in front of you. Short of staring fixedly at the ground and finding the exercise machines by feel, it is impossible not to look.

I was once accosted in the gym by an irate lady who angrily demanded to know what I was staring at. Since I was struggling to release myself at the time from an overweighted pecs machine that was threatening to dislocate my shoulders, I found it hard to gather my thoughts.

"You," I said bluntly. "Your scantily dressed body that leaves nothing to the imagination, that keeps leaping into view wherever I go. What did you think I was staring at?"

Well, that's what I would have liked to say instead of spluttering a mortified apology, feeling my face blush with shame. To be honest, I don't think I had been staring. In fact I think I was in one of those aerobically bored vacuous states that the gyms induce. She stalked indignantly away, and I felt too embarrassed to ask her if she could help me retrieve my elbows, which were touching behind my head. To me, it seems a bit unfair to confront us with virtual nakedness and then accuse us of disgustingly lewd thoughts. All I was trying to do was torture myself in a gym.

It seems that the prim and proper message is that such garments are worn not to be sexy, but because they make the wearer feel good. They simply display the wearer's confidence in herself. Well, that's as may be, but it strikes me they display a damn sight more than that, and to deny it is plain self-delusion. I'm not easily offended or prudish in any way, far from it, but I do resent being a victim of a dishonest conspiracy. If these clothes are the uniform of the post-feminist woman, as I've heard said, and are about woman's empowerment and not men's desires, then I'm a wildebeest.

To wear outrageously enticing apparel and at the same time profess the sensibilities of a sentimentalized Victorian spinster is shamelessly deceitful. Sure, I'm not allowed to touch. I know that. But faced with spread-eagle semi-nakedness, can't I just leer a little? It might help both sexes if they took all the mirrors away. The men wouldn't be ambushed by horny visions at moments of muscle-ripping effort and the women wouldn't be reminded of how beautifully empowered and confident they are.

However, all things being equal, I'd much rather cope with the women's sense of gym fashion than that of the average male. Wobbling beer bellies straining through unwashed, sweat-stained tee-shirts are bad enough, but it doesn't stop there. It is odd the way men bare their arms in tank tops, all the better to show off their bulging biceps and allow them to conveniently forget about the blubbery sphere of fat quivering above the tight belt of their shorts. Some wear wide leather weight-lifting belts, either to look tough or more probably to restrain the verandah above their toyshops, as the Australians so delightfully describe beer bellies.

The worst gym I've known was attended by four huge bouncers from a now bankrupt Sheffield night club. They were big both in height and musculature, but they were not honed into the sort of symmetry, however unnatural, that body builders acquire—broad shoulders, small "V-shaped" waist and powerful legs. These guys were utter slobs. They went in for bench-pressing horrendous stacks of steel, curling dumbbells so heavy that I doubted I could lift one off the floor with both hands, making animal grunting noises, and sweating profusely. When not displaying their awesomely pointless machismo, they glared around the gym, exuding an atmosphere of raw violence.

There was something truly repulsive about their flabby white arms and shoulders, biceps as thick as my thighs, short bull necks with ludicrously small cropped pinheads balanced on top. They walked with muscle-bound ponderous gaits. I had seen them in action in the club and listened to their monosyllabic conversations in the changing room. These consisted almost entirely of accounts of the unfortunate wretches battered into a pulp the previous night. If they changed the subject at all, it was to discuss the relative merits of various different steroids and body-building drugs. In time I developed a keen sense of disgust whenever I met them and tried to avoid eye contact in case their walnut-size brains suddenly recognized my impudence.

So it was with the same horror that I found myself trapped by their hulking presence in a six-foot by six-foot sauna. It was the first and last time I will ever go into one of those hellholes. They barged in just as I came to the decision to leave.

"Can't take the heat?" one of the slobs sneered as he laid his towel on the slatted wooden bench and lowered his vast naked buttocks on to it.

"Are you wimping out, youth?" his mate said as he thrust a leg the size of a tree trunk against the door.

"No, no," I said quietly. "I've had my go."

"Have you heck as like," pinhead in the corner snarled. "That's been two minutes. What's the problem? Too hot for you, or are you just scared?"

"Scared? Scared of what?"

They laughed and I sat down disconsolately.

"I'll show you what's hot, lad." Pinhead leaned forward and began ladling water onto the coals. Steam erupted and the temperature soared. At least it hid the sight of their gross bodies. I was tempted to point and laugh at their miniscule genitals squashed like chipolatas between the bulge of their thighs and bellies, but I decided that I quite liked my arm in one piece and bit my lip. Instead I bowed my head and breathed slowly, feeling the dry burning steam in my throat. What a bunch of wankers! I thought.

When they grew bored with the heat competition, they took to shaving and squeezing the mass of pimples covering their heavy rounded shoulders and broad backs. I wondered if it was the steroids that caused the body acne.

"I fancy that bint in red," pinhead growled as his mate dug his nails into the white-headed pustules on the back of his neck.

"Aye, I'd give her one."

Give her one? You'd crush her to death, I almost yelped and bit my lip. I edged toward the door.

"Going somewhere, kid"

"Er . . . no, no. Just adding some more water. Not hot enough yet."

". . . bet she'd go," pinhead continued his fantasy. ". . . like the shit house door in a gale." He roared with laughter.

"Bet you wouldn't find your dick," I murmured under my breath.

"Yer what?"

"Nothing, nothing. Just talking to myself," I said hastily.

"Best shave you can have," pinhead's companion announced with satisfaction as he dragged the disposable razor across his unlathered cheek. A rash of beheaded spots began to bleed copiously. He wiped the stubble from the blade with his thumb and smeared it on the wall.

"Right, I'd better be off," I said brightly and grabbed the door handle. I had it open and was half-out before the thigh came across the jamb. I hopped over it and slammed the door, cutting short the rant about "poncey fooking students."

I changed as fast as possible and was heading outside when I spotted the broom in the corner. I glanced at the sauna door with its tiny window-pane and back at the broom. The door had a stout wooden loop handle and opened inwards. It was the work of seconds to slide the broom through the handle and across the door, jamming it firmly in place. I sprinted out, half expecting to hear insane bellowing and the sound of splintering pine doors. I ran from the gym, never to return and never to set foot in their nightclub again.

Now, at last, I have found a pleasant, friendly gym in the YMCA and train there three times a week. I still dislike the monotony of it, but I go all the same. Without building the strength in my legs, particularly around my knee, I know the doctors' dire warnings would very soon come true.

"How's things?" Clive asked as he handed me my membership card. "Haven't seen you for a while."

"No, I've been in Tibet and Nepal, trying Cho Oyo."

"How did it go?"

"Five topped out, so that was good, but I got a chest infections and had to give up."

"That's bad luck after giving up smoking."

"Yeah, tell me about it."

"Where to next?"

"Peru," I said. "Next week."

"Well, have a good one." He smiled.

"Yeah, thanks. I will."

I had been back from Nepal for less than three weeks, barely enough time to shake off whatever had infected my chest and resume my usual twenty-a-day smoking habit. I was due to guide three clients for a Sheffield-based trekking company in the Cordillera Blanca. It was to be my first time in Peru since the dreadful accident on Siula Grande in the Cordillera Huayhuash had crippled me nine years before.

The bell rang time as Richard came back from the bar with two foaming pints of bitter.

"How do you feel about going back?" he asked as he handed me a pint.

"Oh, it'll be great," I replied airily. "Why do you ask?"

"Well, you know. Bad memories, that sort of thing."

"Oh, no, I'm looking forward to it, and I'm being paid. Anyway, it wasn't Peru that did me, or even the mountains. It could have happened anywhere. I have been on ten trips since then, you know, and the medics said I'd never go again. No, I feel okay about it."

I had accepted Bob Lancaster's offer to lead a party in the Cordillera Blanca for his trekking company High Places. Ric Potter and I would guide on various acclimatization peaks before attempting Huascaran (6768 meters), the highest mountain in the Tropics and the fourth highest in South America. After the trip, Ric and I planned to do some climbing for ourselves.

"Just easy routes, okay?" I had warned him. "Nothing hard, nothing new, all right? I'm not getting into any more epics, ever again."

"Sure," he said, "but good easy ones. Alpamayo, perhaps, or Artesonraju."

A week later, as Heathrow approached and Sheffield faded down a long ribbon of gray motorway, I was feeling less sure of myself. I felt superstitious, as if I might be tempting fate, as if going back could be the end of a journey.

I knew it was irrational, and tried not to believe that I could be closing the circle of life I had been blessed with since Siula Grande, but the sudden rush of apprehension was hard to dispel.

"Don't be stupid," I kept telling myself. But the feeling absorbed me and wouldn't go away. I lit a cigarette and watched a Jumbo defy logic as it hung in the empty sky above the terminal.

"Are you okay?" Pat asked as she pulled into the Terminal 1 car park.

"Yes, of course I am," I snapped defensively. "Why shouldn't I be?"

"Just checking. You look a bit tense, that's all."

"Oh, it's nothing. Just the thought of flying," I lied fluently, and she smiled, knowing it wasn't true.

"It'll be fine. There's nothing to worry about," I said as I lifted the rucksacks out of the back of the car.

"I wasn't worrying. You're the one who's worrying." She laughed at the look of surprise on my face.

"Well, just a little, I suppose," I admitted and felt my heart skip a beat. I swallowed nervously and headed toward the check-in desks.

"TALES FROM THE GRIPPED"

FROM
Sherman Exposed
BY JOHN SHERMAN

JOHN SHERMAN'S IRREVERENT STYLE AND SLIGHTLY RIBALD VIEW OF the climbing milieu was well received when his column first appeared. His approach mirrors the attitude that often drives traditionally iconoclastic climbers. Sherman, who earned the name "Sherman the Vermin" from one of his high school teachers, has said he thinks that not only climbing should be fun, but "climbing writing" can be fun, or thought provoking, just not boring. So the humorist is content to be the "squeaky cog in the mighty media machine."

"Tales from the Gripped" is the story of Sherman's lengthy quest to climb the Mystery Towers, three desert spires not far from Moab, Utah. Like other Sherman accounts, this one is hilarious, but pays homage as well to some cool history of desert climbing and of pioneering personalities such as Layton Kor.

Written in 1993 for *Climbing* magazine, the venue of Sherman's often satiric columns, the piece chronicles Sherman's multiple attempts on the towers: Gothic Nightmare, Doric Column, and the Citadel. "Tales from the Gripped" captures varied aspects of desert climbing, including 200-mile beer runs to avoid the ubiquitous near beer of Utah, rock so hot it burns the hands, and torrential rains. Sherman skillfully overlays the humor of the story with a requiem for the lost solitude of the desert—"the Mystery Towers are a mystery no more"—and the establishment of a latter-day outdoor scene in Moab that has changed the place entirely.

As Sherman recounts multiple near-death experiences hanging from marginal aid in these towers made of mud, he eloquently describes the nature of desert climbing and it's unusual techniques, such as banging lost arrows into bolt holes, or "rock" so useless that putting weight on a three-and-a-half inch bolt blows it out. The stuff is so shaky that on the Citadel Sherman can feel the tower vibrate as his partner Rob Slater cleans the pitch forty feet below.

If the piece resonates with the hasty promises made by those facing their imminent demise, in this case by climbers hanging off a bolt that's oozing out as they watch it ("just get me down to my last piece and I'll give this up forever ... "), the great thing about the story may be that, in the end, Sherman climbs the towers. All three of them. It's like the guy who has the moxie to get back on the horse after a nasty fall, even if Sherman applies a healthy does of authentic climbing reality: "I knew if I didn't go back up, I'd be chickenshit forever." As usual, it's Sherman's honesty that makes his stories fun.

"Tales from the Gripped" was reprinted in *Sherman Exposed,* on pages 155–165.

T his is not negotiable."

Tom Cosgriff was on the line, feeding me some bull.

"Listen, we had a deal," I said. "Remember? We were going to climb illegal desert spires until we got caught or you had to go back to Norway."

"No. We gotta climb A5 in the Fisher Towers." Cosgriff was adamant.

"Tom, you aren't getting me anywhere near those petrified turds. Besides, they're legal. What fun will that be?"

"This is not negotiable. We're going to the Fishers."

Damn him. How could I say no? He never does. Like the first climb we did together—Gorilla's Delight, a classic 5.9 in Boulder Canyon—me with a knee that bent only 60 degrees, Cosgriff with a cast on his wrist. No problem. Now the poor bastard spends most of the year stuck behind a desk in Norway, eyeing some plump blond secretary gobbed in makeup. I relented. Nevertheless, deep down I knew this was his way of getting even for that time I visited him in the Yosemite jail, the time I asked if I could borrow his haulbag, since he wouldn't need it for awhile.

He did bend an iota, though, and I got my sentence reduced. We'd climb the 350-foot Gothic Nightmare, hidden far behind the Titan in the Mystery Towers group of the Fishers. Endwise, it looks like one of the Coneheads wearing a jester's cap, dangly bells sprouting out of the top. From the side it resembles a sailfish fin. The Gothic was still unrepeated after two decades, a fact that appealed to Cosgriff. It was rated only A3, a fact that appealed to me.

There was one hitch: we needed gear, lots of it. Hence my descent into the abode of the Evil Doctor, Tom's pal, *Climbing* magazine's gear editor, Duane Raleigh.

Had I not been with Tom, Raleigh would surely have never let an arch-traditionalist like me in his house. As it was, Duane was nervously trying to keep an eye on me, his gear, and his wife, all at the same time. Back in the spare room I found his chisel collection and actually touched one of the grade reducers. It moved me to eloquence better left unprinted. My comments were not well taken. Duane pulled Tom aside and whispered the doctor's orders: "Make him suffer."

At first, the suffering was limited to humping gear up the long approach, dumping it at the base, and hiking out. Then it intensified when we went for beer and pizza at Moab's famous Poplar Place. The jalapeño, garlic, and green pepper combo was, said Tom, "the most evil pizza I've ever had." Tougher to swallow was the wimpy 3.2 stout. The waitress assured us, "A lot of people are really happy to find beer like this in Utah." Yeah, that's like the happiness one feels when he's in jail, and only gets "befriended" by the little guy.

The next morning we both passed a hibachi's worth of glowing briquettes. We tried a new, uglier approach through several inches of snow. Conditions on the Gothic were wretched. All around, the snow was melting, loosening stones. Those stones hit others, until thunderous rock slides ripped down the walls of the Mystery Towers cirque.

We had reached the base, and were now committed to bucking out double loads in defeat. We hadn't climbed an inch. There was no sense in lugging out the beer, so we sat in the saddle between the Citadel and the Gothic Nightmare and swilled. By the time we had split a six of King Cobra tallboys, tons of debris had worked its way down, and our psyche had worked its way up. Tom started leading.

Only the thought that Tom was suffering more than I was made the shady north-face belay stance bearable. He beat knife blades into millimeter-thick calcite seams. With enough pounding they'd go to the hilt and hold body weight. Stepping on a drilled pin, he blew the hole apart. This was Tom's idea of a great vacation.

A few hours later he was at the belay, and I was following. I could've cleaned the pitch with a Fisher-Price hammer. Now it was my lead.

"Dammit. This isn't funny." My yelps only made Cosgriff laugh harder. "Shit shit shit shit shit." My voice was getting higher. "Watch me." It was 20 degrees Fahrenheit, I was in tennis shoes and thin wool gloves, and I was free-climbing vertical mud. Not out of my own free will. The perfect #3 Friend placement I had excavated from the mud, jump-tested, and moved up on had just exploded, leaving a depression the size and shape of a chili bowl. The only reason I hadn't fallen was that one foot was stemmed onto a knob. Now I was stuck: one foot on the knob and my shoulder pressed against the opposite wall of the dihedral. All the nearby holds were covered in dirt from my attempts to excavate the next placement. The pump flooded in.

Every piece was a time bomb, and if I fell, it would be onto the anchor. Earlier, Tom had stopped me climbing so he could tie off the belay line. He hastily punched another bolt in the anchor because the old ones were oozing out under his weight.

"If I get down to that last piece, I will lower off, let Tom finish this, and retire from aid climbing forever." Such were my thoughts, and "What if I don't?"

I reached down below my feet to the last piece, my balance big-rack, clothes-bundled, tilt-out awkward. My hands and feet were slipping on the dirt. I could grab the stem of the Friend, but knew that it would rotate out if I tried to lower onto it. My only hope was to clip on some aiders and step in.

I clipped aiders to the placement, but couldn't reach down far enough to guide one over my foot. I had one lousy inch of nylon to step through but it was lying flat against the wall like it was glued there. I tried to flick the aider away from the wall and kick my foot through, usually an easy trick, but not with the top step. The curses spilled out of my mouth in angry tones, plaintive tones, and tearful pleas.

One lousy inch of nylon.

The pump clock was ticking down. Then, like in some MacGyver script, when he defuses a nuclear device with a pocket knife as the timer reads one second left, my foot slid through. I eased my way down, clipped into the piece, and rested my helmet against the wall.

The panic vanished, replaced by a nervousness about the piece I was resting on. Then came a bigger fear. Not the threat of imminent injury, but the fear that if I didn't go back up, I would be a chickenshit forever.

I can't remember how long I hung there, regrouping mentally, forcing the decision, willing courage. Finally, I stood up, grabbed my hammer, and started gouging at the crack through the mud, waiting to hear that scraping sound when I reached real rock, my mind focused on one thing: making that next piece stick.

The summit ridge offered sunshine and snow and no evidence of how Bill

Forrest and Don Briggs traversed it to its faraway high point. All we found was a hawser-laid rap sling encircling a pile of rubble; twenty years ago it was a sturdy pinnacle. We sat on the ridge, with nothing to do but listen to the intermittent rumble of the towers and walls eroding around us. Four trips in and out, a 200-mile beer run to Grand Junction, and two short, frigid pitches on the north face were all for naught—we bailed.

What possessed me to go back? Or should I say, who? Not Cosgriff. He was pecking his keyboard, sneaking peeks at chunky hips and painted lips, and suffering through economically induced sobriety (seven bucks a beer) in Norway. No, only one other person could drag me back to the fudge-brownie and stale-bread summits of the Mystery Towers. My partner of countless Eldo epics; the man who sent me on my first heading and hooking lead on El Cap (without telling me the first ascensionist decked on the same pitch); The Provider who lent me a faulty portaledge that sent me on a headfirst, 4 A.M. wake-up call a third of the way up El Cap; Mr. Confidence, Mr. Cockiness, and lover of all that is ovine—Robbie Slater. The Team was back together.

This time it was June. The beauty of the maroon-walled, Roadrunner-Coyote approach canyon was lost in the heat, loose sand, and shoe-sucking quicksand.

Our objective was all three Mystery Towers: the Doric Column, the Citadel, and the Gothic Nightmare.

First was the Doric. Say it fast and it sounds like Dork, which is just what it looks like.

Kor was first to try it, but backed off when he saw how much drilling would be required. Forrest and George Hurley then bagged the first ascent in 1969, sneaking onto the summit while their British partner Rod Chuck, tired of being bombarded at the belays, rested on the ground. The Yanks pulled their ropes on the way down. Chuck was not amused. Twenty-three years later, a fellow Brit, Steve "Crusher" Bartlett, avenged the injustice, making the second ascent with George "Chip" Wilson.

The first pitch was mostly free climbing. A 5.7 dirt mantel gave me brief pause, half an hour or so, for reflection. It wouldn't have taken so long if I didn't keep glancing down to see our half-naked companion sunbathing at the base. Knowing Rob's penchant for flat-chested blonds, I had no worries about him being distracted from his belay duties.

Soon, the anchor was cause for thought. Crusher's bolts, now two months old, were already coming loose in the soft rock. I drilled another, feeling the vibrations through my feet. Later, I could feel Rob clean pins forty feet below.

The next three pitches climbed a mud-encrusted chimney/groove that resembled the inside of a giant gutted fish. Here, the second-ascent crew had freshly riveted Forrest's bolt and bathook ladder for us, so progress was quick and easy for the leader. For the belayer, it could never be quick enough. Mud clods bombarded the belayer's helmet every few minutes, and goggles, bandannas, and long-sleeved shirts couldn't keep the dirt from grinding against the teeth, plugging the ears, and invading every pore. Days after the ascent my nose continued to produce twin strands of red-brown mucus.

On top we basked in the late-afternoon sun, strolling about the spacious summit, clambering up the boulder marking the high point. Forrest and Hurley, not having known they'd bag it the day they did, had not left a register. Crusher had, however, with a note that said, "The Citadel is next."

The Citadel and the Gothic—both unrepeated, both prizes, both tottering piles of choss you could piss a bolt hole into. Crusher might come back any day, so the Citadel was next.

The Citadel looks like an Olympic medals stand viewed in a fun-house mirror, the kind that would make Danny DeVito look like Manute Bol. The first pitch appeared to be a casual dirt scramble, so I volunteered for the lead.

Off-route from the start, I had soon paddled across a dirt slab I dared not reverse. I had no gear in, and below was a series of 35-degree dirt shelves with six-foot drops between them. It would be an ugly fall, like rolling a 165-pound baseball down ten flights of stairs.

As the dirt under my feet continuously gave way, I slowly walked in place. I desperately needed pro, but the only weakness in the rock slab at my chest was a seam thinner than a pencil line. I had no RURPs, so I pounded two knife blades in. One actually went in half an inch, before it busted off the side of the seam. I tied off and equalized the pins, then agonized over the flexing mantel shelf in front of me for another fifteen minutes.

I figured I'd rather fall going up than going down and figured I had little choice. What I didn't figure was that the dirt above was dark brown, facing south, and now heated to over 100 degrees. When I got there it was too hot to hang onto. Fortunately, the angle was low enough that I could chop steps with my hammer, like ice climbing in the Sahara.

A hundred feet of zigzag climbing had netted me only forty feet in elevation. The next anchor was half a rope away so it was decided—I don't remember by whom—that I should lead up to it and get us a full rope off the ground. Had I read Hurley's 1970 article on the Mystery Towers in *Climbing* prior to our ascent, this would surely have been Rob's lead. In it, Forrest recounts the fall he took on this pitch when a quarter-inch bolt broke under his weight. He had removed the bathooks below, and the only pro left between him and a lengthy fall was a fold he tied off in the mud curtain. Miraculously, the thread held.

I had read about the Mystery Towers in the guidebook, however, and was aware of certain tricks used to ascend them: the curtain tie-offs for one, pins forced in calcite veins for another, and angles driven into the mud tent-stake style. Within thirty feet I had employed techniques two and three, as well as some steps gouged in the mud. I reached a bolt and promptly backed it up with the worst bolt I ever placed.

Next came a blank section. The only hint of passage was a couple of millimeter-deep dimples, the remnants of bathook holes. Given that most of the old bolts were now hanging about an inch out from the rock due to erosion, I figured that Forrest drilled bathook holes roughly an inch deep. At first I tried to preserve Forrest's pattern: two to three holes, then a bolt. In the last two decades, however, not only had the rock changed, but so had the technology. Bathooks were no longer in vogue, so as Crusher had done on the Doric, I put rivets in my freshly drilled inch-deep holes. An ethical quandary ensued. Forrest had taken more risk—his hook holes were empty after he passed them. He had nothing to stop a fall except a bolt every fifteen feet or so—small consolation in this rock. At least I had eight cents worth of soft steel carriage bolt plugging every hole, plus thicker bolts backing up his quarter-inch coffin nails. It didn't seem sporting, even if my rivets were the weakest money could buy.

I stopped backing up Forrest's bolts, and began tying off their exposed shanks and using them as rivets—the ones that didn't pull out in my fingers, that is. I nailed whenever possible. Fifty feet above my last bolt, I shuddered, looking down at the string of bent rivets and shaky pins beneath me. A long stretch and I hooked the pick end of my hammer through the rotting belay slings and gingerly pulled up on the anchor.

Slater chuckled up the next pitch, in the process performing the impossible—he fixed a pin in the Fisher Towers. Half an hour of pounding wouldn't get it out. Half a year of erosion probably will.

We were keeping the same pace as the first ascent—100 feet per day. In the guidebook, the Citadel is listed as Grade V, even though it is only 400 feet tall. At the rate we were going, it would be a Grade VI. Every bit of work done by the first-ascent party had to be redone. The old pin scars and bathook holes had long since eroded away, and only a handful of original bolts still supported body weight.

Day three on the Citadel. We started up the fixed lines early—the thermometer read a mere 95 degrees. The long summit pitch was mine, the endless belay session Rob's. The first eighty feet was mostly putting in rivets, the only fun coming when I plucked out the old bolts—some in only a quarter-inch—with my fingers.

I reached a shoulder on the arête and balanced across a doormat-width mud gangplank to the final headwall. Sheer walls dropped away on either side. If the ridge should crumble, I thought, I have to fling myself over the opposite side, so the rope would catch me. At the base of the headwall, I clipped the old bolt anchor, gratefully. I had plenty of rope left so, after hauling up some water, I kept going.

Above, the rock was so decomposed that it was turning into mud in situ. I went to work on a ¾-inch crack. A few taps sent in a 1-inch angle. Fingers pulled it out. Ditto for the 1½. Ditto for the 2-inch. Ditto for the 3-inch bong. Now I had a fist-sized hole in the crack pouring sand. I might as well have been nailing a giant sugar cube.

Twenty-five feet up was a three-bolt ladder to the solid capstone summit crack. The only way up would be to nail the mud curtain. I grabbed the 3-inch Longware bong, a historic borrowed piece of iron, angled it down slightly, and pounded it in until only the sling on the eye poked out through the mud. It went in like a dull knife punched into a jack-o'-lantern.

Pounding in the next bong, I could feel the whole curtain shake. I returned to the ridge to test it, a pattern I would keep up as long as my chain of aiders would reach.

The line went straight up, and a fall would certainly intercept the ridge; I would end up draped and broken over it. Either that or I'd pound onto it then fly down the exposed face on the right or ricochet down the steep flute on the left.

The last twelve feet had taken four hours. I had drained the water bottle at the ridge. We had enough light to make the summit, but I didn't have enough nerves left. In my exhausted and dehydrated state, it would be easy to blow it. Day three ended twenty feet shy of the top.

The next day I went back up, shoving a few of the placements back in with my hands. Soon I was grabbing the rappel slings snaking through the crack at the summit. They came free in my hands, rotted through by twenty-three years of sunshine and wind.

As Rob pulled over the lip, he declared it the coolest summit in the desert. Just like he had with the Doric Column. Just like he had on every spire he'd climbed. We sent the temptingest trundle in celebration.

We had run out of time. The Gothic Nightmare would have to wait for another trip.

Eleven months later it was a race. With the exception of the Titan, the Fisher Towers had been virtually ignored for two decades. Now they had become trendy among some of the Boulder crowd. Rob had ticked nearly every Fisher Tower in the guide, and in his outspoken way, had declared his intention to be first to top them all. Others soon declared their intention to beat Rob, then begged him for beta and pin lists. "The race will be over when I finish," was all Rob would tell them, "no sooner."

I just wanted to do the three Mystery Towers and in the process settle my score with the Gothic, preferably with the second ascent.

Rob had been in the Fishers every weekend for four months. Loyal to The Team, he had been saving the Gothic to do with me. Our experience on the Citadel convinced us this would be more than a weekend project, and Rob had a Monday-through-Friday job. Hence we extended honorary Team membership to Mike O'Donnell, Rob's Sea of Dreams partner. A soft-spoken, red-haired brute from Boulder, Mike had a list of wild escapades rivaled by few, including a failed attempt at the Gothic in which an expanding flake both he and I had previously nailed came loose on its own, fell twenty-five feet, clocked the retreating Mike in the head, and split his helmet from one end to the other. Mike and I would fix up to the summit ridge, then Rob would meet us and triumphantly lead to the top.

The changes a year makes. The popularity of the Moab area had spread like a cancer, and Onion Creek had been "discovered" by the hoi polloi. Tents and campers filled every turnout. Mountain bikes jammed the road. Little TP prayer flags fluttered in the bushes—signs of the reverence Joe Six-pack pays the wilderness.

When Cosgriff and I had approached the Mystery Towers two years before, we saw not a single footprint. The canyon was wild, the approach inobvious, the directions in the guidebook poor, the towers hidden from sight until halfway in. It felt as if nobody had walked this wash since Forrest and crew had rolled in the wheelbarrows supporting their ballsacks.

Now Mike and I followed numerous foot- and pawprints up the approach. Mike explained that this had become a popular day hike for the "Kumbaya-ers," the crowd of hippie mountain bikers who now call Moab their own. He started mimicking their behavior, whistling as if calling a dog, and saying, "Dark Star, come here, boy."

We turned the corner where you get the first view of the Doric, and saw a party rapping down—the fifth ascent in less than a year. The Mystery Towers were a mystery no more.

The rock on the Gothic makes the Titan look like granite. Once again I drew the first pitch, which entailed tied-off knife blades, expanding blocks, and dirt-dagger free climbing. I hadn't nailed for a year and was pretty spooked. In the South, they'd say I was shaking like a dog shitting peach pits, but this was more like a dog passing sea urchins. Fortunately, it was a short pitch.

Mike methodically worked out the next pitch, knocking off loads of mud and rotten rock. Most fell to the side of me, but one chunk exploded on my belay plate, making me happy I hadn't opted for a hip belay.

After nailing the expanding mud-block traverse the first-ascent party had bathooked, Mike started chain-smoking. Belaying me on the next lead didn't help matters, though I did my best to help him quit; from twenty feet up I dislodged a chunk of rock that whistled down to knock Mike's "twitch stick" from his lips.

I wriggled into a short chimney between two narrow ridges. It was like chimneying between slightly open scissor blades, and I could easily peer down both the north and south faces. O'Donnell was belaying on the north side. The chimney expanded on the south side. I said, "Listen to this," planted my left foot on the north face, then shoved lightly with my right. A portion of wall the size of my body slowly tipped off like a tree being felled, then traveled 300 feet before creating a thunder that echoed through the valley for minute after satisfying minute. A fine trundle is a rare and beautiful thing. I was reminded of Kor's words when asked why he climbed the desert towers: "Not so much because they're there, but rather because they may not be there much longer."

Even more of the Gothic disappeared when I groveled on top of the knife-edge ridge the next day. I punched and shoved until the ridge was a foot lower, and the medium I would mantel onto resembled rock. A short stroll along the dirt ridge, similar, but wider than the Citadel's gangplank, got me to the anchor and the end of my leading commitment.

Now Rob had joined us, and went to work. After sixty feet, he stopped at a saddle between two gargoyles, midway along what the first ascent dubbed "The Traverse of the Goblins." The saddle was composed entirely of cobbles, a three-foot-thick layer, every one of which you could pull out with your fingers. No way to nail it or drill it, and free climbing would be nuts. Luckily for Rob, a storm was moving in, and his partners called for a retreat.

The weekend was over. We sat in a Mexican restaurant discussing our plight. I wasn't about to leave. O'Donnell felt likewise. Outside, the streets of Moab were flooding. This, and a job commitment, convinced Rob to flee. He drove us out to the Onion Creek road, where my van was parked. It was a moonless night and still raining. He dropped us at the first stream crossing, then left us to die.

The first crossing turned out to be an insignificant tributary we had never seen water in. We didn't know this until we reached the real Onion Creek. We stood on the bank—what was left of the road—and listened to boulders rolling down the torrent. It was so dark I wondered if we were listening to my van floating by. We stood in tee shirts, shorts, and flip-flops, me with a bag of provisions, Mike with a borrowed tent, and Rob long gone with the tent poles.

I wrapped myself in the tent, Mike wrapped himself in the fly, and we hiked back to the highway. No cars. Was it flooded now, too? Closed for the night? The Rob-left-us-to-die jokes turned into serious talk about what to do next.

I'm not one to throw away beers, even if they are Utah 3.2 road-pops, but I ditched the sixer, something I would do only in the most dire circumstances. The nearest ranch house was seven miles distant. We started hiking.

Finally, a caravan of rafters drove by and took pity on us, two drowned rats wrapped up like nuns with tents over our heads.

"What are you doing out here?" they asked.

"Rock climbing," we replied.

"Climbers? That explains it."

They dropped us off in Moab, where, once again, we knocked on the door of the patron saint of Moab mud-nailers, Kyle Copeland. If it weren't for his hospitality and gear, we would have never gotten into this mess.

Betrayal. The Team ripped asunder by filthy lucre. Rob knew that next Friday was the only day I could go back. O'Donnell was going to be there. I told Rob he must call in sick, especially since he'd already told his competitors that the second ascent was a done deal.

"You've got to wait until Saturday," Rob pleaded. "I'll lose 6,000 dollars if I don't go to work on Friday."

"Don't give me this bullshit about chicken feed. This is the second ascent of the Gothic we're talking about."

O'Donnell and I went back alone. Forrest had told Slater that from the summit ridge up it was all drilling. Indeed, the only pins he placed were lost arrows pounded into bolt holes; the rock was so bad in places that inch-and-a-half long bolts wouldn't cut it. I finished Slater's lead. Mike led to the glorious summit.

The very top is the size of a park bench, and perfect to sit on. It was time to lift a Mount Everest malt liquor, toast the first ascensionists Forrest and Briggs, toast ourselves, toast Rob who would jug up the next day, and toast all those who have sought adventure in these most stupendous of choss heaps.

"Here's mud in your eye."

(Robbie showed up later with Pancho Torrisi to bag the third ascent of the Gothic.)

"THE ART OF CLIMBING DOWN GRACEFULLY: A SYMPOSIUM OF COMMONLY USED PLOYS...."

FROM
One Man's Mountains
BY TOM PATEY

AT THE SAME TIME TOM PATEY WAS ESTABLISHING THE BENCHMARK for hard Scottish ice climbs, big alpine routes, and Himalayan first ascents, he found another calling as well: the eloquent voice of climbing. Before his untimely death in 1970, Patey wrote a series of articles for Great Britain's *Mountain* magazine. "The Art of Climbing Down Gracefully," which became one of the most beloved pieces in mountaineering literature, was one of his best. It was published shortly after Patey was killed rappelling off a sea stack on the Scottish coast.

Patey's record of climbing achievements in the decades before his death was unsurpassed. He symbolized the very soul of hard winter climbing in Scotland with the first ascent of Zero Gully and the first winter traverse of the Cuillins, not to mention almost all the sea stacks off the coast of the Northern Highlands. With first ascents in the Himalaya, including the Mustagh Tower in the Karakoram in 1956 and Rakoposhi in 1958, and a decade of new routes in the Alps with Joe Brown, Patey was firmly established in the climbing elite. But it is his writing that has kept Patey's spirit alive.

With this story in particular, Patey struck a chord among his readers. The piece is so dead on that it makes even climbers uncomfortable. Patey's descriptions of the ploys that climbers use to avoid climbing are so recognizable, so universal, they have become archetypes. At one time or another, every climber, after arriving at his intended objective and actually seeing for the first time what he's come to climb, has been aghast. But backing out without appearing to chicken out isn't easy. Every climber who has spent a night in the tent, wide-awake and praying for rain (or some other act of God that will make climbing impossible) will recognize himself in this amusing look at the human condition.

"The Art of Climbing Down Gracefully" is in *One Man's Mountains*, on pages 131–140.

Modern climbing is becoming fiercely competitive. Every year marks the fall of another Last Great Problem, or the fall of the Last Great Problem Climber. Amid this seething anthill, one must not overlook the importance of Staying Alive.

This is why I propose to devote a few lines to "The Art of Climbing Down Gracefully"—the long, dedicated Decline to Dignified Decrepitude.

I have had another title suggested, viz: "How to be a top climber without actually climbing." This is not only misleading—it makes a travesty of this article. One must assume that respect has been earned honorably on the field of battle and not by mere subterfuge. It is in order to maintain this respect, that one employs certain little subtleties that would ill befit a brash impostor.

In short, this is a symposium for Mountaineers—not mountebanks!

1. THE "OFF-FORM" PLOY

This one is as old as the hills but still widely used. Few climbers will admit to being "on form." Everyone would feel uneasy if they did. Again, a climber who was "on form" during the morning can be feeling "off-form" by early afternoon. If an interval of forty-eight hours or so has elapsed between climbs, he may talk of being "out of condition." If the interval is a month or longer, he may justifiably consider himself to be "out of training." Unfortunately so many climbers take their training seriously nowadays (with press-ups, dumbbells, running up the down escalators in tube stations, etc.)—that it is unwise to be out of training when in the company of dedicated mountaineers. A friendly invitation to Bowles Mountaineering Gymnasium can be the natural outcome of such a remark.

2. THE "TOO MUCH LIKE HARD WORK" PLOY

This is the Englishman's favorite gambit when climbing (or not climbing) North of the Border. Many Scottish cliffs are admittedly remote by comparison with Shepherd's Crag, but I have heard this sort of generalization directed at Glencoe, where you can scarcely leave the main road without bumping your head against an overhang. No, this simply will not do! Far more effective is the Sassenach Second Choice Gambit, viz.:

3. THE "CHOSSY CLIMB" PLOY

"Poxy," "Chossy," "Spastic," and "Rubbish" are all terms characteristically used by English and Welsh climbers to denigrate Scottish routes which they have either failed to climb or failed to find (without searching too minutely).

Eyewitness reports could in fact reveal that Spiderman made repeated attempts to overcome the crux, before he was ignominiously repulsed and left hanging in a tangle of slings and étriers, but this is completely at variance with the official Party Line, which stresses Spiderman's disgust on finding the initial holds cloaked in greenery. His aesthetic senses had been so offended that he had instantly abandoned the climb and spent the day more profitably in a nearby hostelry.

Spiderman's reputation remains untarnished. It is the luckless pioneers who are singled out for derision just as they were preparing to crow over his downfall—a neat demonstration of how to convert defeat into a moral triumph. A really selective "route gourmet" like Spiderman can sometimes spend years in a fruitless quest for perfection without ever finding a climb to which he can justifiably or morally commit himself.

4. THE "ICE-MAN" PLOY

This is the exiled Scotsman's counter-ploy when lured on to English outcrops. "I'm a Snow and Ice Man myself!" is a fairly safe assertion at Harrison's, where it is highly unlikely that you will be given the opportunity to demonstrate your skills.

Oddly enough the first time I heard this line it was spoken by an Englishman. The scene was an alpine hut, at that time (1952) almost entirely populated by Oxbridge types—pleasant fellows, although all unmistakably tarred with the same brush, and handicapped by their common background. Amid this select group one particular rank outsider stuck out like a sore thumb. I was captivated by his facility for saying the wrong thing at the wrong time. ("I say! You two lads have got definite promise. If one of you gets himself killed would the other please look me up? I'm looking for a partner for the Brenva.")

This man had swallowed Smythe and Murray piecemeal and could regurgitate selected phrases from either author with gay abandon. His impact on the Establishment was shattering: "All this talk of VIs and A3s bores me to tears," he would announce in a loud voice, addressing no one in particular. "Show me the Englishman—Yes; show me the Englishman, I say—who can stand upright in his steps, square set to the slope, and hit home hard and true, striking from the shoulder! There must be very few of us Ice-Men left around. Ice-Manship may be a forgotten craft but it's still the Cornerstone of Mountaineering. Never forget that! Any fool can monkey about on rock over-hangs but *it takes craft and cunning to beat the Brenva!*"

He got away with it too. The "Great Mixed Routes" are so seldom in con-dition that a dedicated Ice-man can remain in semi-permanent cold storage without much fear of exposure.

5. THE "SECRET CLIFF" PLOY

This dark horse is seldom seen in the Pass, but makes a belated appearance at closing time. He speaks slowly and reluctantly with a faraway look in his eyes. "We've been sizing up a new crag," he eventually admits after much prob-ing, "amazing why nobody ever spotted it before, but then climbers don't get around much nowadays. . . . We're not giving away any details of course until we've worked it out. . . . Should be good for at least twenty more top-grade routes. . . . " etcetera.

None of these routes ever appear in print, but this too can be explained away at a later day by the Anti-Guidebook ploy: "Why deprive others of the joys of original exploration? We don't want such a superb crag to suffer the fate of Cloggy, and become vulgarized by meaningless variations."

Evasiveness can be finely pointed.

"What route did you climb today then?"

"Dunno, we haven't named it yet!"—is perhaps one of the most spectacular.

All these ploys find their ideal medium in the "Solo Man" Gambit.

6. THE "SOLO MAN" GAMBIT

The subtlety of this ploy is that no one, apart from Solo Man, knows how he spent the day. From the moment he disappears at the double over the first convenient hillock his movements are shrouded in mystery. He needs no ac-complice, and he holds all the aces.

"Had a look at Vector today. . . . Quite thin. . . ." (Solo Man had indeed looked at Vector. He did not like what he saw.) Or: "Forgot the Guidebook. . . . No idea where I was . . . damned good route all the same! . . . Yes, it probably was a first ascent, but I won't be entering it. You can't expect me to remember details: one route is just the same as another as far as I'm concerned." Or: "Found the Tension Traverse pretty tricky . . . a rope would have been quite useful. . . . "

7. THE "RESPONSIBLE FAMILY MAN" PLOY

This is the most stereotyped of all the non-climbing ploys. How often has the marriage altar (halter?) proved the graveyard of a mountaineer's ambitions? The little camp-follower who cooked the meals and darned everybody's socks is suddenly transformed into an all-demanding, insatiable virago whose grim disapproval makes strong men wilt in their *kletterschuhe*. Climbing weekends become less and less frequent and, despite well-meant advice from climbing friends on the benefits of "the Pill," it is only a year before the union is blessed with child. In many cases this is the natural end of all things, but a few diehards still put in an annual appearance—pale shrunken ghosts, who glance nervously over their shoulders before they speak.

"Don't seem to get away much nowadays," they mutter despondently. "Can't take the same risks—unfair on the kids." So saying, they leap into their Volvos or Mini-Coopers and become power-crazy charioteers, mowing down crash-barriers and terrorizing the walking populace. Back home they scream to a halt in a cloud of dust and shrink back into normal dimensions.

"Sorry you had to wait up for me, Dear—just dropped in for a quick one with the lads and got a bit carried away."

This is very effective because it contains an element of pathos, and brings a lump to the throat of the most hardened of Hard-Men. Some aging climbers, no longer able to make the grade on the crags, have been known to contemplate matrimony as the only honorable way out.

8. THE "WRONG GEAR" PLOY

With a little foresight it is always an easy matter to bring the wrong equipment for the day, and then allow everyone to share your vexation. Such a man will turn up for a winter assault on Point Five Gully, wearing brand new P.A.s.

"Great God! I didn't expect to find snow on the Ben this late. Just my luck. . . . "

For a weekend's climbing at Harrison's he will have borrowed a pair of High Altitude Everest Boots.

"Just breaking them in for the Real Thing. Not much use on the small hold stuff but jolly good for the South Col."

I remember an American climber who survived an entire summer at Chamonix by means of this ploy.

"You're missing all the fine weather," we told him.

"I'm an Aid-man," he explained, "and I'm stuck here till my hardwear arrives. It was crated up in New York three weeks ago and the last I heard it was in Paris."

The elusive crate, in fact, never reached its destination. First it was in Cherbourg, then Paris, finally Chamonix. From Chamonix it was redirected to Paris, before the owner could stake his claim. We left him a month later still propping up the Juke Box in the Bar National.

"Some guys have all the goddammed luck," he complained bitterly.

9. THE "GAMMY LEG" PLOY

A permanent physical disability can be a useful handicap, but before it can be turned to advantage it must be something immediately obvious. A wooden leg, for example. (Winthrop Young climbed the Grépon with a wooden leg, but he was unusual.)

Any lesser incapacity is scarcely worth the discomfort it entails. Everyone knows by now that Don Whillans used to perform with a whimsical knee joint that was so unstable it dislocated every time he turned in his bed, but the same knee joint carried him to Gaurisankar and back, with only occasional halts for realignment. Joe Brown, when not putting up new Extremes at Gogarth, slipped a disc in his back garden. Raymond Lambert, the Swiss Guide, climbed even better when all his toes had been amputated. This brought his center of gravity nearer the footholds. There are many more tales of courage or triumph over adversity. Too many, in fact. Extracting sympathy from the present younger generation is like wringing blood from a stone. So if you still sport an old War Wound from the Dardenelles, your best bet is to suffer in silence.

10. THE "FAULTY ALARM CLOCK" PLOY

Somebody ought to manufacture Faulty Alarm Clocks for weekend climbers. Far better to blame an inanimate object for your misfortunes, than to inculpate your companions. . . .

One acquaintance of mine, a Mr. X., always made a point of discussing the next morning's breakfast before turning in for the night. Companions, who assumed that he intended to rise and breakfast himself, were dismayed to waken at 10 A.M. to the sight of an irate Mr. X. pointing accusingly toward an alarm clock that had mysteriously appeared at their bedside overnight.

"You promised to waken me when the alarm went off!" he thundered, "and here I've been, lying awake, not knowing the time, and now it's too late to attempt anything worthwhile! Really, this is too bad!" etcetera.

11. THE "FÖHN WIND" AND OTHER BAD WEATHER PLOYS

Writes René Desmaison with spine-chilling candor, "I have heard it said that it takes more courage to retreat than to advance. I cannot share these sentiments!" M. Desmaison is of course a Frenchman writing for Frenchmen, but he would scarcely get away with this sort of remark in the British Alpine Journal. Not by a long chalk. It strikes at the very foundations of British Alpinism and undermines our most deep-rooted traditional ploy—"Giving the Mountain Best."

It was during my first alpine season that I came into contact with the ever popular Zermatt gambit. An elderly gentleman, wearing knickerbockers and armed with alpenstock, would totter out on to his hotel balcony, raising aloft one pre-moistened, trembling index finger.

"Aha!—I thought as much," he would chuckle grimly. "The Föhn Wind is in the offing! No climbing for you young fellow, for a week at least!"

I was a bit frustrated by this and the next time I went up to a hut I determined to follow the advice of local Alpine Guides. If they don't know, who does? Thirty-two Guides slept at the Couvercle Hut that night, and they all got up at 2 A.M. like a major volcanic eruption. One Guide, with an attractive female client in tow, walked out, prodded the snow with an ice ax, sniffed the night air, and without a word retired to his bed. It later transpired that this was the celebrated X.X. Thirty-one silent Guides looked at each other, shook their heads, and retired likewise. We woke at 8 A.M. to find brilliant sunshine.

"Pourquoi?" I demanded wrathfully of one, "Pourquoi?" (It was one of the few French words at my disposal, so I used it twice.)

"X.X. a dit!" he said reverently, mentally crossing himself, "C'est trop dangereux!"

"Pourquoi?" I demanded again, not without reason.

"X.X. a dit!" he repeated, waving his arms toward a cloudless horizon, "Tempête de neige, qui va venir bientôt sans doubt."

The last time I saw X.X. he was heading for the valley with the attractive blonde in close attendance. It was the first day of what proved to be a ten-day record heat wave. I remembered the time-honored Victorian advice, "Follow the Old Guide—he knows best!" There was more than a grain of truth in that statement. . . .

In the hands of a reliable weather-lore expert the Bad Weather ploy can be practically infallible. Such a man can spend an entire alpine season without setting boot to rock, simply by following the bad weather around, and consistently turning up in the wrong place at the wrong time.

12. THE "GREATER RANGES" PLOY

Historians tell us that Frank Smythe only began to function properly above 20,000 feet. This adds up to a pretty considerable handicap, when you consider how much of his life must have been spent at lower altitudes. It is all part of the mystique that surrounds The Men who are expected to Go High.

For this ploy some previous Himalayan experience is essential; it may involve a tourist weekend in Katmandu, a transcendental meditation with the Maharishi. Once the aura has formed, you can hardly go wrong. You can patrol the foot of Stanage with all the invested authority of an Everester. No one expects you to climb. It is enough that you retain a soft spot for your humble origins.

"This is all very different from the South Col!" you can remark crisply, as you watch bikini-clad girls swarming over the rock like chameleons. Any off-the-cuff comment of this nature goes down well, and gives them something to talk about after you have moved on. As I said before, nobody really expects a man who has survived the South Col to risk his neck on a paltry outcrop.

"I'm a Gritstone Man myself!" you can admit with pride, and then proceed to qualify the statement, "But let us keep our sense of proportion, and remember that British crags are not an end in themselves but a Springboard to the Greater Ranges. The Battle of Waterloo was won on the playing fields of Eton! That is something we must all remember. . . . "

Old Winthrop Young summed it all up in his Valedictory Address to the Alpine Club: "These armies of young boys and girls practicing their wholesome open-air calisthenics, flooding the valleys in hale and hearty chase of pins-and-needles upon which to thread their athletic limbs upside down. . . . What was their love to ours? . . . the pursuit of the distant white Domes . . . etc. . . . etc. . . . etc."

13. THE "BASE CAMP MARTYR" PLOY

This philanthropic character always contrives to be the Odd Man Out.

"Look here, chaps! Let's be sensible about this. A rope of two makes much faster time than a threesome, and I'm only going to hold you back. It's the team effort that counts, after all. If we get Two Men to the Top we will not have failed! I may be kicking my heels at base camp but I'll be with you in spirit: you both know that. Good Luck and Good Hunting!"

14. THE "OLD MAN OF THE MOUNTAINS" PLOY

The essence of this ploy is that you cannot teach an Old Dog new tricks, viz:

"Play up, and play the game—but learn the rules first. Ignore the rules, and the game is no longer worth playing. Present-day rock acrobats don't accept exposure as part of the game. They protect themselves every yard of the way with ridiculous little gadgets of all shapes and sizes. The designations are unimportant—they are un-British in name and un-British in nature! Gone are the days of Kirkus and Edwards, when a leader had sufficient moral conviction to run out 150 feet of lightweight hemp before taking a hitch! Who wants to join the clanking Slab queues to witness the crucifixion of a long-loved friend. I found *this* at Abraham's Ledge on the Crowberry last week!" (unwrapping a rusty piton which he carries around for this purpose). "Covet it young man at your peril! My race may be run, but never let it be said that I helped beget a generation of Cream-Puff climbers."

To qualify for the Hob-Nail Brigade the speaker need not have reached the allotted three-score-and-ten, but he should at least cultivate an aura of venerability and familiarize himself with the appropriate vocabulary, viz.:

Acrobats, monkeys, engineers, technicians, and steeple-jacks	the Modern Generation
hare-brained escapade	a new route
Munich mechanization	artificial climbing
Death-or-Glory fanatics	Hard-men
Dangle-and-Whack merchants	Aid-men
The Golden Age	pre-1930
The Iron Age	post-1930
A sound climber	an old climber
A cautious climber	a very slow climber
A mature climber	an aging incompetent
A die-hard traditionalist	a rude old man
Unjustifiable	perhaps quite hard
Utterly unjustifiable	quite hard
A great mixed route	a snow plod
A courageous decision	chickening out
An Alpine Start	the time to leave the Bar National

PERMISSIONS

ACKNOWLEDGEMENTS

Extraordinary thanks to Bill Fortney, Geoffrey Nichols, and Connie Pius.

ABOUT THE EDITOR

Journalist Peter Potterfield has covered wilderness adventure and mountaineering for newspapers, magazines, books, and online publishing. He served as editor and publisher of MountainZone.com from 1996 to 2000, where he pioneered live reporting of Everest expeditions and other real-time mountaineering events from remote locations. Potterfield has made a specialty of covering mountaineering and wilderness adventure for the popular press, and he has written on these subjects for *Outside, Reader's Digest, Summit, Backpacker, Conde Nast Traveler,* and other national publications. He is the author of four books on mountaineering, including the critically acclaimed *In the Zone* (The Mountaineers Books, 1996) and *The High Himalaya* (The Mountaineers Books, 2001).

ABOUT THE FOREWORD WRITER

Greg Child is an Australian-born climber and writer. He's made new routes on El Capitan, on Alaskan peaks, and on remote crags all over the world. On numerous Himalayan expeditions he has successfully climbed Everest and K2, as well as Gasherbrum IV, Trango Tower, and Shipton Spire, the latter three by new routes. His writing has appeared in *Climbing, Outside,* and *National Geographic.* He has authored six books, the most recent being *Over the Edge* (Villard). In addition, Child was awarded an Emmy for his video work on the National Geographic documentary *Hitting the Wall,* about the first ascent of a big wall route on Baffin Island in the Canadian Arctic. He lives in southeast Utah.

THE MOUNTAINEERS, founded in 1906, is a nonprofit outdoor activity and conservation club, whose mission is "to explore, study, preserve, and enjoy the natural beauty of the outdoors. . . . " Based in Seattle, Washington, the club is now the third-largest such organization in the United States, with 15,000 members and five branches throughout Washington State.

The Mountaineers sponsors both classes and year-round outdoor activities in the Pacific Northwest, which include hiking, mountain climbing, ski-touring, snowshoeing, bicycling, camping, kayaking and canoeing, nature study, sailing, and adventure travel. The club's conservation division supports environmental causes through educational activities, sponsoring legislation, and presenting informational programs. All club activities are led by skilled, experienced volunteers, who are dedicated to promoting safe and responsible enjoyment and preservation of the outdoors.

If you would like to participate in these organized outdoor activities or the club's programs, consider a membership in The Mountaineers. For information and an application, write or call The Mountaineers, Club Headquarters, 300 Third Avenue West, Seattle, WA 98119; 206-284-6310.

The Mountaineers Books, an active, nonprofit publishing program of the club, produces guidebooks, instructional texts, historical works, natural history guides, and works on environmental conservation. All books produced by The Mountaineers Books fulfill the club's mission.

Send or call for our catalog of more than 500 outdoor titles:

The Mountaineers Books
1001 SW Klickitat Way, Suite 201
Seattle, WA 98134
800-553-4453
mbooks@mountaineersbooks.org
www.mountaineersbooks.org

The Mountaineers Books is proud to be a corporate sponsor of Leave No Trace, whose mission is to promote and inspire responsible outdoor recreation through education, research, and partnerships. The Leave No Trace program is focused specifically on human-powered (nonmotorized) recreation.

Leave No Trace strives to educate visitors about the nature of their recreational impacts, as well as offer techniques to prevent and minimize such impacts. Leave No Trace is best understood as an educational and ethical program, not as a set of rules and regulations.

For more information, visit *www.LNT.org,* or call 800-332-4100.